NO SUBSTITUTE FOR VICTORY

NO SUBSTITUTE FOR VICTORY

SUCCESSFUL AMERICAN MILITARY STRATEGIES FROM THE REVOLUTIONARY WAR TO THE PRESENT DAY

David Rigby

Carrel Books may be purchased in bulk at special discounts for sales promotion, corporate gifts, fund-raising, or educational purposes. Special editions can also be created to specifications. For details, contact the Special Sales Department, Carrel Books, 307 West 36th Street, 11th Floor, New York, NY 10018 or carrelbooks@skyhorsepublishing.com.

Carrel Books® is a registered trademark of Skyhorse Publishing, Inc.®, a Delaware corporation.

Visit our website at www.carrelbooks.com.

10 9 8 7 6 5 4 3 2 1

Library of Congress Cataloging-in-Publication Data is available on file.

Print ISBN: 978-1-63144-005-2
Ebook ISBN: 978-1-63144-018-2

Printed in the United States of America

For my siblings—Judy, Sue, Tom, and Rick

CONTENTS

PREFACE

Douglas MacArthur coined the phrase "No Substitute for Victory," which I have appropriated for the title of this book. General MacArthur spoke these words to a joint session of the US Congress on April 19, 1951 in which he expressed the frustrations he had encountered as the commander of United Nations forces fighting a limited war in Korea. MacArthur's expression of anguish seems particularly apt for the title of a book which describes the difficulties that American political and military leaders have encountered throughout the nation's history as they tried to formulate effective military strategies.

ACKNOWLEDGMENTS

I would like to thank Nick Lyons for always being willing to do a favor for a fellow salmon fisherman. I would also like to thank the following friends and colleagues, and one of my nephews, who were kind enough to read parts of this manuscript: Aaron Hiltner, Brianne Keith, Charles Gallagher, S.J., Cindy O'Neill, and Graham Rigby. I take complete and sole responsibility for any errors in this book. I would also like to thank my sister, Sue, whose lifelong support of my endeavors began when she taught me how to ride a bicycle when I was six years old.

INTRODUCTION

This book is about American military strategies that have led to American victory in war. In describing how narrow the margin of victory in war can sometimes be, historian Richard Overy has written in regard to the most important naval battle of World War II that for the Americans "the decisive engagement at Midway Island was won because ten American bombs out of the hundreds dropped fell on the right target;"[1] that target being on the decks of four Japanese aircraft carriers. Overy is quite right, of course, but an additional reason why the Americans won the battle of Midway in June 1942 is that the Japanese failed to concentrate their forces at the right place at the right time. The Japanese deployed a total of eight aircraft carriers, and dozens of other warships, for the descent on Midway Island and a concurrent attack on the Aleutian Islands. However, those eight carriers were dispersed amongst four widely scattered Japanese task forces. Thus, only four Japanese aircraft carriers were close to Midway Island on the morning of June 4, 1942, the only place that mattered that day, and the Americans sank all four. The Americans had three aircraft carriers available for the Midway battle and all three of them operated close to Midway Island in a superb position to intervene.

Concentrating all available forces at the decisive point is one successful American military strategy described in this book. Another is that the adage "the best defense is a good offense" is not always true on the battlefield. American forces have won important victories (Midway being one) by adopting a defensive posture; waiting for a strong enemy force to attack; and then launching a powerful local counterattack.

---

[1] Richard Overy. *Why the Allies Won*. (New York: Norton, 1995): 320.

The value of defensive victory and concentration of forces are covered in Chapter One of this volume. The Battle of Gettysburg in 1863 is here compared to Midway as another battle in which the United States (in this case, the Union) fought and won from a defensive standpoint. The second chapter describes the manner in which the battle for hearts and minds is overwhelmingly important in geostrategic terms. If hearts and minds can be won over, the United States can actually attain a strategic objective without fighting. The examples highlighted here are the Berlin Airlift and the Marshall Plan; specifically that it was American good intentions that gave birth to the Berlin Airlift and to the Marshall Plan with which the Airlift was closely associated, and that those good intentions were personified by Gail Halvorsen, the "Candy Bombing" American pilot who took to dropping chocolate bars tied to tiny parachutes to the children who gathered to watch American transport planes land in Berlin during the Airlift. I have tried to illustrate how the Marshall Plan, the Berlin Airlift, and the "chocolate offensive" waged by Gail Halvorsen and other American Airlift pilots represented the most effective implementation of the strategy of containment during the entirety of the Cold War.

The third chapter stresses that America's armed forces are far more likely to win wars when the nation's war aims are clear, rational, and consistent. The primary examples described here are, respectively, the ruthless simplicity of President James K. Polk's aims during the Mexican War and the fact that President Lincoln's Emancipation Proclamation during the American Civil War was really a logical part of Lincoln's strategy of reuniting the nation rather than a departure from that strategy. The incoherence of American aims in the Vietnam War that led to disaster in that conflict is discussed here as a touchstone for what happens when America's armed forces fight in accordance with a bad strategy; or even with no strategy.

Chapter Four is devoted to occasions when American forces have benefited greatly from mistakes made by the enemy. Examples include mistakes made by Germany and Japan, respectively, in World War II; but the bulk of this chapter is devoted to the battles of the Saratoga campaign in the summer and fall of 1777. During the Saratoga campaign, the British made so many serious mistakes that they practically defeated themselves. The victory at Saratoga in October 1777 is one of the most important military victories in American history. Saratoga allowed the infant American Republic to survive; it convinced the French government to join the war as an ally to the Americans; and it proved to be a pivotal event in the eventual American victory in the War of the Revolution.

The fifth and final chapter focuses on the necessity for unity of command. In this chapter, I explain how the unity of command obtained by the British and the Americans in World War II allowed General Eisenhower to run Supreme Headquarters Allied Expeditionary Force (SHAEF) smoothly despite the sometimes difficult subordinate commanders he was forced to work with. Also described is the way in which a unified theater command in the Central Pacific during World War II enabled the American ground force commander for the Central Pacific Drive, Lieutenant General Holland M. Smith, a marine, to fire an army divisional commander during the Marianas campaign. The bulk of this chapter, however, focuses on the manner in which Union forces in the American Civil War did a much better job of attaining a unified command structure than did the Confederacy. Examples from the Civil War include the manner in which General Ulysses S. Grant worked closely with naval river gunboats to win victories such as that at Fort Henry in February 1862 and at Vicksburg in July 1863. Grant's willingness to develop good working relationships with his naval counterparts such as Rear Admiral David Dixon Porter at a time when the United States did not yet have a Secretary of Defense who could give orders to officers of both services were examples of the personal qualities Grant possessed which convinced President Lincoln in March 1864 to make General Grant the supreme commander of all Union land forces.

Andrew Roberts has written that "Because Nazi Germany was an autocracy, Hitler was able to impose a grand strategy on his generals that a few at the beginning, but many by the middle and almost all by the end, thought suicidal."[2] Roberts is correct that dictators are unfettered by the kinds of limits that democracy imposes upon what an American president can do in time of war. However, the Vietnam War proves that just because the United States is the world's greatest democracy this is

---

[2] Andrew Roberts. *Masters and Commanders: How Four Titans Won the War in the West, 1941–1945*. (New York: HarperCollins, 2009): 576.

not a guarantee that American military strategy will always be logical and coherent or even that a war the United States finds itself in will be a "just" war.

Nevertheless, the most successful American military strategies tend to be employed when and where the United States is fighting a just war, or at least when the American people feel that they are fighting a just war. Richard Overy writes in regard to World War II that "whatever the rights or wrongs of the case, the Allies were successful in winning the moral high ground throughout the war. . . . The Allied populations fought what they saw as a just war against aggression."[3] When the American people offer widespread support for a war, such as World War II or the Gulf War of 1991, American political and military leaders can allow American military forces to fight with no holds barred. Most of the strategies described in this volume have in common the idea that while democracy does impose limits on what the United States can do in time of war, a government of the people is actually a great source of strength in time of war.

---

[3] Overy, *Why the Allies Won*, 22.

CHAPTER 1

CONCENTRATE ONE'S STRENGTH AT THE DECISIVE POINT, ESPECIALLY WHEN FIGHTING DEFENSIVELY

The defining characteristic of a defensive battle is that the defender reacts to moves initiated by an attacking force. In his classic treatise *On War*, Carl von Clausewitz emphasizes that a defensive battle can yield a surprisingly decisive victory for the party doing the defending. Clausewitz goes so far as to state that "the form of warfare that we call defense not only offers greater probability of victory than attack, but . . . its victories can attain the same proportions and results."[1] Armies and navies fight from a defensive standpoint sometimes by choice but usually in desperation when no other option is available.

The Battle of Gettysburg in 1863 and the Battle of Midway in 1942 were both *defensive* victories for the United States and in both cases the victorious force fought defensively more out of desperation than by choice. One of the best examples of a defensive victory obtained by voluntarily ceding the initiative to the enemy is Kursk in July 1943. By the summer of 1943, the Red Army and air force were stronger and held the initiative over German forces on the Russian front. Intelligence data had

---

[1] Carl von Clausewitz. *On War*. Michael Howard and Peter Paret, eds. and trans. (Princeton, NJ: Princeton University Press, 1976): 392.

informed the Russians that the Germans were planning to attack the Kursk salient. The Russians decided to let the Germans attack first and concentrated on building up the Russian defenses in the Kursk area. Only after the Germans had worn themselves out by attacking the strongly fortified Russian position did the Russians go over onto the offensive at Kursk, with excellent results for the Russians. At both Gettysburg and Midway, the defending forces did not hold the initiative and had no choice but to fight defensively. A common characteristic shared by the victor at Gettysburg and at Midway, the Union Army of the Potomac and the United States Navy, respectively, is that in each battle the victor concentrated virtually all of its strength at the decisive point while their respective opponents (particularly the Japanese at Midway) failed to do so. The Civil War presents a peculiar and tragic situation in that it was Americans fighting against other Americans. However, Gettysburg was a victory for the United States Army because the victorious Union Army of the Potomac was serving the national government in Washington, DC. The Confederate Army of Northern Virginia, which was defeated at Gettysburg, was serving a confederacy of eleven states which were in active rebellion against the government of the United States.

Gettysburg exemplifies the fact that defensive battles are not always the result of the defender being the weaker party. The Union Army of the Potomac was larger and better equipped than was the Confederate Army of Northern Virginia. Union forces fought defensively at Gettysburg because, prior to that battle, the successive commanders of the Army of the Potomac had been consistently outgeneraled by Robert E. Lee, resulting in a crisis of confidence in the high command of the Army of the Potomac and a consequent determination by President Abraham Lincoln that that army should stand on the defensive for the time being. In the weeks leading up to the Battle of Gettysburg, Lincoln was still casting about for the right commander for the Army of the Potomac and for the right strategy for the war as a whole. By way of contrast, American forces fought defensively in the Battle of Midway in June 1942 because they were weaker than the enemy. At that time, Japan's navy was more powerful than the US Pacific fleet and the Japanese held the strategic initiative.

When searching for a Civil War comparison to the Battle of Midway, Chancellorsville seems the obvious first choice as an example of the victor reacting brilliantly in defense in order to defeat a larger attacking force. At Chancellorsville in May 1863, the Army of the Potomac, then under the command of Major General Joseph Hooker, advanced southwards toward Richmond with some 120,000 troops—more than twice what General Robert E. Lee had available in the Confederate Army of Northern Virginia to face Hooker. Although outnumbered two to one, Lee and his ablest field commander, Lieutenant General Thomas "Stonewall" Jackson, inflicted a brilliantly executed and very sharp defeat on the Union forces. Lee was always outnumbered, but prior to Gettysburg he had often been able to achieve "local" superiority. For instance, at Chancellorsville, the superior generalship of Lee and Jackson ensured that only a small fraction of the Union forces actually got into the battle while the entire Confederate force saw action. Chancellorsville was very much a defensive victory for the Confederacy. The Chancellorsville battle is also why General Hooker is better known today for lending his name as a synonym for the prostitutes he allowed to do a brisk business quite close to his army encampments than as a military commander.

General Lee would be outnumbered again at Gettysburg, but he nonetheless held the momentum and the initiative coming out of the Chancellorsville campaign. Lee's veterans in the Army of Northern Virginia seemed invincible and the movement of such a force into northern territory was perceived by President Lincoln, his cabinet, and Union General-in-Chief Henry W. Halleck not as a potential opportunity, but instead as a worst nightmare coming true. Lee had another reason besides holding the initiative for undertaking a second invasion of northern territory. He knew that time was not on the side of the Confederacy. From the moment Lee took command of the Army of Northern Virginia on June 1, 1862, he knew that aggressive attack, not static defense, was the only way for the Confederacy to prevail due to the much greater economic and manpower resources of the North.[2] In this, Lee faced the same conundrum that Admiral Yamamoto Isoroku, commander of the Japanese Combined Fleet and the architect of the Pearl Harbor and Midway operations, would confront seventy-nine years later

---

[2] Jeffry D. Wert. *The Sword of Lincoln: The Army of the Potomac.* (New York: Simon & Schuster, 2005): 95–96.

in the months leading up to the Battle of Midway. Namely, Yamamoto in 1942 knew that his superiority over the US Pacific Fleet was only temporary and that the industrial might of the United States would make it impossible for Japan to win a long war. Like Lee at Gettysburg, Yamamoto at Midway needed a knockout blow, and he needed it fast.

When writing, historians are often confronted with the problem that history almost always defies neat packaging. Thus, at the risk of fitting a square peg into a round hole, it seems worthwhile in a book about successful American military strategies to compare Gettysburg, not Chancellorsville, with the Battle of Midway as examples of defensive victories for the United States. Unlike Chancellorsville, the victorious forces at both Gettysburg and Midway were, as the United States Constitution intended, under the command of the president of the United States. Also, there are numerous parallels between the two battles. At Gettysburg and Midway, American forces received a new senior commander just before the fighting began. There are lingering allegations that American forces failed to follow up each victory with appropriate vigor. Both battles presented the respective American commanders with a similar dual responsibility.

At Midway in June 1942, Admiral Chester W. Nimitz, Commander-in-Chief of the US Pacific Fleet, was expected to both defend a piece of territory from invasion—the two islets that form Midway itself—and to defeat the attacking Japanese naval fleet. In the weeks leading up to Gettysburg, the Union Army of the Potomac was expected to defend the capital and drive back the invading rebels. As Lee's Army of Northern Virginia moved north in June 1863, General Hooker, prior to being relieved of the command of the Army of the Potomac on June 28, 1863, was told by Lincoln and Halleck simply to keep the Army of the Potomac between Lee and Washington, DC—very much a defensive stance for Lincoln and Halleck to adopt.[3] Those instructions were passed on essentially intact to Hooker's replacement at the head of the Army of the Potomac, Union Major General George Gordon Meade, who was expected to defend Washington, DC, and Baltimore while also defeating the invading Confederates. This was made clear to Meade in a message

---

[3] Brooks D. Simpson, ed. *The Civil War: The Third Year Told by Those Who Lived It.* (New York: Library of America, 2013): 285.

from General Halleck that accompanied President Lincoln's formal letter appointing Meade to the command of the Army of the Potomac. Halleck first promised not to meddle in Meade's business, but then immediately began to micromanage shamelessly:

> You will not be hampered by any minute instructions from these headquarters. Your army is free to act as you may deem proper under the circumstances as they arise. You will, however, keep in view the important fact that the Army of the Potomac is the covering army of Washington as well as the army of operation against the invading forces of the rebels. You will, therefore, maneuver and fight in such a manner as to cover the capital and also Baltimore, as far as circumstances will admit.[4]

Another parallel between the two battles is that while there would be limited offensives undertaken by other Confederate armies after Gettysburg, Lee's Army of Northern Virginia was generally forced, after July 1863, to take on a defensive posture for the remainder of the war,[5] as were the Japanese in the Pacific after the Battle of Midway. Also, at both Midway and Gettysburg, American forces had to "exorcise ghosts" from the past.[6] In June 1942, the United States Navy and the American public were still reeling from the shock of the Pearl Harbor attack that had taken place six months earlier and which had made the Japanese Navy appear to be invincible. Similarly, according to Jeffry D. Wert, "at Gettysburg, the Army of the Potomac confronted its past, a record of defeats unmatched by any American army since the American Revolution."[7]

Admiral Nimitz did not "want" to fight the battle of Midway. That is, while Nimitz never lacked for offensive spirit, he knew that he was

---

[4] Halleck to Meade. June 27, 1863. *The War of the Rebellion: A Compilation of the Official Records of the Union and Confederate Armies.* Series 1, Vol. 27, Part 1—Reports. Volume Editor—Lieutenant Colonel Robert N. Scott, Third U.S. Artillery. Washington, DC: Government Printing Office, 1889): 61.

[5] Wert, *The Sword of Lincoln*, 310–311, 316–319.

[6] See Wert, *The Sword of Lincoln*, 288 for the expression "exorcise ghosts" used in reference to the new and improved Army of the Potomac that fought at Gettysburg.

[7] Wert, *The Sword of Lincoln*, 304.

not ready for a major battle in June 1942. None of the new *Essex* class aircraft carriers were yet available, and the carriers he did have had been taking a beating. The fleet favorite USS *Lexington* had just been sunk by Japanese air attack during the Battle of the Coral Sea in May 1942. *Yorktown* had sustained bomb damage in the same battle and did not make it back to Pearl Harbor for repairs until May 27th. *Saratoga* spent most of 1942 on the sidelines having torpedo damage repaired. Indeed, *Saratoga* seemed to attract Japanese submarines, which resulted in the big carrier being torpedoed on January 11, 1942 and then, after lengthy repairs had been completed, again in late August 1942. Indeed, *Saratoga* was beginning to get a reputation as a bad luck ship. The aircraft carriers *Ranger* and *Wasp* were in the Atlantic.[8] Likewise, the new *South Dakota* and *North Carolina* class battleships were unavailable, either working up after their recent commissioning or already earmarked for other duty. The USS *Washington*, for instance, was operating with the British Home Fleet at the time of Midway. The battleships Nimitz did have access to in summer 1942 were too old and slow to operate with aircraft carriers. They were also highly vulnerable to air attack.[9] The older American battleships dated from World War I and the early 1920s, when the threat to ships from aircraft was not yet fully appreciated. Thus, the half dozen old American battleships that had not been at Pearl Harbor on December 7, 1941, and were thus technically ready for duty, were not yet bristling with anti-aircraft guns as the newer American battleships would be later in the war. Nimitz would fight at Midway without battleships. Because of the way the battle unfolded, that was actually not a serious disadvantage. The various Japanese fleets that sortied for the Battle of Midway deployed between them no fewer than eleven battleships, but the Japanese were defeated anyway. Midway was to be a carrier battle in which naval air power would reign supreme.

---

[8] Samuel Eliot Morison. *History of United States Naval Operations in World War II.* Vol. 4. *Coral Sea, Midway and Submarine Actions: May 1942–August 1942.* (Edison, NJ: Castle Books—by arrangement with Little, Brown and Company, Inc., 1949, 2001): 10–11 *n*, 81 text and note. Edward Stafford. *The Big E: The Story of the U.S.S. Enterprise.* (Annapolis, MD Naval Institute Press, 1962): 170, 251.

[9] Morison, *Coral Sea, Midway and Submarine Actions*, 82.

Courtesy: Library of Congress, Prints and Photographs Division. Negative Number LC-USZ62-15191

The American aircraft carrier USS *Yorktown*, moving from right to left in the photo, is struck by a Japanese aerial torpedo on June 4, 1942 during the Battle of Midway. The light puff of smoke is the explosion of the torpedo striking the hull. The dark puffs are bursting anti-aircraft shells. The ship is in a high speed turn to the right, which has caused the ship to lean left. Note the boiling water of the wake to the right in the photo.

Two years later the situation was quite different. By the summer of 1944, Nimitz and his Pacific fleet commanders were very eager for a fight, wanting nothing better than to bring the Japanese fleet into a decisive battle with the by then greatly augmented US Pacific Fleet. In 1944, the United States Navy was no longer reacting; it was *acting*. June 1942 was a very different time. During its first full year as a combatant, the United States was forced to fight a "come as you are" war. That is, the Americans had to get through 1942 primarily with the weapons that had been available at the time of Pearl Harbor.[10] Nothing exemplifies this more

---

[10] Craig L. Symonds. *The Battle of Midway.* (New York: Oxford University Press, 2011): 19–24.

poignantly and tragically than the fact that while the US Navy possessed an excellent dive bomber at Midway, the Douglas SBD Dauntless (indeed, the finest dive bomber in the world at that time), all of the American Navy pilots who flew torpedo planes from aircraft carriers at Midway had to make do with the hopelessly obsolete Douglas TBD Devastator. Lumbering along at just over one hundred miles per hour, barely enough speed to remain airborne, the Devastator had difficulty even in catching up to a fast surface ship that was steaming away from it (such as the Japanese aircraft carrier *Kaga*, which was chased by torpedo planes from the USS *Enterprise* approaching from astern on June 4, 1942) and had absolutely no chance of evading Japanese fighter planes. The agonizingly long, slow approach required for the *Enterprise* Devastators to get close enough to the *Kaga* to drop their torpedoes at Midway enabled Japanese fighter aircraft and anti-aircraft fire from Japanese ships to shoot down ten of the fourteen *Enterprise* torpedo planes.[11] Similarly, all fifteen of the torpedo planes in the *Hornet*'s Torpedo Squadron Eight were shot down while attacking the Japanese aircraft carriers at Midway. In all, thirty-seven out of forty-one American carrier-based torpedo planes were shot from the sky in the Battle of Midway without inflicting any damage on the Japanese fleet.[12]

In addition to possessing the superb SBD Dauntless dive bomber, the Americans did have in 1942 one other crucial weapons-related advantage that the Japanese lacked: radar. Had even one of the Japanese ships in the Midway battle, say the flagship carrier *Akagi*, been equipped with an air search radar and an operator who knew how to read and evaluate radar data, the results of the battle might have been quite different. Without radar, the Japanese were forced to rely solely on visual sightings to detect the incoming waves of attacking American aircraft. These American attacks, by carrier-based torpedo planes and by Midway-based marine, army air forces, and naval aircraft came in so fast and furiously from several different directions on the morning of June 4, 1942, that the

---

[11] Alvin Kernan. *The Unknown Battle of Midway: The Destruction of the American Torpedo Squadrons*. (New Haven, CT: Yale University Press, 2005): 155. Stafford, *The Big E*, 98–99.

[12] Symonds, *The Battle of Midway*, 287.

Japanese carrier striking fleet was forced temporarily into a situation in which the Japanese developed a dangerous sort of tunnel vision, focusing on beating off the immediate attacks and ceasing to think of what lay beyond the horizon. If just one of the ships in Vice Admiral Nagumo Chuichi's advanced carrier striking force had had an air search radar on its masthead and an operator trained to use it, the forty-nine *Enterprise* and *Yorktown* dive bombers that won the battle for the Americans by delivering mortal blows to three of the four Japanese aircraft carriers in a stunning ten minute attack that began at 10:20 a.m. (local time) on June 4, 1942, could have been detected and perhaps dealt with long before they got close enough to attack.[13]

New American ships and aircraft were in the pipeline, but were arriving in a trickle during 1942; a trickle that would become a flood in 1943. However, once intelligence data made it clear that the Japanese were preparing to invade Midway Island, Nimitz realized that he had to concentrate his limited resources at the decisive point. His dilemma in the spring of 1942 was that, as historians Jonathan Parshall and Anthony Tully have stated, in the months immediately following the Pearl Harbor attack, the US Pacific Fleet "had not yet recovered the ability to launch strategically meaningful operations of its own—it could only react to Japanese moves. The Japanese held the intiative everywhere."[14] In short, Nimitz needed to do to the Japanese at Midway exactly what Lee and Jackson had done to Hooker at Chancellorsville. Nimitz had to react to moves initiated by his enemy and he needed to concentrate his numerically inferior forces at the decisive point. This he did, and brilliantly, but Nimitz had first had to get past the formidable Admiral Ernest J. King, Commander-in-Chief, US Fleet and Chief of Naval Operations. King was obsessed with the South Pacific and had ordered Nimitz to keep two aircraft carriers south of the equator at all times. Nimitz knew he needed to bring all three of his available carriers, the *Enterprise*, *Yorktown*, and *Hornet*, back to Pearl Harbor to prepare for Midway. It was an uphill, but

---

[13] Jonathan Parshall and Anthony Tully. *Shattered Sword: The Untold Story of the Battle of Midway.* (Washington, DC: Potomac Books, 2005): 136, 186–188. Morison, *Coral Sea, Midway and Submarine Actions*, 83.

[14] Parshall and Tully, *Shattered Sword*, 22.

ultimately successful, struggle for Nimitz to get the necessary permission for this from King.[15]

The weeks leading up to the Battle of Gettysburg were equally tumultuous for the force that would do the defending there, the Union Army of the Potomac. The peevish General Hooker's resignation in late June 1863, which was eagerly accepted by President Lincoln, cleared the way for Lincoln to give the Army of the Potomac its first competent commander in the person of the aforementioned Major General George Gordon Meade just three days before the fighting began at Gettysburg. Nobody in the Union camp from President Lincoln down to the lowliest foot soldier had any confidence in Joe Hooker after Chancellorsville. Regarding the replacement of Hooker by Meade at the head of the Army of the Potomac, Union divisional commander Brigadier General Alpheus S. Williams pulled no punches when he wrote to his daughters on June 29, 1863, just before the curtain rose at Gettysburg that

> "For myself, I am rejoiced at the change of commanders. . . . I had no confidence in Hooker after Chancellorsville. I can say now, that if we had had a commander of even ordinary merit at that place the army of Jackson would have been annihilated. I cannot conceive of greater imbecility and weakness than characterized that campaign from the moment Hooker reached Chancellorsville and took command."[16]

The Union rank and file were equally enraged at Hooker's incompetence. So many Union troops had done nothing but march and countermarch during the Chancellorsville campaign without ever coming to grips with their enemy that the level of frustration amongst the infantry was at an

---

[15] Parshall and Tully, *Shattered Sword*, 93. Thomas B. Buell. *Master of Sea Power: A Biography of Admiral Ernest J. King.* (Annapolis, MD: Naval Institute Press, 1980): 199–202. E.B. Potter. *Nimitz.* (Annapolis, MD: Naval Institute Press, 1975, 1987): 76–86. John B. Lundstrom. *Black Shoe Carrier Admiral: Frank Jack Fletcher at Coral Sea, Midway, and Guadalcanal.* (Annapolis, MD: Naval Institute Press, 2006): 209–212, 215–216.

[16] Alpheus S. Williams to his Daughters, June 29, 1863, in Simpson, ed., *The Civil War: The Third Year*, 286.

all-time high after the battle. Indeed, Bruce Catton has written of the mindset of Union troops toward Hooker after Chancellorsville that "his soldiers were angrily inquiring how they had lost a battle in which so many of them had not even had a chance to fight."[17]

The change in command prior to the Battle of Midway was due to illness, not incompetence. Vice Admiral William F. Halsey, Jr. spent the period of the Battle of Midway in hospital at Pearl Harbor recovering from a severe skin rash. He was replaced for the Midway battle by Rear Admiral Raymond Spruance, who would command Task Force 16 which comprised the aircraft carriers USS *Enterprise* and USS *Hornet* as well as a handful of cruisers and destroyers. The overall American commander for the Battle of Midway would be Rear Admiral Frank Jack Fletcher whose flagship carrier, *Yorktown,* would lead Task Force 17. Neither Spruance nor Fletcher was a pilot, but Fletcher had experience commanding aircraft carriers in the Battle of the Coral Sea.

While there was an element of accidental collision involved when the two armies met at Gettysburg on July 1, 1863, the ground can be said to have been chosen far more by General Lee than by General Meade, the latter still settling in to his new billet. While he was new to the command of the entire Army of the Potomac, Meade was a highly experienced army officer. An 1835 West Point graduate, Meade had seen plenty of combat in the Civil War already as a divisional, and then a corps, commander. Nevertheless, the timing and circumstances surrounding his promotion to command the entire Army of the Potomac must have come as a rude shock to Meade. General Lee had invaded the north in the summer of 1863 and knew he would have to fight a battle as a result. Meade, on the other hand, had had only days to get used to being an army commander instead of a corps commander. Meade's brief was far more defensive in nature—to drive back the invading force; or, at the very least, to keep Lee away from Washington, DC.

Lee was outnumbered again at Gettysburg. Although the exact troop totals involved at Gettysburg are still subject to some debate, it seems that there were approximately 75,000 Confederate troops involved in the

---

[17] Bruce Catton. *This Hallowed Ground: The Story of the Union Side of the Civil War.* (Garden City, NY: Doubleday, 1956): 243.

battle, while the Union Army of the Potomac deployed from 83,000–88,000 troops at Gettysburg.[18] The difference at Gettysburg, however, was that there would be no local superiority for Lee. A former surveyor who had an excellent eye for terrain (a talent shared by his subordinates Buford, Reynolds, and Hancock), General Meade also saw to it that Lee would have to fight the entire Army of the Potomac at Gettysburg, not just part of it. No Union soldier who was at Gettysburg and survived ever needed to complain afterwards that his services had not been utilized to the full.

Fighting defensively allows one to use internal and thus shorter lines of communication while the enemy's lines of communication are lengthy and vulnerable. Even if the Japanese had succeeded in capturing Midway Island in the summer of 1942, they would have found it extremely difficult to hold indefinitely. The supply lines to and from a Japanese-occupied Midway would have been very long and very vulnerable to American naval and air attack. For the Americans on the other hand fighting at, and in the waters around, Midway was relatively easy from a logistical standpoint. Technically part of the Hawaiian chain, Midway lies 1,000 miles northwest of Oahu—a relatively short distance given the immense size of the Pacific theater as a whole. The Japanese would be fighting far from home because, while holding the initiative is highly advantageous in war, it does have its drawbacks. One of these is that you have to go out and find the enemy in order to bring him to battle. Later in the war, when the Americans took the offensive in the Central Pacific, they would be faced with the same problem of operating far from home. The Americans, however, had done a much better job between the wars of preparing for this eventuality than had the Japanese. Many historians have noted that the Americans relied heavily on the "Orange" plans formulated at the US Naval War College in Newport, Rhode Island during the 1920s for guidance when fighting the war in the Pacific twenty years later. The Orange Plans accepted as gospel that in case of war against Japan, the United States would have to seize forward island operating bases in the western

---

[18] Simpson, ed., *The Civil War: The Third Year*, 292. *Encyclopædia Britannica Online*, s.v. "Battle of Gettysburg". http://www.britannica.com/EBchecked/topic/232210/Battle-of-Gettysburg. Accessed October 17, 2013.

Pacific.[19] What is less well known is that the "fortification clause" of the Washington Naval Treaty of 1922 prohibited the United States from building elaborate defensive fortifications on its prewar island possessions in the Pacific, such as Wake or Guam. Historian John T. Kuehn has pointed out that the fortification clause caused American naval planners in the 1920s to develop elaborate and ingenious methods to give the United States Navy an extremely high level of mobility through such techniques as the construction of floating dry docks which could be, and indeed were, towed out to forward bases in the Central Pacific such as Eniwetok or Ulithi during the war. This meant that an enormous *Iowa* class battleship could, during World War II, have its hull scraped, painted, and perhaps even have a propeller replaced without having to leave the combat zone in the western Pacific to return to Pearl Harbor.[20] Other means by which the US Pacific fleet was given long "legs" during the war included that the *Fletcher* class of destroyers were designed to be extremely long-range vessels for ships of their size. The Americans also saw to it that there were plenty of American tankers wandering the far reaches of the Pacific during the war so as to be available when American ships did have to refuel. The Americans refueled their warships at sea far more frequently and with far greater success than did any other navy in World War II.

At Gettysburg, General Meade benefited greatly from fighting on internal lines of communication in both a macro and a micro sense. Meade fought in the North. Lee had to come and get him. Also, by the morning of July 2, 1863, the second day of the battle, the Federals were concentrated on Cemetery Ridge south of the village of Gettysburg. This gave the Union forces a very compact area within which to operate. Knowing he was in an excellent defensive position, Meade wisely waited for Lee to attack. Lee's Confederate forces on the other hand were spread out along a lengthy perimeter. Lee's army was smaller than that of his

---

[19] David Rigby. *Allied Master Strategists: The Combined Chiefs of Staff in World War II.* (Annapolis, MD: Naval Institute Press, 2012): 79–80.

[20] John T. Kuehn. *Agents of Innovation: The General Board and the Design of the Fleet that Defeated the Japanese Navy.* (Annapolis, MD: Naval Institute Press, 2008): 127–143.

opponent's and thus Lee could not afford to be stretched so thin. Meade was able to operate on interior lines of communication both in the sense that he was much closer to his bases of supply than was Lee, and in that within the battlefield Meade was able to shift reinforcements easily from one part of the Union position to another.[21]

Admiral Nimitz also benefited, in ways large and small, from internal lines of communication during the Midway battle. Nimitz concentrated all of his carrier strength at Midway to face Japanese Vice Admiral Nagumo Chuichi's aircraft carrier striking force and American pilots basically ignored any target except the all-important Japanese aircraft carriers. Like Meade at Gettysburg, Nimitz at Midway was fighting close to home, much closer to home than American forces had been during the Battle of the Coral Sea a month prior to Midway. The Japanese carrier striking force under Nagumo had to come all the way across the Pacific to get at the Americans. Midway is close enough to Oahu that the two places were connected by a submarine cable which gave the Americans a completely secure means of communication. That submarine cable between Midway and Oahu was a critical advantage for the Americans prior to the Midway battle. Vital orders regarding dispositions and supplies were sent via the cable without increasing the volume of radio traffic emanating from Midway. The Japanese had not had much success cracking American codes, but a major increase in the volume of radio traffic coming from Midway itself would have been a dead giveaway to the Japanese that the Americans were aware that "something was up."[22]

Meade and Nimitz each, in their respective battles, ignored what was unimportant. Meade was not bothered by the fact that the Confederates occupied the village of Gettysburg itself on July 1, 1863. He, or rather his subordinates Brigadier General John Buford and Major General John Reynolds, realized on the first day at Gettysburg that until the entire Army of the Potomac could arrive, the temporarily outnumbered Union troops would have to abandon the village of Gettysburg and fall back on

---

[21] Catton, *This Hallowed Ground*, 252. Douglas Southall Freeman. *R.E. Lee: A Biography*. Vol. 3. (New York: Charles Scribner's Sons, 1935): 148–149.

[22] Morison, *Coral Sea, Midway, and Submarine Actions*, 71, 83.

the high ground just south of the town.[23] This high ground, centered on Cemetery Ridge, was the key to the entire battle. In Buford and Reynolds, Meade was served by talented subordinates. Meade himself did not arrive at Gettysburg until late in the evening on July 1. Major General Winfield Scott Hancock, commander of the Union Second Corps, would also prove to be a tower of strength for Meade at Gettysburg.

The Japanese attack on the Aleutian Islands in June 1942 was undertaken concurrently with the Midway battle. To counter the Japanese northern strike, Nimitz assigned Rear Admiral Robert A. Theobald a modest force of cruisers and destroyers with which to attempt to break up the Japanese landings in the Aleutians. Admiral Theobald never got close enough to the Japanese northern force to engage in a surface action, and the Japanese did occupy two islands in the Aleutians—Attu and Kiska. Theobald had no aircraft carriers, but he did have five cruisers and thirteen destroyers; the latter arrayed in two groups—of four and nine, respectively. Perhaps those destroyers would have been put to better use if they had been given to Fletcher and Spruance. Had a few extra destroyers been available to guard the stricken carrier *Yorktown*, which had absorbed three bomb and two torpedo hits in the Japanese attacks on June 4, perhaps the Japanese submarine *I-168* would not have been able to get close enough on June 6, 1942 to fire the torpedoes that finished the *Yorktown* off.[24] Nimitz did reserve his three precious aircraft carriers for the main battle, which he knew would occur near Midway.

Not only did Nimitz succeed in concentrating almost all of his forces at the decisive point, he also succeeded in inculcating into the minds of his pilots what was vital and what was not. The American pilots focused exclusively on the Japanese aircraft carriers. The Japanese employed more than one hundred ships in the Midway and Aleutians operations. The Americans sank only five of them. While the Americans did not sink a lot of enemy ships at Midway, they did sink the *right* ships—the four big aircraft carriers and a heavy cruiser. By surgically removing the heart of the Japanese fleet by sinking the four carriers, the Americans forced

---

[23] Catton, *This Hallowed Ground*, 250–252.

[24] Morison, *Coral Sea, Midway and Submarine Actions*, 155–156, 166–167, 173–174. Symonds, *The Battle of Midway*, 201–205, 357–358.

the "extremities," meaning all of the dozens of other Japanese warships Admiral Yamamoto had deployed all over the Pacific, to withdraw.[25]

An intelligence failure crippled both Lee at Gettysburg and the Japanese at Midway. In June 1863, in the weeks leading up to Gettysburg, the brilliant cavalry commander Major General Jeb Stuart, who was General Lee's "eyes," lost track of the Army of the Potomac. Stuart compounded this difficulty by attempting to ride all the way around the Union force, which kept him out of touch with Lee in the critical week prior to the battle.[26] Similarly, the Japanese had no idea that three American aircraft carriers were lying in wait for them northeast of Midway in June 1942.

During Stuart's absence, it appears that the first hard intelligence Robert E. Lee had that hinted at the true location of the bulk of the Army of the Potomac came from a Confederate spy who informed Lieutenant General James Longstreet and General Lee on June 28, 1863, just a few hours after General Meade had learned that he (Meade) was now an army commander, that the Federals were already across the Potomac and heading north. It appears to have come as quite a shock for Lee to learn that the Union high command had discerned his (Lee's) intentions and had reacted so swiftly.[27] Rapid and logical action was not something that Lee had come to expect from his enemy. In all fairness, much of the credit for getting the Union Army moving north so quickly must be given to General Hooker. The move north was well underway by the time Meade was appointed to succeed Hooker. The Army of the Potomac was on the "inside," moving north but remaining between Lee and Washington, DC. Consequently, as both armies converged on Gettysburg, the southerners actually approached the town from the north and the east, while the northerners approached Gettysburg from the southeast.

---

[25] Barrie Pitt, Consultant Ed., *The Military History of World War II.* (NY: The Military Press, 1986): 107—see caption accompanying image of SBD dive bomber.

[26] Bruce Catton. *The Army of the Potomac: Glory Road.* (Garden City, NY: Doubleday, 1952): 253–254. H.W. Brands. *The Man Who Saved the Union: Ulysses Grant in War and Peace.* (New York: Doubleday, 2012): 325.

[27] Wert, *The Sword of Lincoln,* 272–273.

The extreme ambivalence with which the Japanese approached the chore of launching search planes as the Japanese carrier striking force neared Midway shows clearly that the Japanese were not expecting company.[28] Japanese naval doctrine in World War II stipulated that search duties were to be carried out by cruiser floatplanes that were launched from catapults, thus leaving all the carrier aircraft available for striking, not searching. Indeed, two of the heavy cruisers Japan built in the 1930s, *Tone* and *Chikuma*, were designed with this specific purpose in mind. Pound for pound, this pair may have been the finest cruisers fielded by any navy during World War II. Each retained the full firepower expected of a heavy cruiser; eight 8-inch guns, but the four twin 8-inch turrets were all concentrated on an elongated forward deck. This meant that some 200 feet of deck space behind the superstructure could be devoted entirely to the handling of aircraft. The result was two cruisers ideally suited for scouting purposes while retaining plenty of offensive firepower. The afterdeck on *Tone* and *Chikuma*, respectively, was covered with an elaborate system of rails on which floatplanes could be moved on dollies. There was on each ship an enormous crane amidships for pulling aircraft around on deck, hoisting them onto the two catapults each ship carried and, most importantly, lifting floatplanes out of the water once they had landed alongside after a mission.[29] The overall length of each of these fine ships, 661 feet, made each of them almost as long as an American *South Dakota* class battleship.

The scouting advantage delivered to the Japanese fleet by *Tone* and *Chikuma* was not a result of carrying huge numbers of aircraft. Each of these two cruisers normally carried five floatplanes, while each of the other sixteen heavy cruisers in the Imperial Japanese Navy, despite having a more conventional fore and aft layout of the 8-inch gun turrets, was able to carry at least two and often three floatplanes. Rather, the clear deck space, the rails, and the giant crane were supposed to enable *Tone* and *Chikuma* to launch and recover aircraft much faster than any other cruiser. Things did not work out quite that way at Midway, at least for

---

[28] Symonds, *The Battle of Midway*, 222.

[29] Mark Stille. *Imperial Japanese Navy Heavy Cruisers 1941–45*. (Long Island City, NY: Osprey Publishing, 2011): 40–44. Parshall and Tully, *Shattered Sword*, 18.

Tone. The launch of the No. 4 search plane from *Tone,* the plane that first spotted American surface forces, was delayed by a half hour on the morning of June 4, 1942. Apparently, the pilot altered his search plan to make up for the delay by shortening his outward search leg. Thus, the delay in launching may not have actually delayed the warning Nagumo received of the presence of American surface ships.[30] However, the *attitude* of that pilot, Petty Officer Amari Hiroshi, did make a difference in that his contact reports were maddeningly vague and slow in coming.[31] At 7:28 a.m. (local time), Amari reported that he had sighted ten American surface ships. Forty minutes later, he was more specific, stating that the American ships were cruisers and destroyers. Then, at 8:20 a.m., almost a full hour after his initial contact report, Amari stunned Nagumo by reporting that one of the American ships was a carrier.[32]

Every historian who has written about the Battle of Midway agrees that this report altered the entire landscape of the battle by throwing Nagumo into a crisis. Should he launch a partial strike against the American ships with those dive bombers and torpedo planes that had already been loaded with anti-shipping ordnance? Should he instead allow his Combat Air Patrol (CAP) fighters and the strike aircraft returning after bombing Midway Island to land first and then rearm, refuel, and launch everything except his CAP fighters for a massive strike against the American ships? Historians have noted that Nagumo's peace of mind during this period was not improved by the fact that while he was trying to decide what to do about the American ships he had to listen to the deafening roar of anti-aircraft fire as his own ships, under persistent attack by American Midway-based aircraft, were forced to undertake wild evasive maneuvers.[33]

[30] Symonds, *The Battle of Midway,* 224, 238–239.

[31] Parshall and Tully, *Shattered Sword,* 146–148, 198. Morison, *Coral Sea, Midway and Submarine Actions,* 106–110.

[32] Parshall and Tully, *Shattered Sword,* 183–184. Morison, *Coral Sea, Midway and Submarine Actions,* 106–110.

[33] See, for instance Parshall and Tully, *Shattered Sword,* 186–188.

Amongst the other Japanese failures in the area of reconnaissance was that Japanese search planes flew too high at Midway, making it easy for cloud cover to obscure targets. This is apparently the only reason that a *Chikuma* search plane failed to sight the Americans at Midway. American search aircraft at Midway flew below the clouds, which contributed to American success in spotting Japanese ships.[34] The real problem for the Japanese in regard to reconnaissance at Midway, however, seems to have been hubris. Nagumo should have had two dozen aircraft out searching continuously for the enemy once he got to within 500 miles of Midway Island, not the half dozen or so airplanes that he did get out. Samuel Eliot Morison was undoubtedly correct when he described Nagumo's search plane operations on the morning of June 4, 1942 as "almost perfunctory."[35] Exactly what search pattern Amari flew that day and why his reports were so vague and tardy are issues still being debated by historians;[36] but it is safe to say that Nagumo should have had four or five search aircraft covering such a vital quadrant—almost due east of the Japanese carriers—not just Amari alone. Indeed, Nagumo would have benefited by sending a few dive bombers out to search this area instead of just one essentially unarmed cruiser floatplane. The Americans often used carrier-based dive bombers for scouting purposes, and the US Navy had a wise regulation during the war that any American dive bomber taking off anywhere in the Pacific theater at any time for whatever purpose (even a training mission in the Hawaiian Islands) had to be carrying at least one 500 lb. bomb so that a pilot would never find himself over a target without ordnance. Thus, during the Battle of the Santa Cruz Islands on October 26, 1942, that policy paid off when two American SBD dive bombers from the carrier *Enterprise* that had been searching for a Japanese carrier force were able to home in on a contact report from another pair of *Enterprise* SBDs and make an attack in which both planes scored direct hits with 500 lb. bombs on the Japanese carrier *Zuiho*—even though their primary purpose that day had been scouting, not attacking.

---

[34] Symonds, *The Battle of Midway*, 224.

[35] Morison, *Coral Sea, Midway and Submarine Actions*, 106.

[36] Parshall and Tully, *Shattered Sword*, 146–148, 183–184.

Unfortunately for the Americans on this occasion, the bombs struck near the stern and *Zuiho* had not been in the process of arming and fueling her planes. Thus, there was no massive secondary explosion of the type that had destroyed the four Japanese carriers sunk at Midway.[37]

It should be noted, however, that American aerial reconnaissance during the Midway battle was far from perfect. Admiral Fletcher did use some of his dive bombers for scouting purposes, and it would be a *Yorktown* dive bomber that on the afternoon of June 4, 1942 located the elusive *Hiryu*, the only Japanese carrier to escape the attack by American dive bombers that morning. Admiral Spruance, who emerged as the American hero of the Midway battle, had an attitude toward searching that can only be described as laggard. Even Spruance's biographer Thomas B. Buell has found it to be more than passing strange that on June 4, 1942 Spruance did not use any of his dive bombers or cruiser floatplanes to search for the Japanese.[38] Fletcher located the *Hiryu*, and it had been a Midway-based PBY Catalina that had located the Japanese striking force early on the morning of June 4. (Unlike Spruance, Fletcher at least had had dive bombers out searching for the Japanese when that PBY contact report came in.) Regarding the lackadaisical attitude Spruance showed regarding air searches, Buell concludes that "apparently he [Spruance] was content to wait for someone else to find the enemy."[39] Fletcher's diligence in searching actively for the Japanese is one reason some historians feel that Admiral Fletcher does not get enough of the credit for the American victory at Midway.

In the days leading up to the Battle of Gettysburg, General Lee was also unaware of his enemy's exact whereabouts, largely due to the week-long absence of Jeb Stuart and his cavalry. Just as the Japanese did not seem to believe it was possible in June 1942 that the Americans had broken enough Japanese code to know that an attack against Midway was impending and thus might be preparing to ambush the Japanese

---

[37] Stafford, *The Big E*, 119–120, 178–182.

[38] Thomas B. Buell. *The Quiet Warrior: A Biography of Admiral Raymond A. Spruance.* (Annapolis, MD: Naval Institute Press, 1974, 1987): 144, 152–153, 156.

[39] Buell, *The Quiet Warrior*, 152.

striking force, Lee does not seem to have thought it possible in late June 1863 that the Federals would be able to concentrate the entire Army of the Potomac in southern Pennsylvania in the near future. While Nagumo should have used more search planes in 1942, perhaps Lee would have been wiser in 1863 on his move northwards to have halted on the south bank of the Potomac river and waited until Jeb Stuart returned and could tell Lee exactly where the Federals were, and in what strength. Lee apparently had harsh words for Stuart when the young cavalry general finally reached Gettysburg on July 2, 1863.[40] However, Lee's contempt for his enemy's abilities was the more likely culprit in explaining why Lee found himself outnumbered and occupying the low ground instead of the high ground at Gettysburg. In the habit of winning, Lee seems to have grown somewhat complacent in that he did not seem to feel that he needed accurate intelligence data heading into the Gettysburg battle. Lee's behavior in this regard is similar to the way in which he broke his own rule by abandoning the tactics of maneuver at which he excelled and instead settled for frontal assaults once the battle began. According to Confederate Major General Henry Heth, heading into the Gettysburg campaign "General Lee believed that the Army of Northern Virginia, as it then existed, could accomplish anything."[41]

The Japanese made several other errors at Midway to compound their deficient intelligence gathering and inadequate aerial reconnaissance. These errors had one thing in common: the Japanese were unable to concentrate their vastly superior forces at the decisive point at the decisive time. The simultaneous Japanese attack in the Aleutian Islands did not distract Nimitz, who decided based on code decrypts that this was a feint—although historians Jonathan Parshall and Anthony Tully have recently challenged the idea that the Aleutians operation was intended by the Japanese to be a diversion.[42] Even Samuel Eliot Morison, writing in 1949, suggested that part of the Japanese motivation to land troops in the Aleutians went beyond diversion into being an effort to block a potential

---

[40] Wert, *The Sword of Lincoln*, 300–301.

[41] Heth, as quoted in Freeman, *R.E. Lee: A Biography*, Vol. 3, 23.

[42] Parshall and Tully. *Shattered Sword*, 43–44.

northern invasion route that the United States might use to advance towards Japan.[43] The fact that Admiral Yamamoto kept the main body of his fleet 300 miles behind Admiral Nagumo's advanced carrier striking force meant that Yamamoto could not hope to be on the scene until after the battle had already been decided. Most importantly, overconfidence had convinced Yamamoto and Nagumo that the Japanese carrier striking force could sail without its two newest units, the modern carriers *Shokaku* and *Zuikaku*, which were back in Japan undergoing repairs and replacing a depleted air group, respectively, as a result of the Battle of the Coral Sea. Nagumo's striking power was thus reduced by one third. Having six aircraft carriers at Midway instead of only four would undoubtedly have made a big difference for the Japanese. Historians Jonathan Parshall and Anthony Tully have demonstrated that if the Japanese had really tried, they could have found enough replacement aircraft and pilots to make *Zuikaku* operational in time to participate in the Midway battle.[44] Doing so would have given the Japanese five carriers at Midway to the American three. Indeed, Parshall and Tully state that at Midway the Japanese, by scattering their fleets; by sending the aircraft carriers *Ryujo* and *Junyo* to the Aleutians and assigning the carrier *Zuiho* to the Midway invasion fleet instead of giving those hulls to Nagumo;[45] and especially by failing to make *Zuikaku* ready for battle, had recklessly abandoned the doctrine of "operational mass" that had served them so well in the Pearl Harbor attack. They note that on December 7, 1941 and later in the Indian Ocean, the Japanese Navy, by keeping its six large carriers together to operate as a unit, "had presented its opponents with an insuperable tactical problem. Japan had won not because of its racial superiority, or *Yamato damashii*, but because the Imperial Navy brought *more* flight decks and *more* aircraft

---

[43] Morison, *Coral Sea, Midway and Submarine Actions*, 161–162, 181.

[44] Parshall and Tully, *Shattered Sword*, 65–66. See also Symonds, *The Battle of Midway*, 181, 199.

[45] Parshall and Tully seem somewhat torn as to whether or not *Ryujo* and *Junyo*, because they were small and slow, would have been of any real use to Nagumo. For their views on that question and on the placement of the more valuable *Zuiho*, see *Shattered Sword*, 46–47, 49, 270, 418–419.

to the point of contact than its enemies could muster in return."[46] The Japanese would forget this important lesson at Midway.

The fact that there would only be four large Japanese aircraft carriers in the vicinity of Midway Island gave Admiral Nimitz a chance to win using his three available American aircraft carriers.[47] Even if the Aleutians were not a diversion, but a primary Japanese strategic objective, the fact remains that the Aleutians operation drew away two Japanese aircraft carriers that would be unable to support Nagumo when the Battle of Midway suddenly turned against the Japanese when American dive bombers from *Enterprise* and *Yorktown* struck at 10:20 a.m. (local time) on the morning of June 4, 1942. Also, if the Japanese had not committed *Shokaku* and *Zuikaku* to support the Port Moresby invasion operation in May 1942, both of those fine carriers would have been available for the Midway battle. In explaining the Battle of Midway, its Coral Sea preliminary, and the Aleutians adventure, Parshall and Tully state that "the [Japanese] Navy ultimately ended up committing its carriers in support of more operations than they could handle, with disastrous consequences. The circuitous path by which it shouldered these disparate and contradictory commitments was a misadventure of truly epic proportions."[48]

With the exception of the Japanese Army's abortive drive on Imphal in India in 1944—a sideshow that ended disastrously for Japan, Midway was the last time that the Japanese chose the time and the place for a battle in World War II. After Midway, it would be the United States that decided when and where to fight the Japanese. The war in the Pacific would thenceforth be fought on an American schedule.

If the Japanese were overconfident heading into the Midway battle, it was because Japan's navy had swept everything before it in the six months since the Pearl Harbor attack. Nagumo's carriers had raided the Indian Ocean in the late winter and spring of 1942. Nagumo reminded the people of Australia just how close the war now was to them by using his carrier-based aircraft to bomb the port of Darwin in northern Australia

---

[46] Parshall and Tully, *Shattered Sword*, 405.

[47] Parshall and Tully, *Shattered Sword*, 405–406.

[48] Parshall and Tully, *Shattered Sword*, 26.

on February 19, 1942. The Japanese also won notable victories against American, British, Dutch, and Australian (ABDA) naval forces at this time. During the Battle of the Java Sea in late February 1942 and a sweep through the Indian Ocean a month later, Nagumo's carrier pilots and their escorting cruisers sank the ancient American aircraft carrier USS *Langley*, the equally antiquated British carrier HMS *Hermes*, the Allied heavy cruisers HMAS *Perth*, HMS *Exeter*, HMS *Cornwall*, HMS *Dorsetshire*, and USS *Houston*, as well as the Dutch light cruiser *De Ruyter*. The Japanese also destroyed upwards of two dozen Allied merchant ships in the Indian Ocean at this time.[49]

If the Japanese were overconfident prior to Midway, Robert E. Lee seems to have been overconfident going into battle at Gettysburg. Lee's overconfidence was nowhere more apparent than in the overall fact that he accepted an unfavorable tactical situation. By the morning of July 2, 1863, the second day of the Battle of Gettysburg, Meade's Union forces had occupied the high ground south of the town of Gettysburg—Cemetery Ridge, Culp's Hill, and the Round Tops. Lee did assail Meade's flanks, but he attacked those flanks essentially head on instead of trying to get around them. Confederate troops vigorously attacked the Little Round Top on the Union left (on July 2) and Culp's Hill (on July 2 and again the next morning) which anchored the Union right wing, respectively. After the failure of these flank attacks, Lee settled on the idea of a frontal assault on the Union center on July 3—Pickett's famous charge. For all its heroism and grandeur, however, the reality was that Pickett's charge meant that, at Gettysburg, Lee made the same mistake that Union Major General Ambrose Burnside had made at Fredericksburg; namely Lee chose to make a frontal assault uphill against a well-entrenched enemy in broad daylight.[50] Like the Japanese at Midway, Lee at Gettysburg seemed to have forgotten everything his previous victories had taught him. You do not charge uphill over open ground against a well-entrenched and positioned enemy. Instead you try to make the enemy employ that tactic against you so you can slaughter his forces.

---

[49] Pitt, Consultant Ed. *The Military History of World War II*, 95.

[50] Catton, *Glory Road*, 286.

If one stands today on the Gettysburg battlefield near the equestrian statue built where Lee is thought to have stood while watching the events of the third of July unfold and looks across the battlefield to the Union position, it becomes apparent that Cemetery Ridge is what a surveyor would call a "low gradient" incline—the ridge rises gently, not steeply. Perhaps the gradual nature of the incline helped Lee decide that the ridge could be stormed. Nevertheless, Pickett's division would have to cover a mile of gently rising and very open ground just to reach the Federal position. It seems incredible that an officer of Lee's brilliance actually believed that his troops could succeed in taking such a position using the same tactics that had led to disaster for Burnside at Fredericksburg.

Meade was no Burnside, who could be hash-housed and shouldered aside. Meade wisely chose to stand on the defensive and absorb Lee's frontal assaults, first on each Union flank and then in the center. Lee's tactics at Gettysburg were somewhat like the unsuccessful tactics employed by Napoleon at Waterloo on June 18, 1815 where Napoleon too discarded the tactics of maneuver that had served him so well in the past and opted for a series of frontal assaults against Wellington's center—which, as at Gettysburg forty-eight years later, was on a hilltop. Also as at Waterloo, Meade at Gettysburg employed Wellington's "reverse slope" technique of keeping his reserves sheltered on the back side of Cemetery Ridge—although Meade's employment of this tactic does not appear to have had quite as much finesse as when Wellington employed the tactic.[51] Historian Bruce Catton describes what the back side of Cemetery Ridge looked like on the evening of July 2, 1863: "Behind the ridge there was a great tangle of men and animals and equipment, jammed together like the debris of a hopelessly defeated army. On the hillsides, beaten regiments and brigades tried to reassemble."[52]

Lee's troops had manhandled Union forces on so many previous occasions that he and his subordinate commanders had no reason to

---

[51] Andrew Roberts. *Waterloo, June 18, 1815: The Battle for Modern Europe.* (New York: Harper Perennial, 2005): *passim.*

[52] Catton, *Glory Road,* 301.

expect that Gettysburg would be any different.[53] Perhaps hubris explains why Lee's tactics at Gettysburg were so much less imaginative than his plan of campaign had been earlier at Chancellorsville. Why waste time with sophisticated tactics if one's enemy is incompetent? Lee did not pay enough attention to the Union flanks—although the Union troops on the Little Round Top on the Union left flank who were being badly shot up by the Confederates who got into the "Devil's Den" on July 2 probably did not think there was anything half-hearted about the rebel attacks on the flanks. Nevertheless, Gettysburg is not a particularly large battlefield. Why was an army—Lee's—which was famous for its ability to move quickly, never able to get around behind Meade? Indeed, at Gettysburg, Lee seems to have ignored repeated pleas from his second in command, Lieutenant General James Longstreet, that Confederate forces make more of an effort to outflank the Federals instead of under-taking frontal assaults.[54] As we have seen, Confederate troops did attack the flanks; hitting both Union flanks hard on July 2 and sending 9,000 rebel troops against Culp's Hill, which anchored the Union right, on the morning of July 3, the final day of the Battle of Gettysburg.[55] However, these were still essentially frontal assaults against parts of the Union line which Lee had hoped might be weakly held rather than attempts to actually get around the flanks of the Federals. Wooded terrain certainly helped the Federals to protect their respective flanks. There were trees on and behind the Round Tops on the Union left. Culp's Hill, anchoring the Union right was also wooded in 1863, perhaps even more densely than were the Round Tops. There exist many photographs of the Gettysburg battlefield that were taken in the immediate aftermath of the battle by

---

[53] Diary of (British) Lieutenant Colonel Arthur James Lyon Freemantle (who was with Lee's army at Gettysburg as an observer), July 4, 1863, in Simpson, ed., *The Civil War: The Third Year*, 295, 306.

[54] Wert, *The Sword of Lincoln*, 285, 296–297. Bruce Catton. *The Centennial History of the Civil War*. Vol. 3. *Never Call Retreat*. (Garden City, NY: Doubleday, 1965): 184–185, 187. Freeman, *R.E. Lee*, Vol. 3, 73–76, 87–89, 107.

[55] Wert, *The Sword of Lincoln*, 287–290, 293, 295–296.

photographers such as Mathew Brady.[56] However, photographs of the Gettysburg region from *before* the battle for comparison are much harder to come by. A great many trees in and around the Union positions were knocked down by Confederate artillery fire. Thus, it is difficult to say based on the Brady post-battle photographs just how thick the woods were in areas like the Round Tops and Culp's Hill during the battle. Most likely, those wooded areas were probably at least as dense when the battle began as they are today. However, it seems safe to say that none of the wooded acreage around Gettysburg in July 1863 could possibly have been denser than the forests through which Stonewall Jackson's troops had maneuvered and attacked with relative ease at Chancellorsville. Thus, the existence of wooded terrain does not fully explain the Confederate failure to get around behind Meade.[57] Of course the Round Tops and Culp's Hill were, and are, high ground, but that was all the more reason for Lee to try to get around them rather than sending his troops up such murderous slopes. Lee had been willing to use a daring flanking movement at Chancellorsville, but then he had had Stonewall Jackson to carry out the maneuver. That Jackson was killed at Chancellorsville was a terrible loss for the Confederacy. At Gettysburg, Lee does not seem to have had had enough confidence in General Longstreet's ability to succeed in a maneuver similar to what Jackson had done at Chancellorsville. Longstreet was learning the hard way just how deeply symbiotic had been the working relationship between General Lee and Stonewall Jackson. Lee had treated Jackson as an equal, but as far as Lee was concerned, General Longstreet was strictly a subordinate.[58]

Confederate Major General John B. Hood apparently also became convinced that the Union left flank could be turned instead of assaulted

---

[56] For an excellent series of immediate post-battle photos of the Gettysburg battle-field, see Henry W. Elson (text); James Barnes (captions). *The Photographic History of the Civil War in Ten Volumes*. Vol. 2. *Two Years of Grim War*. (New York: The Review of Reviews Co., 1911): 227–267.

[57] Wert, *The Sword of Lincoln*, 285–290, 295–297.

[58] Catton, *Never Call Retreat*, 184–185.

head on. Hood's division was on the far right of the Confederate lines, and it would be Hood's men who suffered the bulk of the Confederate casualties in the Confederate attack against the Little Round Top on July 2. Lee's biographer Douglas Southall Freeman claims that by the time Hood made his concerns known to Longstreet, the latter was in such a blue funk because his earlier requests to Lee that he, Longstreet, be allowed to outflank, rather than attack, the Union right had been rejected that Longstreet had now done an about face. Longstreet, says Freeman, ordered Hood to follow Lee's orders to the letter—not because Longstreet believed they were good orders but because Longstreet supposedly wanted to teach Lee a lesson for not heeding Longstreet's earlier cautions. This view should be taken with a grain of salt. Freeman's early biography of Lee did win a Pulitzer prize in 1935. However, Freeman's account of the Battle of Gettysburg places a great deal of the blame for the Confederate defeat, perhaps too much, on Longstreet. It does seem true that General Longstreet was not at his best during that battle, but he may not have been quite as uncooperative, moody, rebellious, and rum-soaked as Freeman makes him out to have been.[59]

By contrast, General Meade had great faith in his subordinates. Since Meade himself did not arrive at Gettysburg until late in the evening of July 1, his subordinates directed the battle for him on the first day—and they directed it well. Meade had thought that the coming battle would be fought in northern Maryland, but he sent Major General John F. Reynolds and the Union First Corps to Gettysburg to have a look around as a precaution. What Reynolds found at Gettysburg on July 1, of course, were Confederate troops—lots of them. It would be Reynolds (who was tragically killed that day) and Union Cavalry commander Brigadier General John Buford who would set the scene for Meade. Unlike Lee, who does not seem to have fully trusted Longstreet, Meade allowed Reynolds to decide whether or not Meade should bring the entire army to Gettysburg. Reynolds quickly decided on the morning of July 1 that this should be done, and when the courier Reynolds sent reached Meade with the news that Lee was concentrating at Gettysburg,

---

[59] Freeman, *R.E. Lee*, Vol. 3, 73–76, 87–89, 92, 94–95, 97–99, 132.

Meade immediately set his entire army moving towards Gettysburg.[60] That is, upon finding out where the enemy was, Meade moved immediately to get at him. General Hooker never would have done that. As Bruce Catton writes: "The qualms that had paralyzed Joe Hooker when he found himself facing the Army of Northern Virginia had no place in Meade's makeup."[61]

Unfortunately for Meade, one of his subordinates was completely unworthy of any kind of trust. Major General Daniel E. Sickles, in command of the Union Third Corps at Gettysburg, was an insubordinate and mentally unstable officer who had been promoted far beyond his abilities due to his political connections. The unauthorized move in which Sickles, on his own initiative, placed his troops in the Peach Orchard along the Emmitsburg Road was an act of sheer lunacy that undoubtedly caused the overall Union casualty figures at Gettysburg to be far higher than they had to be.

The subordinate Meade trusted the most was the highly capable Major General Winfield Scott Hancock, the commander of the Union Second Corps. To Hancock, Meade assigned the critical task of holding the center of the Union position on Cemetery Ridge. Hancock's presence on the battlefield was a steadying influence of the first order and a very welcome contrast to the antics of Dan Sickles, whose troops were adjacent to Hancock's in the front lines. A distinguished looking man, just the sight of Hancock on horseback riding up to a group of Union infantry who seemed to be wavering seemed to help put spirit into the men. Hancock's role was far more than symbolic however. He adroitly funneled reinforcements into threatened sections of the line. Hancock was a general who men would fight for, a fact that dispels the myth that George McClellan was the only Union general that the rank and file ever had any real affection for. On July 2, 1863, Hancock ordered the First Minnesota regiment of infantry to counterattack a Confederate force which was advancing up Cemetery Ridge in a sort of precursor to what would happen the following day during Pickett's charge. The

---

[60] Catton, *Never Call Retreat*, 180–181.

[61] Catton, *Never Call Retreat*, 184.

Minnesotans did their job; the rebels were evicted from Cemetery Ridge for the time being after a very tough fight.[62] Of the fighting qualities of the First Minnesota and its fearful losses in this savage little chapter in the Gettysburg battle, Bruce Catton writes:

> What was left of the Minnesota regiment came back to reorganize. It had taken 262 men into action and it had 47 men left, and the survivors boasted that while the casualties amounted to 82 percent (which seems to have been a record for the Union Army for the entire war) there was not a straggler or a prisoner of war on the entire list.[63]

Constantly placing himself in the line of fire, Hancock was badly wounded at Gettysburg. Every Civil War historian agrees that his services were invaluable. It would be Hancock's troops who would beat back Pickett's charge on July 3.[64] It is undeniable that at Gettysburg for the first time in the war the way that Meade and his subordinate generals (with the notable exception of the deranged Sickles) supported each other and trusted each other gave the foot soldiers of the Army of the Potomac something to which they were not accustomed—a smoothly functioning command team.[65]

Both victorious commanders, Meade at Gettysburg and Spruance at Midway, were second-guessed for supposedly not following up vigorously enough after winning a victory. Meade was informed by telegraph from Halleck on July 14, 1863 that President Lincoln was greatly distressed that Lee's army had been allowed to escape. Meade bristled and offered to resign. Lincoln wrote a letter the same day expressing his disappointment that Meade had failed to attack Lee when the latter was

---

[62] George Gordon Meade, ed. *The Life and Letters of George Gordon Meade: Major-General, United States Army.* Vol. 2. (New York: Charles Scribner's Sons, 1913): 88—narrative section apparently written by Meade's son; also named George.

[63] Catton, *Glory Road*, 300.

[64] Catton, *Never Call Retreat*, 188.

[65] Wert, *The Sword of Lincoln*, 304–305.

delayed in his retreat by the high water of the flooded Potomac. Even though Lincoln wisely decided not to send this letter, Meade knew the gist of it from Halleck's telegram, which Meade did receive. Lincoln's letter is strongly worded and claims that Meade had it within his power to destroy the Confederacy once and for all and that because of Meade's failure to finish off Lee north of the Potomac "the war will be prolonged indefinitely."[66] That was a heavy accusation to make, given that Lincoln had not seen fit to give Meade more than three days to get used to being the army commander prior to the opening of the battle. Indeed, just after Gettysburg, in a letter to his wife describing what his life had been like since taking command of the Army of the Potomac, it becomes clear that it is a credit to Meade that he was able to accomplish as much as he did at Gettysburg. Meade writes:

> From the time I took command till to-day, [*sic*] now over ten days, I have not changed my clothes, have not had a regular night's rest, and many nights not a wink of sleep, and for several days did not even wash my face and hands, no regular food, and all the time in a great state of mental anxiety. Indeed, I think I have lived as much in this time as in the last thirty years.[67]

It should be noted that although he did not realize it right away, Lincoln had definitely found in Meade the right commander for the Army of the Potomac. Even after Ulysses S. Grant was promoted Lieutenant General and placed in supreme command of all Union armies in March 1864, he (Grant) retained Meade as the commander of the Army of the Potomac until the end of the war.

Another reason why Lincoln's immediate post-Gettysburg criticism of Meade was unfair is that at that time there were still powerful Confederate armies in Tennessee and Georgia. It took General Grant's later efforts beginning in spring 1864 to get all the Union armies moving to the attack at the same time against every quadrant of the Confederacy

---

[66] Lincoln to Meade, July 14, 1863 (unsent), in Simpson, ed., *The Civil War: The Third Year*, 378–379. See also introductory note on 378.

[67] Meade to Mrs. Meade, July 8, 1863. George Gordon Meade, ed., *The Life and Letters of George Gordon Meade*, Vol. 2, 132.

to give the Union its true winning strategy.[68] The Union was rich in resources and it was proven at Gettysburg that its soldiers could decisively defeat Lee's Army of Northern Virginia. Also, on the day after the Battle of Gettysburg concluded, General Grant accepted the surrender of Confederate forces in far off Vicksburg, Mississippi. Yet, while it could win battles, the Union in 1863 did not yet have a winning *strategy* for the long term, a situation that was more the fault of Lincoln than of Meade.

Like Meade, Admiral Spruance faced criticism about not following up vigorously. These critiques relate to Spruance's actions at Midway on the evening of June 4, 1942. By then, all four of the Japanese aircraft carriers had been turned into flaming, drifting, hulks by American carrier-based dive-bombing attacks. Admiral Fletcher's flagship, carrier *Yorktown*, was out of action due to battle damage. Fletcher felt that what remained of the battle should be directed from an operational aircraft carrier. Thus, Fletcher selflessly transferred overall command to Admiral Spruance. Much has been written since of Spruance's cautious, but ultimately very wise, decision to have the American fleet steam eastwards for five hours that night, turning west again at midnight. His critics have claimed that Spruance's caution cost him the opportunity to destroy more of the Japanese fleet. However, most historians of the Battle of Midway agree that Spruance's refusal to get carried away by being over-aggressive in pursuit were the proper actions for a commander who was fully aware that he was fighting defensively from a position of relative weakness. Had Spruance chased the Japanese westwards all night, he most likely would have encountered a powerful Japanese surface force under Vice Admiral Kondo Nobutake that included four heavy cruisers and two battleships. During the upcoming Guadalcanal campaign, the Japanese would prove that they were highly skilled in fighting nighttime naval battles. Spruance and Meade were shrewd gamblers who knew when to call and when to hold.[69]

---

[68] Bruce Catton. *Grant Takes Command*. (Boston: Little, Brown and Company, 1968): 167–172. Wert, *The Sword of Lincoln*, 331–332.

[69] Morison, *Coral Sea, Midway and Submarine Actions*, 141–143. Stafford, *The Big E*, 105, 109. Buell, *The Quiet Warrior*, 154–155, 174–175.

To re-engage Lee on open ground at the flooded Potomac would have been much more risky for Meade than was his skillful use of the strong defensive fortifications on Cemetery Ridge that had served him so well during the Gettysburg battle. Meade had not had time yet to put his imprint on the army. Indeed, noted Civil War historian Bruce Catton casts aside the "great man" theory of history completely when he notes that replacing Hooker with Meade when the Army of the Potomac was actually on the march to meet the enemy [at Gettysburg] "was an act of sheer desperation" and that "what happened now would be largely up to the men themselves. In effect, they had no leader."[70] The idea that Meade's presence at Gettysburg was irrelevant seems to be more than a bit harsh on Meade. In fact, Confederate Lieutenant General A.P. Hill told a British Army officer who was traveling with the Confederate Army of Northern Virginia as an observer that in Hill's opinion "the Yankees had fought with a determination unusual to them" on the first day at Gettysburg.[71] Perhaps Meade's presence at the helm did stiffen the Union troops. Meade's greatest contribution at Gettysburg may have been simply that he let his troops get at the enemy. The Army of the Potomac had in Meade a commander who was finally willing to let his soldiers fight.

Hooker, on the other hand, had been roundly criticized by his corps commanders and by his ordinary soldiers for an attitude of hesitancy and caution at Chancellorsville that was so extreme and deep that it amounted essentially to inertia. Many men in his own Army of the Potomac were convinced that Hooker's order to retreat from Chancellorsville was premature in the extreme and that the trouble with the Army of the Potomac was not with the fighting spirit of its average soldier, but was instead a debilitating problem with the management.[72]

Similarly, there are historians who say that the real command credit for American victory at Midway lies not with Admiral Spruance, but

---

[70] Catton, *Glory Road*, 259.

[71] Diary of (British) Lieutenant Colonel Arthur James Lyon Freemantle, July 1, 1863, in Simpson, ed. *The Civil War: The Third Year*, 294.

[72] Wert, *The Sword of Lincoln*, 250–254.

rather with Admiral Halsey's seasoned staff, which Spruance inherited when he took command of Task Force 16 just prior to Midway. It has also been said that the real American heroes of the Battle of Midway were the American dive-bombing group leaders, Lt. Cdr. Maxwell Leslie and Lt. Cdr. Clarence W. (Wade) McClusky, Jr., respectively, who each showed great individual initiative by finding the enemy carriers on their own after being given incorrect bearings on the morning of June 4, 1942 prior to takeoff from *Yorktown* and *Enterprise*, respectively. The resourcefulness exhibited by Leslie and McCluskey allowed American dive bomber pilots to deliver mortal blows to three of the four Japanese aircraft carriers in the morning attack. The *Hiryu* would be destroyed in a second dive-bombing attack on the afternoon of June 4, 1942.

In regard to General Meade, the attempted debunking of the "great man" theory of history began almost as soon as the Battle of Gettysburg ended. General Meade was fully aware that President Lincoln and General Halleck had very mixed feelings about Meade's handling of the Army of the Potomac, and by late 1863 Meade expected to be relieved of his command any day.[73] By that time, newspapers had begun to treat Meade as the "forgotten man" of Gettysburg. In a letter to his wife in December 1863, Meade wryly noted that "I see the *Herald* is constantly harping on the assertion that Gettysburg was fought by the corps commanders and the common soldiers, and that no generalship was displayed. I suppose after awhile it will be discovered I was not at Gettysburg at all."[74]

Due to the vastly greater manpower and economic resources enjoyed by the Union over the Confederacy in the Civil War and by the Americans over the Japanese in World War II, there is a tendency to regard the respective American victories at Gettysburg and Midway as convenient but not really essential.[75] In point of fact, Gettysburg and Midway were

---

[73] Meade December 1863 correspondence with Mrs. Meade in Meade, ed., *The Life and Letters of General George Gordon Meade*, Vol. 2, 159–160. See also Wert, *The Sword of Lincoln*, 318, 321–322.

[74] Meade to Mrs. Meade, December 7, 1863, in Meade, ed., *The Life and Letters of General George Gordon Meade*, Vol. 2, 160.

[75] See, for instance, Parshall and Tully, *Shattered Sword*, 427–428.

critical victories that the United States had to have. Victory at Gettysburg against the Confederacy's best general proved to the world that the Union rank and file were just as highly motivated and dedicated as were their Confederate counterparts. Winning big at Gettysburg and Vicksburg in the same week also had important international ramifications for the Union cause. For instance, on October 9, 1863 the British government finally ceased turning a blind eye to the fact that British shipyards had been flagrantly violating Britain's supposed neutrality in the American Civil War by building warships for the Confederacy when it seized the two most advanced of these warships—large, steam-powered vessels with iron rams affixed to their bows—before those ships could leave British waters. These British-built steam-powered rams were intended for use in destroying the wooden hulled warships that the US Navy was using to blockade southern ports. There is even some evidence that at the time of Gettysburg there was talk in the British Parliament about Britain perhaps acting as intermediary to sound out other European nations regarding the possibility of those nations and Britain extending diplomatic recognition of the Confederacy as an independent nation—something that ultimately never happened. The victories at Gettysburg and Vicksburg played a large part in helping to convince the British government that permanent estrangement from Washington was a very bad idea.[76]

The American victory in the Battle of Midway was equally critical for the United States. Midway destroyed the myth of Japanese invincibility. According to Omer Bartov, when Hitler attacked France in 1940, German "victory was anything but a foregone conclusion" in that campaign.[77] The French people, or at least their political and military leaders, had lost hope when German tanks broke through the Ardennes forest into northern France in the early summer of 1940. The title of French historian Marc Bloch's account of that campaign, *Strange Defeat*, is highly appropriate. With American desire for revenge for the Pearl Harbor attack running at a very high pitch in the summer of 1942, it is

---

[76] David Rigby. *The C.S.S. Alabama and British Neutrality During the American Civil War*. Unpublished paper, 1991, 12. Freeman, *R.E. Lee*, Vol. 3, 118.

[77] Omer Bartov. *Hitler's Army: Soldiers, Nazis, and War in the Third Reich*. (New York: Oxford University Press, 1992): 13.

far less likely that the American people would have completely lost hope had American forces been defeated at Midway. Nevertheless, and despite all the new construction that would give the United States by war's end the largest navy in world history, an American defeat at Midway would have been catastrophic. It would have given the Japanese an outpost just 1,000 miles from Pearl Harbor and could well have been accompanied by the destruction of much of America's remaining naval strength.

How much of America's resources should be devoted to the war against Japan as opposed to the war in Europe was one of the most contentious issues over which the Americans argued with their British allies in the eighteen months following the Pearl Harbor attack. Until late summer 1943 the British pressed relentlessly for the Americans to severely limit the Pacific commitment until after the defeat of Germany. The American victory at Midway showed that great things could be accomplished in the Pacific war with relatively modest resources.[78] Even taking the atomic bombs into account, World War II in the Pacific could not have ended until Japan's navy, air force, and merchant marine had been completely destroyed. The Battle of Midway was the first step in that essential process.

Richard Overy has written that "the Allies won the Second World War because they turned their economic strength into effective fighting power, and turned the moral energies of their people into an effective will to win."[79] The importance of the "will to win" cannot be overstated. The French did not have it in 1940. In countries where the will to win existed, it had to be fed. The Russians had to have a relatively early victory against Hitler. They got it at Moscow in December 1941. The Americans had to have a relatively early victory against the Japanese. They got it at Midway in June 1942. In the Civil War, the people of the North and the soldiers of their most important fighting force, the Army of the Potomac, needed a sign that Robert E. Lee's Army of Northern Virginia was beatable. They got that sign at Gettysburg in July 1863.

---

[78] Rigby, *Allied Master Strategists*, 73–83.

[79] Richard Overy. *Why the Allies Won*. (New York: Norton, 1995): 325.

CHAPTER 2

SUCCESSFUL STRATEGY INVOLVES FAR MORE THAN MILITARY POWER

The greatest practitioner of the doctrine of containment during the Cold War was not John Foster Dulles, Henry Kissinger, or Ronald Reagan; but rather a young American air force pilot named Gail Halvorsen whose weapon of choice was candy, not bombs.[1] The chocolate bars and sticks of chewing gum dropped to the children of Berlin by Gail Halvorsen and other US Air Force pilots is perhaps the happiest chapter in the well-known Berlin Airlift, which took place from June 1948 to May 1949. The Berlin Airlift was closely associated with the Marshall Plan, formally known as the European Recovery Program (ERP).

The Marshall Plan was George Kennan's favorite "tool" of containment. Probably the most misunderstood aspect of George Kennan and the policy of Cold War containment is that Kennan *did not* fear that Russian tanks were going to roll into Paris in the late 1940s. What Kennan *did* fear was that if western Europe was allowed to remain an economic ruin after World War II, the Communist party in say, France,

---

[1] See Andrei Cherny. *The Candy Bombers: The Untold Story of the Berlin Airlift and America's Finest Hour.* (New York: G.P. Putnam's Sons, 2008): 475.

might gain enough seats in the National Assembly to put a communist government legally in power in France.[2]

The Cold War provides perhaps the best example of the necessity for any national security strategy to extend well beyond military power. George Kennan, as architect of the doctrine of containment, felt that containing communism involved three major types of activity, only one of which was military. In addition to maintaining a strong military posture, Kennan was convinced that American policy makers needed to focus heavily on economics and psychology as equally critical aspects of containment as a strategy. Unfortunately, Kennan did not try hard enough to "sell" his nonmilitary ideas about containment to the American people.[3] Kennan seemed to personify the adage of "be careful what you wish for." With his Long Telegram of February 1946, and his subsequent "X" article published in *Foreign Affairs* in July 1947 at long last gaining him the influence he had craved for so long, Kennan found that his natural reclusiveness made him uncomfortable with many aspects of his unexpected notoriety as he was suddenly thrust into the spotlight in Washington, DC. In the twenty-one years Kennan had spent as a career diplomat representing the United States abroad in places like Lisbon, Berlin, and Moscow prior to writing the Long Telegram, he had never had to worry about, or deal with, public opinion. In fact Kennan had been completely unknown outside the State Department until 1946, at which time he was forty-two years old. His tenure as the first head of the Policy Planning Staff at the State Department in the late 1940s was therefore an eye-opening experience that left Kennan with a deep distrust of the US Congress and of the political atmosphere of Washington, DC in general. A passage from Kennan's biographer John Lewis Gaddis illustrates Kennan's conviction during this period that "'my specialty,' [Kennan] noted angrily in January 1948, 'was the defense of US interests against others, not against our own representatives.'"[4]

---

[2] John Lewis Gaddis, *Strategies of Containment: A Critical Appraisal of American National Security Policy During the Cold War.* (New York: Oxford University Press, 1982, 2005): 33–34, 35, 38. John Lewis Gaddis. *The Cold War: A New History.* (New York: Penguin, 2005): 31–32.

[3] Gaddis, *Strategies of Containment*, 49–51.

[4] Gaddis, *Strategies of Containment*, 51.

Like Woodrow Wilson and Jimmy Carter, George Kennan found out how difficult it is to get anything done in Washington when one attempts to stay "above" politics. Kennan gave up trying to influence foreign policy directly when he resigned as head of the Policy Planning Staff effective January 1, 1950. For a man who is remembered for formulating a strategy by which the United States could successfully grapple with a totalitarian power, the USSR, Kennan seems to have had a surprisingly deep distrust of the cumbersome nature of democratic government and a curious fascination with, even envy for, the way dictators can run their governments with an efficiency born out of a complete absence of any need to answer to public opinion.[5] For instance, Kennan made a statement to an audience at the National War College in September 1948 which can only be classified as odd and disturbing when he said "there was a great deal in Hitler's so called new order which would have made sense if the guiding spirit behind it had not been Hitler."[6] Late in his long life Kennan evinced an admiration (albeit somewhat tepid) for Russian strong man Vladimir Putin.[7]

Containment became, from the late 1940s, the official but poorly understood American national security policy. Presidents from Dwight D. Eisenhower to Richard Nixon placed far too much emphasis on the military aspects of containment at the expense of all else. It is interesting to note that George Kennan's idea of the true meaning of containment in practice was the Marshall Plan, which was all about economics and restoring hope and had nothing overtly military about it. Kennan himself and the Policy Planning Staff he headed at the State Department drafted many of the details of the Marshall Plan.[8] The Marshall Plan linked economics with psychology—the latter in the form of restoring hope to the peoples of western Europe. By rebuilding the economies of

---

[5] Gaddis, *Strategies of Containment*, 49–50.

[6] Kennan, as quoted in Gaddis, *Strategies of Containment*, 32 *n*.

[7] Mark Feeney. "American Sage Making History as Well as Writing It: George F. Kennan Masters a Century." *Boston Globe*, October 26, 2000, D1.

[8] George F. Kennan. *Memoirs: 1925–1950*. (Boston: Little, Brown and Company, 1967): 343.

western European nations, the Marshall Plan convinced Europeans that they could have a better future under democratic, free market economies than they could if they turned to radical, totalitarian political "solutions."[9] Kennan realized instinctively that the Cold War was a conflict in which the battle to win over hearts and minds would be more important than military strength.

The Marshall Plan is of course named after George C. Marshall, who became American Secretary of State in January 1947. Although best known to most Americans due to the Marshall Plan which bears his name, George C. Marshall was also one of only five men ever to attain five-star rank in the US Army. General Marshall had served with great distinction as US Army Chief of Staff during World War II, in which capacity he became President Roosevelt's premier military advisor. Famous World War II generals such as Eisenhower, Patton, and Bradley became known to the public (and to the enemy) only because General Marshall, as Army Chief of Staff, had replaced the Army's seniority system with the much better method of promoting officers based upon merit alone. Marshall refused to continue the hitherto common practice of promoting mediocre officers simply because they had long service in the army. Instead, he retired scores of mediocrities and promoted bright officers who had shown talent, not just long service. Sometimes Marshall promoted bright young officers. Other officers promoted by General Marshall were, like Eisenhower, no longer young men but had spent long years trapped in the middle ranks before Marshall became Chief of Staff and made room at the top by forcing the high ranking mediocrities to retire.[10] General Marshall was well known and respected in Great Britain as well as in his native land due to his wartime service as a principal member of the British-American Combined Chiefs of Staff.

General Marshall often spoke of the United States as a land of "citizen soldiers," by which he meant that Americans are a peace-loving people who would rather not maintain a large standing army. But, in time of war, Americans are quite good at trading in their civilian clothing

---

[9] Gaddis, *Strategies of Containment*, 33–34, 35, 38. Gaddis, *The Cold War*, 31–32.

[10] Forrest C. Pogue. *George C. Marshall*. Vol. 2. *Ordeal and Hope 1939–1942*. (New York: Viking, 1966): 91–99.

for military uniforms (sometimes with conscription to help them make up their minds) and enabling the nation to build up its military strength quite rapidly. The general himself was an excellent example of the citizen-soldier concept. Upon his retirement from the military after forty-five years as a career army officer, General Marshall effortlessly made the transition to a civilian job, Secretary of State, which required him to don a business suit every day instead of a general's uniform. George Kennan praised General Marshall

> for his unshakable integrity; his consistent courtesy and gentle-manliness of conduct; his ironclad sense of duty; his imperturb-ability—the imperturbability of a good conscience—in the face of harassments, pressures, and criticisms; his deliberateness and conscientiousness of decision . . . his lack of petty vanity or ambition.[11]

The Marshall Plan was introduced to the American public in rough outline form via the speech made by Secretary Marshall at Harvard University on June 5, 1947—commencement day at Harvard. Although he is now described as Harvard's official "Commencement Speaker" for that year,[12] that was not quite the case in fact. The Harvard speech was organized hastily since General Marshall had scheduling and press of work difficulties in the weeks leading up to Harvard's commencement day. Thus, he was not actually the keynote speaker at the Commencement which took place in the morning on June 5. That duty was divided up amongst three graduating seniors who took turns speaking before the degree-granting ceremony. Marshall received an honorary doctorate-of-laws degree at the morning ceremony. The venue at which Marshall actually spoke was in the afternoon to a meeting of the graduating class ("graduated" would be more accurate; since they had received their degrees that morning) and the alumni, which was traditionally an occasion for a less formal speech than that for the morning's Commencement exercises.

---

[11] Kennan, *Memoirs, 1925–1950*, 345.

[12] See for example, the list of Harvard Commencement speakers over the years posted on Harvard's web site.

The details of Marshall's speech were kept tightly under wraps until the day before it was delivered, when journalists were allowed to see the text. President Truman was fully in accord with Marshall and Kennan that some kind of American aid package for Europe needed to be cobbled together quickly. However, even Truman did not know the contents of Marshall's speech until after it was delivered. President Truman's surprise at the speech was, however, a pleasant surprise. Truman liked the speech and said so to Marshall soon after.[13]

Despite the secrecy, Harvard President James B. Conant seemed to have an inkling that something big was coming. Conant and Laird Bell, the President of the Harvard Alumni Association, hit on the idea of having Marshall speak in the afternoon to the alumni instead of at the morning Commencement as a way to ease Marshall's fears that he, Marshall, had not had time to prepare a formal Commencement address.[14] It seems that Conant knew that at whatever time of the day he actually spoke, General Marshall would be the main event. That is probably why Conant deliberately did not bring in a big name keynote speaker for the official morning Commencement ceremony. It should also be noted that other prominent people, including Army General Omar N. Bradley, spoke at the afternoon ceremony.[15] In fact, it was not until a week before the event that Marshall could know for sure that his schedule would permit him to make it to Harvard. According to Marshall's biographer Forrest Pogue:

> By May 28, [Marshall] informed Conant of the decision he had made nearly a week earlier. He could come, he said, but would not

---

[13] Marshall to Dean Acheson and Robert Lovett. June 16, 1947. *The Papers of George Catlett Marshall.* Vol. 6. *The Whole World Hangs in the Balance: January 8, 1947–September 30, 1949.* Larry I. Bland and Mark A. Stoler, eds. Sharon Ritenour Stevens, Assoc. Ed. (Baltimore: The Johns Hopkins University Press, 2013): 153. (Hereinafter *Marshall Papers*, Vol. 6.) See also, Forrest C. Pogue. *George C. Marshall.* Vol. 4. *Statesman 1945–1959.* (New York: Viking Penguin, 1987): 210–211 on secrecy.

[14] Pogue, *Statesman*, 208–209, 210–212. *Daily Boston Globe*, June 6, 1947. "2185 Harvard Graduates Join 'Fellowship of Educated Men,'" 4.

[15] Pogue, *Statesman*, 212.

promise a formal address. However, he would be pleased to make a few remarks and perhaps 'a little more' at the alumni meeting. The 'little more' was to have global reverberations.[16]

It was not a long speech—just over twelve minutes—but Pogue is correct that it did indeed have worldwide implications.[17] In the Harvard speech, General Marshall laid out the situation in the common sense, practical sort of language that was typical of him, saying that:

> It is logical that the United States should do whatever it is able to do to assist in the return of normal economic health in the world, without which there can be no political stability and no assured peace. Our policy is directed not against any country or doctrine but against hunger, poverty, desperation and chaos. Its purpose should be the revival of a working economy in the world so as to permit the emergence of political and social conditions in which free institutions can exist.[18]

The Berlin Airlift, although an emergency measure planned far more hastily than the Marshall Plan, provides another example of how providing hope is definitely a war winning strategy. The Airlift might have occurred even had there been no Marshall Plan, although the two were in fact closely related. The Berlin Blockade, which began on June 24, 1948 and which necessitated the Airlift, was the most visible feature of Stalin's anger that western Europe was beginning to stir out of its postwar devastation-induced torpor and move toward economic recovery. Europeans were moving on with their lives and Stalin did not like that. The fact that the Airlift and the Marshall Plan began to operate simultaneously meant that in many ways the Airlift crystallized what the Marshall Plan was all about—hope. Shortly after it began in June 1948, the Berlin Airlift accidentally acquired a very friendly face in the person of Gail Halvorsen. Halvorsen, a young American air force pilot became known

---

[16] Pogue, *Statesman*, 209.

[17] Bland and Stoler, eds. Ritenour Stevens, Assoc. Ed., *Marshall Papers*, Vol. 6, 149–150 *n*.

[18] Bland and Stoler, eds. Ritenour Stevens, Assoc. Ed., *Marshall Papers*, Vol. 6, 148.

as the legendary "Chocolate Bomber" by dropping bags of candy to the children of Berlin during the airlift as he made his approaches to the runway at Tempelhof Airfield in Berlin at the controls of a Douglas C-54 Skymaster transport plane.

Although Halvorsen's story has been told many times, it is worthwhile to trace the serendipitous manner in which the Berlin Airlift seemed to grow out of the Marshall Plan; and then how the best intentions of the political, economic, and military leaders who orchestrated the Marshall Plan and the Airlift became personified by the unique bond Halvorsen formed with the children of Berlin, who of course represented the future. The Marshall Plan, the Airlift, and Gail Halvorsen did much to ensure that the future of those Berlin children, and other children all over western Europe, would be one of hope and possibility instead of one of misery and despair.[19]

Gail Halvorsen was only one of hundreds of American and British pilots who participated in the Berlin Airlift. Each four-engined C-54 aircraft that arrived in Berlin during the Airlift carried over seven tons of meat, coffee, vegetables, fuel, medical supplies, and other urgent necessities of life for the inhabitants of Berlin. But it was that candy that Berliners remembered the most. Other pilots followed Halvorsen's example and the dropping of candy to children in Berlin quickly became a big business. The photographs of German children standing atop piles of wartime rubble watching as American aircraft come in for landings and hoping that some candy will fall to them have become the iconic images of the Berlin Airlift. As the representative of everything that was right about the Marshall Plan and the Airlift, it can be convincingly argued that Gail Halvorsen and the candy he delivered to the children of Berlin did more to keep Communism in check than did the entire Vietnam War.

Regarding the Vietnam War, John Lewis Gaddis, Kennan's biographer, demonstrates how far the United States had by then strayed from the true meaning and purpose of containment:

---

[19] See Cherny, *The Candy Bombers*, 389, for how American candy manufacturing executives got involved not simply to burnish their respective corporate images, but because they realized that Berlin's children needed a future of hope.

Kennan had sought to maintain the global balance of power by applying a combination of political, economic, military, and psychological leverage in carefully selected pivotal areas; [President Lyndon B.] Johnson by 1965 was relying almost exclusively on the use of military force in a theater chosen by adversaries.[20]

Gaddis has repeatedly noted that George Kennan also believed in matching American strengths against enemy weaknesses.[21] The Marshall Plan did just that. Because the American people, through their elected representatives, voted to fund the Marshall Plan, that plan represented an act of national will. The American people wanted to see economic recovery in Europe. By way of contrast, Stalin and his entourage at the head of the Soviet regime in Moscow, because they had no legitimacy, had no idea what the Russian people wanted for Europe.

The Airlift itself was a powerful reminder of American strength. Russia had by the end of World War II a very powerful air force, but it was strictly tactical; comprised of fighters and small twin-engined bombers designed for direct support of ground troops. Large aircraft were almost entirely lacking from the Russian inventory in the late 1940s. The Russians had nothing like the fleets of four-engined C-54s which carried out the Airlift. Even though the Airlift planes were unarmed transports, the display of them flying into and out of Berlin like clockwork twenty-four hours per day, seven days a week could not but have helped to make a deep impression on Stalin, who had always liked big airplanes. The only thing Stalin had envied the western Allies during the war were the fleets of long-range, four-engine bombers such as the Boeing B-17 and the Avro Lancaster that the Americans and the British, respectively, possessed in abundance by war's end.

That all of the American aircraft used in the Airlift were unarmed transport planes was an excellent reminder that to rely on military force to the exclusion of all else is actually the antithesis of containment. Gaddis dwells on the irony of the fact that after the Johnson administration

---

[20] Gaddis, *Strategies of Containment*, 236–237.

[21] Gaddis, *Strategies of Containment*, 236–238. John Lewis Gaddis. *George F. Kennan: An American Life*. (New York: Penguin, 2011): 287.

got the United States bogged down in Vietnam via an overdependence on military force alone, the main reason behind the sophisticated diplomacy of Henry Kissinger and President Richard Nixon in reaching out to mainland China and to the Russians, the latter being "the original target of containment," was to try to find an exit strategy from Vietnam. Coordinating diplomacy with the war effort, something Johnson had never done, actually enhanced Nixon's military options while decreasing the risk of direct Chinese or Russian intervention in Vietnam.[22]

Gail Halvorsen grew up poor on a struggling farm in Utah. He became a ferry pilot during World War II, hauling cargo in transport aircraft and sometimes delivering a brand new bomber to a combat zone. As a cargo pilot in the Air Transport Command (ATC), Halvorsen's World War II service was distinctly unglamorous. He was hard working and very obedient, which is undoubtedly why the powers that be in the army air forces had Halvorsen flying large aircraft rather than training him to be a fighter pilot. Halvorsen's conformist nature is often attributed to his Mormon upbringing, but perhaps it was simply his natural personality.[23]

His by-the-book nature made it all the more surprising that it would be Halvorsen who would defy regulations by deviating from the strict instructions laid down for Airlift pilots that there were to be absolutely no "cowboy" stunts such as buzzing the home of one's girlfriend. Standing orders for American pilots were to fly in a straight line from Rhein-Main Air Force Base near Wiesbaden to either Tempelhof or one of two other fields in Berlin; wait while the plane was unloaded; take on fuel if needed and then return to Rhein-Main for another load. Halvorsen disobeyed these standing orders. That takes courage as well as a subtle confidence in one's own judgment that is somewhat rare. It is much easier to follow orders even when they don't seem to make sense, but following orders to the letter sometimes just does not get the job done. For instance, during the First World War, British Rear Admiral Sir Archibald Moore dutifully followed orders when, owing mainly to a communications mishap with signal flags, he stopped with his powerful

---

[22] Gaddis, *Strategies of Containment*, 237, 297. The quote is on 237.

[23] Cherny, *The Candy Bombers*, 64.

force of British battlecruisers, as he felt he had been ordered to do by his commanding officer Rear Admiral Sir David Beatty, to sink the German armored cruiser *Blücher*, which was damaged and dead in the water, during the battle of the Dogger Bank in January 1915 while three much more valuable targets—the German battlecruisers *Moltke, Derfflinger,* and *Seydlitz* escaped.[24] British First Sea Lord Admiral Sir John "Jackie" Fisher erupted in a rage when he learned that the Royal Navy had blown an excellent opportunity to destroy three of the most valuable units in the German Navy. Fisher was especially angry with Captain Henry Pelly of the battlecruiser HMS *Tiger,* which was closest to the German battle-cruisers after Beatty's flagship, the battlecruiser HMS *Lion,* had to break off the fight after sustaining heavy battle damage. Although he had been advised that Moore and Pelly had faithfully obeyed what they sincerely thought Beatty's wishes had been when they broke off the chase in order to pummel the hapless *Blücher*, Fisher refused to be mollified. Regarding Pelly's failure to pursue the German battlecruisers, Fisher said "Like Nelson at Copenhagen and St. Vincent! In war the first principle is to disobey orders. *Any fool can obey orders!*"[25]

Early in the Berlin Airlift, Halvorsen spoke to some children who had gathered outside the Templehof Airfield perimeter fence where they watched the planes land and take off. They were obviously hungry, but they asked for nothing. The sight of polite children with no joy in their faces struck a chord with Halvorsen. He had two sticks of chewing gum, which he tore in half and gave to the children. The somber faces of the children immediately lit up, but there was not enough to go around, so Halvorsen promised that he would drop some candy on his landing approach the next day. He told the children that they would know which plane was his because he would rock the wings gently from side to side as he approached the airfield. Thus, what was perhaps the best known of his many nicknames, "Uncle Wiggly Wings," was born. The other nicknames by which Halvorsen was addressed in letters written by grateful children included "Chocolate Pilot" and "Angel from the Heavens." Halvorsen

---

[24] Robert K. Massie. *Castles of Steel: Britain, Germany, and the Winning of the Great War at Sea.* (New York: Random House, 2003): 396–406.

[25] Massie, *Castles of Steel,* 414–415. The quote is on 415.

began attaching packets of candy to handkerchiefs that served as miniature parachutes. Without meaning to, designers at Douglas Aircraft had provided Halvorsen with the perfect method for launching the chutes by placing a flare tube immediately behind the pilot's seat in the C-54 cockpit. Other pilots began to donate their chocolate rations to the effort and several other pilots also began making candy "drops." Halvorsen's spontaneous act of kindness became an immediate sensation—on the ground in Berlin and in the American media. The air force quickly had to assign him two secretaries to handle the truckloads of mail he was receiving from the children of Berlin. Wives of other American pilots at Rhein-Main Air Force Base in West Germany began stitching together miniature parachutes, and candy donations began to pour in from all over the United States—from individuals and from American candy manufacturers.[26]

The magnitude of what Halvorsen and the other "candy bombing" pilots who followed his example accomplished in mitigating the scars of war in the minds of the children of Berlin would be difficult to overstate. Three years before the Airlift, the Russian Army that advanced into Germany in early 1945 was an army bent on revenge. The savagery with which the German Army treated Russian civilians in occupied areas of the USSR during the war might well rank as the bloodiest aspect of the very bloody twentieth century. As the Red Army advanced after the decisive battle of Kursk in July 1943 and began liberating village after village in Russia, its troops found mass graves, farms and even entire villages burned to the ground, and other evidence of the brutality endured by Russian civilians under German occupation. Some 13,000,000 Russian civilians were murdered by the German Army or died of exposure and starvation after their villages had been burned down by the invading German troops. The rape of Russian women by German soldiers was commonplace throughout the German occupation of European Russia.[27]

---

[26] Alec MacGillis. "Uncle Wigglywings to take to skies again: Candy Dropper to help mark Berlin airlift." *Boston Globe*, May 3, 1998, A2. Richard Collier. *Bridge Across the Sky: The Berlin Blockade and Airlift, 1948–1949*. (New York: McGraw-Hill, 1978): 86–89, 105–107. Cherny, *The Candy Bombers*, 388–389, 590.

[27] David Rigby. *Allied Master Strategists: The Combined Chiefs of Staff in World War II*. (Annapolis, MD: Naval Institute Press, 2012): 135–136.

In the last months of the Third Reich, Red Army soldiers were in no mood to show any compassion for German civilians. Historian Antony Beevor has estimated that something like 2,000,000 German women were raped by Russian soldiers during the Red Army's advance into Germany in 1945.[28] Knowing what had happened to their mothers and sisters, and perhaps to themselves, the children of Berlin were deeply traumatized by the time of the blockade. Even after the violence subsided, there was still the difficulty of survival in a city destroyed by wartime Russian artillery fire during the battle of Berlin in April 1945 and by Anglo-American bombing raids. The Airlift, and especially the candy delivered by parachute, provided a psychological antidote to children who had seen and experienced things that no child should ever see. According to Andrei Cherny: "They had been the children who played the game of 'rape.' Now social workers observed that a new game was dominant amid the craters and rubble-strewn streets of Berlin. The city's children were playing the game of 'Airlift.'"[29]

US Air Force Major General William H. Tunner, the commander of the Berlin Airlift, was a humorless man but an organizational genius and logistics expert. He was determined to transform the Airlift into an assembly line operation. In doing so, he definitely did not want any cowboy pilots.[30] Tunner had no hobbies and actually enjoyed working eighteen hour days. He had become America's premier airlift expert due to his expert handling of the extraordinarily difficult "Hump" airlift in World War II, in which every piece of military equipment needed to keep China "in the war" against Japan had to be loaded into transport aircraft in Assam province in northeastern India and then flown over the Himalaya mountains into China. This route was rightly referred to by pilots as "the aluminum trail" because it became littered with the carcasses of aircraft that had been forced down due to mechanical difficulty, weather, or the occasional prowling Japanese fighter plane. Even if a pilot

---

[28] Antony Beevor. *The Fall of Berlin 1945* (New York: Penguin, 2002): 410; see also 312–313, 326–327.

[29] Cherny, *The Candy Bombers*, 358.

[30] Collier, *Bridge Across the Sky*, 93, 101.

succeeded in bailing out of a stricken aircraft on the Hump route, his chances of survival in such frozen, forbidding terrain were remote indeed.

Upon his arrival in Germany in July 1948, Tunner had immediately begun to make changes in the Airlift to make the operation as efficient as possible. Indeed, Tunner seems to have been an admirer of Frederick Winslow Taylor, the father of "scientific management" and its associated time-motion studies that, like their inventor, came to be hated by American industrial workers. While Tunner was in command, never more than five minutes went by without a supply-laden American transport plane landing at Tempelhof.[31] However, while prizing efficiency, Tunner was actually a very different sort of man than was the founder of "Taylorism." True, Tunner did not want pilots to leave the tarmac when they landed at Tempelhof. Fuel, changes to orders, weather data, and even sandwiches would be brought to them at their aircraft (which is undoubtedly why Halvorsen and his fellow "candy bombers" used parachute drops to deliver the candy, since after landing they could not routinely wander over to the perimeter fence where the children were waiting). Tunner also organized production line maintenance for aircraft, and he gradually weeded out the older C-47 twin-engined transports so that for American pilots the entire Airlift fleet became standardized on the four-engined Douglas C-54 Skymaster, which could haul more than twice the load of a C-47.[32] This much was in keeping with the manner in which Tunner had operated the Hump airlift during the war.

Unlike Frederick Winslow Taylor, however, General Tunner was capable of seeing beyond efficiency to the human element. Tunner himself remained a workaholic, but he had evolved in the three years between the end of World War II and the beginning of the Berlin Airlift. He had come to realize that not everyone was like him; that not everyone could get their only enjoyment in life from working. According to Andrei Cherny: "The

---

[31] Cherny, *The Candy Bombers*, 348. Greg Behrman. *The Most Noble Adventure: The Marshall Plan and the Time When America Helped Save Europe*. (New York: Free Press, 2007): 205.

[32] Cherny, *The Candy Bombers*, 340. Collier, *Bridge Across the Sky*, 102, 124–125, 162–163. The British continued to use C-47s and several other types of aircraft throughout the Airlift.

man who showed up in Germany was different from the one who arrived in India. In the intervening years, [Tunner] had watched helplessly as his wife slowly faded from life [victim of a malignant brain tumor], he had raised two young boys alone, and he had seen his career stall out."[33] As the director of the Berlin Airlift, Tunner still demanded efficiency, but now he also tried to provide diversions for his pilots and air crew. He arranged short-wave radio connections between pilots in Germany and their families in the United States. Tunner also once hosted a daylong "bull" session in which pilots could air their feelings about what was working in the Airlift and what wasn't. At that session, Tunner provided good food and lubricated the discussion by plying the pilots with draft beer.[34] Tunner was somewhat like the character of Gradgrind in Charles Dickens's novel *Hard Times*. Gradgrind starts out as a Benthamite efficiency expert running a "model" school in which children are addressed by their number rather than by their name. However, late in the novel, Gradgrind renounces his system completely when he belatedly realizes with horror that his seemingly perfect system of education has turned his own children into soulless automatons.

Halvorsen, the children of Berlin, the Airlift, and the Marshall Plan were all to benefit from the change in Tunner's personality. Halvorsen thought he was in big trouble when word of his candy deliveries reached General Tunner in mid-August 1948. Halvorsen was summoned to Airlift headquarters in Wiesbaden for what he was sure would be a dressing down for the ages.[35] What actually happened was quite different. Apparently Halvorsen met first with his commanding officer, Lieutenant Colonel James R. Haun and then later in the day with General Tunner. As Richard Collier relates: "'What in the world,' Haun led off, 'have you been doing?' Halvorsen was guileless; 'flying like mad, Colonel.' Haun exploded. 'Look, I am not *stupid*—it's all over the front pages of the Berlin papers. You nearly hit a journalist on the head with that candy.'"[36] Haun's "anger" was feigned, however. In reality, he was delighted, as was

---

[33] Cherny, *The Candy Bombers*, 427.

[34] Cherny, *The Candy Bombers*, 428. Collier, *Bridge Across the Sky*, 110–112.

[35] Cherny, *The Candy Bombers*, 351–352.

[36] Collier, *Bridge Across the Sky*, 105.

General Tunner. Haun and Tunner both knew that they had a public relations winner in Halvorsen and the candy drops. General Tunner congratulated Halvorsen and told him to carry on.[37]

With "Operation Little Vittles," a subsidiary of "Operation Vittles"—the latter being the name given the Airlift as a whole—now a public relations sensation, Halvorsen was allowed to deviate from his normal approach to Tempelhof in order to swing low over areas that were safer and more hospitable places for his "customers" to congregate than were the piles of rubble adjacent to Tempelhof field. Such areas included schoolyards and playing fields.[38] With permission to wander, Halvorsen tried to accommodate special requests. Some of these were quite specific. As Andrei Cherny relates:

> From nine-year-old Peter Zimmerman, Halvorsen received a crudely made parachute, a map, and instructions so that he could drop candy at the Zimmerman home: 'Fly along the big canal . . . at the second bridge, turn right . . . . I live in the bombed out house on the corner. I'll be waiting in the backyard at 2 P.M.' On his next flight, Halvorsen searched for the house in vain. Soon after, he received another note from young Peter: 'No chocolate yet! . . . You're a pilot! . . . I gave you a map! . . . How did you guys win the war anyway?' Halvorsen put a chocolate bar in the mail.[39]

By Christmas, 1948, Berlin had become a bad place for diabetics. General Tunner was allowing Halvorsen and the other "chocolate bomber" pilots to cut back on their "real" payloads in order to carry more and more candy. On Christmas Eve, 1948, Halvorsen piloted a C-54 to Berlin with eight tons of coal aboard. He also had 800 pounds of candy attached in small packets to his now famous miniature handkerchief parachutes to drop on the way in. American candy manufacturers had by then donated more than 5,000,000 chocolate bars to the effort.[40] Without the candy he was carrying that evening, Halvorsen's plane would have been able

---

[37] Ibid, see also Cherny, *The Candy Bombers*, 352.

[38] Cherny, *The Candy Bombers*, 357.

[39] Cherny, *The Candy Bombers*, 411.

[40] Cherny, *The Candy Bombers*, 496.

to carry almost a half ton more coal on that particular delivery than it actually did.

When he started dropping candy, Gail Halvorsen had probably never heard of George Kennan. Likewise, Kennan and his boss, Marshall Plan namesake Secretary of State George C. Marshall, undoubtedly had never heard of the young air force lieutenant who was beginning to drop candy to Berlin's children. (Kennan and Marshall probably did hear about Halvorsen later since the candy drops made Halvorsen a celebrity in the United States; albeit a modest one who never let his sudden fame go to his head.) Nevertheless, all three men were working towards the same goal—Kennan and Marshall by design; Halvorsen by accident.

The announcement by the Russians on March 30, 1948 that rail and road communication with Berlin would be restricted surprised many people, but not George Kennan. As early as November 1947, Kennan

Berlin "Airlift" of 1948-49 broke through Soviet blockade of city by non-stop supply shipments to beleaguered garrisons and 2½ million civilian population of West Berlin.

Courtesy: Library of Congress, Prints and Photographs Division. Negative Number LC-USZ62-136389

Containment done right: A crowd of mostly children standing on a pile of wartime rubble watching an American C-54 Skymaster landing in Berlin during the Airlift—and undoubtedly hoping that the pilot is one of the "candy bombers."

had informed Marshall that the Marshall Plan would provoke a Russian response. Exactly what that response would be remained a mystery for the time being, but Kennan was certain that it would come. Even though the war in Europe had been over for three years before the Marshall Plan began to operate in April 1948, it could be said that in Germany at least, the "postwar era" had not yet begun because recovery had not yet begun. The Marshall Plan meant recovery and thus the beginning of a "postwar era" that was not to Russia's liking. Marshall's biographer explains the Soviet effort to interfere with a western-oriented European recovery thus: "Their purpose would be not to make war but to stop any move of their satellites toward independent action."[41]

June 24, 1948 marked the beginning of the total blockade of Berlin. The western Allied sectors of Berlin had 2,500,000 German citizens who needed to be fed.[42] On June 28, 1948 President Truman informed his top advisors that the United States would not back down on Berlin. At the beginning of the Berlin Airlift, *New York Times* columnist Drew Middleton described the situation thus:

> U.S. airpower throughout Europe is being mobilized for a great shuttle service into Besieged Berlin. U.S. aircraft, which four years ago brought death to the city [in the form of bombing raids], will bring life in the form of food and medicine to the people of the Western sectors, whose food supplies have been cut off by the Russians.[43]

One of the excuses Stalin used for the supposed need to blockade Berlin was the plan of the western Allies to create a West German government. Such an entity was needed because a well-organized aid program like the Marshall Plan needed to have nation-states, not "occupation zones" on its receiving end. There were also east-west currency disputes in which the Russians on the one hand and the British, Americans, and French on the other could not agree on a common currency for Germany as a whole. Currency reform was critical to a West German nation-state

---

[41] Pogue, *Statesman*, 297.

[42] Pogue, *Statesman*, 302.

[43] Drew Middleton, as quoted in Behrman, *The Most Noble Adventure*, 204.

because any nation, especially one recovering from an utterly devastating military defeat, needs a stable currency.[44] Kennan was right, the beginnings of European recovery did indeed provoke a Russian response.

Why would the Russians actually want Europe to remain a physical and economic ruin? There seem to have been two main reasons. Stalin undoubtedly worried that a third German invasion of Russia might occur in his lifetime should German economic and military power be allowed to revive. However, there was more to it than that. Marshall's biographer explains that "Soviet Russia and Communist regimes elsewhere in Europe were opposed to the recovery of Western Europe. Economic distress was to be exploited for political ends."[45] A good example of this was in Italy, where elections were scheduled for April 1948. The local Communist Party in Italy was quite strong and seemed to have a good chance of winning. Secretary of State Marshall had often hastened to reassure Europeans and the US Congress that the Marshall Plan would not interfere with the sovereignty or the internal workings of any of the beneficiary nations.[46] In practice, this was not quite accurate. As the spring of 1948 wore on and the Italian elections loomed on the horizon, Marshall, who was ordinarily the very soul of tact, courtesy, and discretion bluntly informed that Italian people that if they voted themselves a Communist government, they would have to do without Marshall Plan aid.[47] On April 17, 1948, in a multi-party election Italian voters renounced the Communist Party by voting for the Christian Democratic Party headed by Alcide De Gasperi by a healthy plurality of 48.5% of the popular vote compared to a weak 31% for the Communists.[48]

As soon as he was sworn in as Secretary of State in January 1947, General Marshall knew that something drastic had to be done to aid in

---

[44] Pogue, *Statesman*, 308–311. Behrman, *The Most Noble Adventure*, 202–206. Gaddis, *George F. Kennan*, 327.

[45] Pogue, *Statesman*, 241.

[46] Marshall Statement to the Senate Committee on Foreign Relations, January 8, 1948. Bland and Stoler, eds. Ritenour Stevens, Assoc. Ed., *Marshall Papers*, Vol. 6, 315.

[47] Behrman, *The Most Noble Adventure*, 176.

[48] Behrman, *The Most Noble Adventure*, 176–177.

European recovery. Indeed, economic aid to Europe was the first order of business for George Kennan and the Policy Planning Staff when the Planning Staff, a new sort of steering committee for the State Department, opened for business on May 5, 1947. Kennan's preliminary report went to Marshall's deputy, Undersecretary of State Dean Acheson on May 23, 1947. Late in May, Marshall met with Acheson, State Department legal counsel Benjamin Cohen, Charles "Chip" Bohlen, George Kennan, and Undersecretary of State for European Affairs Will Clayton.[49] (Chip Bohlen was the only other person in the State Department at that time besides George Kennan who spoke fluent Russian. As such, Bohlen had provided invaluable service as President Roosevelt's translator at the wartime Tehran and Yalta Conferences.)

The purpose of this meeting was to consider Kennan's memorandum and a report that Clayton had submitted to Acheson upon Clayton's return from an economic conference in Geneva. While in Geneva, Clayton had become appalled at how bad economic conditions were in Europe. Clayton's desire to see the United States take urgent action regarding European revival paralleled Kennan's views on this matter quite closely. Marshall sought the opinions of all present during this meeting. Kennan was certain that a package deal to aid Europe as a whole could work and that Europeans could carry out the bulk of the administration of the program themselves. Acheson, Bohlen, and Cohen had doubts, especially since the plan was going to be offered to all of Europe, even the USSR and its satellites. In fact, nobody involved in the planning actually wanted the Russians to participate, but the United States had to include the Russians in the offer in order to be seen as an honest broker. Russian participation was unlikely given that participation in the Marshall Plan would have required substantive internal changes in the Soviet system of government, something that Kennan's writings had already made clear was unlikely to happen anytime soon under the Kremlin leadership of the time. Marshall himself listened carefully to the views expressed at this meeting but did not announce a decision just yet.[50]

---

[49] Pogue, *Statesman*, 202–205.

[50] Pogue, *Statesman*, 204–207. Behrman, *The Most Noble Adventure*, 63–65. Gaddis, *Strategies of Containment*, 46–49. Kennan, *Memoirs: 1925–1950*, 342–343.

Kennan was confident that the fact that Marshall Plan aid would not be entirely without strings attached would make the Russians balk at joining in. Europeans would be involved in the implementation as much as possible, but Americans would not be entirely absent from the administration aspect of the plan. For instance, American businessman Paul Hoffman was installed in April 1948 as the head of the Economic Cooperation Administration (ECA). Hoffman would be the Washington-based day-to-day manager of the Marshall Plan. The wealthy and multi-talented Averell Harriman was appointed as a "special ambassador" to be stationed in Paris as head of an entity that came to be known as the Office of the Special Representative (OSR). Harriman's responsibilities were loosely defined, but came to include approving the nation plans put forward by countries receiving Marshall aid and countering Russian anti-Marshall Plan propaganda.[51] Thus, despite the fact that General Marshall wanted Europeans to administer the plan as much as possible, there was in fact strong American oversight.

Will Clayton agreed with Kennan that Europe needed a long-term aid plan and that, in the words of Marshall's biographer, the most immediate enemies as Clayton saw them were "starvation and chaos (*not . . . the Russians*)."[52] Clayton was fully aware of the role economic chaos had played in the rise of dictators such as Mussolini and Hitler during the interwar years.[53] Marshall himself was keenly aware that the poverty, hunger, and misery in postwar Europe would be the perfect breeding grounds for new dictators unless something drastic was done quickly to restore hope. He knew that only the United States was in a position to provide this hope; to let Europeans know that they had a potentially bright future.[54] Marshall also knew that European economic recovery would have beneficial effects worldwide, not just in the form of pulling

---

[51] Behrman, *The Most Noble Adventure*, 193–197.

[52] Pogue, *Statesman*, 206–207. The quote bridges the pages. Pogue's italics.

[53] Pogue, *Statesman*, 206.

[54] Marshall Statement to the Senate Committee on Foreign Relations, January 8, 1948. Bland and Stoler, eds. Ritenour Stevens, Assoc. Ed., *Marshall Papers*, Vol. 6, 310.

the rug out from under potential new dictators in Europe, but also because as Marshall told the Pittsburgh Chamber of Commerce in January 1948: "The economies of Latin America and Canada, for example, are organized on the basis of having markets in Europe. If Europe fails to recover, and she certainly cannot do so without our aid, the repercussions will be felt throughout the entire world."[55] Thus, an important aspect of the Marshall Plan was rebuilding the global economy by resurrecting trading partners for the United States and other western hemisphere nations.

The Marshall Plan was officially in effect from April 1948 to December 1951. Seventeen nations received aid. The United States spent $13 billion during the course of the project—and spent it well. General Marshall and his State Department advisors all admitted in later years that exactly who wrote the Harvard speech and who was the guiding spirit behind the Marshall Plan was hard to pin down with any certainty.[56] Marshall's biographer states that:

> Kennan has claimed that his staff contributed three elements of the speech; (1) Europeans should assume responsibility for initiating the program, (2) the offer should be made to all Europe, and (3) a decisive element should be the rehabilitation of the German economy. The dramatic statement of the economic plight of Europe was from Clayton's memorandum.[57]

What is clear is that none of the details had been worked out yet at the time of the Harvard speech.[58] Marshall himself gave credit for the authorship of the Harvard speech in equal parts to George Kennan, Chip Bohlen, and to himself. It was not a long speech; requiring just over twelve minutes to deliver.[59]

---

[55] Marshall Speech to the Pittsburgh Chamber of Commerce. January 15, 1948. Bland and Stoler, eds. Ritenour Stevens, Assoc. Ed., *Marshall Papers*, Vol. 6, 333.

[56] Kennan, *Memoirs: 1925–1950*, 343–345.

[57] Pogue, *Statesman*, 210.

[58] Pogue, *Statesman*, 215.

[59] Bland and Stoler, eds. Ritenour Stevens, Assoc. Ed., *Marshall Papers*, Vol. 6, 149–150 *n*.

That General Marshall himself intended the ERP to be a long-term solution rather than a short-term stopgap is evident in the language of the Harvard speech. That language made clear that the Marshall Plan was actually to be quite different from Lend-Lease, to which it has been compared. The Marshall Plan was not to be a mere Band-Aid.[60] At Harvard, General Marshall stated that "'any assistance that this Government may render in the future should provide a cure rather than a mere palliative' to the ills that had contributed and were contributing to 'hunger, poverty, desperation and chaos.'"[61] The necessity for a long-term solution and for the active participation of Europeans themselves in the plan was continually hammered by Marshall's aides such as Robert A. Lovett, who had replaced Acheson as Under secretary of State in July 1947.[62]

That the speech called for active participation by the European beneficiaries was a brilliant stroke. European participation in administration and planning guaranteed that the Marshall Plan would not seem like a handout. The plan was not imposed on Europeans by a conquering power. General Marshall was determined that while the United States would provide raw materials and finished goods, it would be Europeans who would proudly rebuild their own economies and infrastructure.[63] Striving to involve Europeans in the implementation of the Marshall Plan as much as possible would also counter Russian propaganda. According to Gaddis: "Neither the Soviet Union nor its communist allies could credibly denounce a *European* initiative as 'American imperialism.'"[64]

The ways in which the Marshall Plan allowed Europeans to rebuild their own economies were quite clever. Sometimes, the Marshall Plan

---

[60] Stacy May. "Measuring the Marshall Plan", in *Foreign Affairs*. Vol. 26, No. 3, April 1948, 457. Pogue, *Statesman*, 217.

[61] Marshall Harvard speech excerpts, as quoted in May, "Measuring the Marshall Plan," 457.

[62] Lovett, as quoted in Pogue, *Statesman*, 229.

[63] Pogue, *Statesman*, 215. Gaddis, *Strategies of Containment*, 36. Marshall Statement to the Senate Committee on Foreign Relations, January 8, 1948. Bland and Stoler, eds. Ritenour Stevens, Assoc. Ed., *Marshall Papers*, Vol. 6, 315.

[64] Gaddis, *George F. Kennan*, 278.

breathed life into existing European recovery plans that had been drafted, but not yet fully implemented. For instance, the Monnet Plan for greatly accelerating French industrialization had been drafted and begun prior to the beginning of the Marshall Plan but would have died in the cradle without Marshall aid.[65] One aspect of the Marshall Plan that was particularly ingenious was the use of "counterpart funds" by which Europeans would purchase equipment using their own national currency, but the American manufacturer of say, a brand new blast furnace for a steel mill in Essen, would have already been paid out of Marshall Plan funds. Greg Behrman describes how the process worked, using as an example a hypothetical French farmer who needed an American tractor:

> The U.S. tractor manufacturer was paid with funds appropriated from the Marshall Plan, allowing the French farmer's francs to go to the French government. Counterpart funds thus performed a 'double duty.' The farmer was allowed to purchase a tractor without exacerbating the French balance-of-payments deficit. At the same time, the French government received the value of that tractor in local currency in a fund to be spent on its national recovery.[66]

The Marshall Plan was unique for its lack of corruption and for the fact that it was not just a case of throwing money at a problem in the hope that the problem would go away. This plan was well implemented and it worked.

The participation of Europeans was also a critically important, but sometimes overlooked, aspect of the Berlin Airlift itself. While the Airlift pilots were Americans and Britons, most of the "grunt" work of loading and unloading aircraft was done by Germans. The Airlift, like the Marshall Plan as a whole, did a great deal to heal lingering bad feelings between the western Allies and their former German enemies. As the Airlift grew, a serious shortage of skilled mechanics in Berlin threatened to significantly slow down the turnaround of aircraft. Since the end of the war, the American, British, and French occupying forces in western Germany and in Berlin had been reluctant to use Germans for any type

---

[65] Behrman, *The Most Noble Adventure*, 72, 219–224.

[66] Behrman, *The Most Noble Adventure*, 179.

of highly skilled labor, perhaps due to a fear of sabotage. General Tunner could see that this philosophy needed to change in a hurry. He sought, and received, permission from American Army General Lucius Clay, the Military Governor of the western occupation zone in Germany, to utilize German aircraft mechanics; that is, mechanics who had serviced *Luftwaffe* aircraft in World War II.[67] The results were wildly successful. The German mechanics took to their work with gusto. They knew that the American aircraft they were servicing were being used to help the German people as a whole.

Similarly, thousands of German laborers were employed on an emergency construction project to build a third airfield in Berlin to supplement Tempelhof in the American zone and Gatow in the British zone. The third airfield, named Tegel, was to be built in the French sector of Berlin. It was badly needed so that the Airlift could be expanded and so that enough coal could be hauled in for heating so that Berliners would not freeze to death in the coming winter. Tegel duly opened for business in late October 1948. Its rapid construction would never have been possible without large scale German labor.[68]

The subject of the shortage of coal in postwar Europe came up continually in the deliberations of Marshall as Secretary of State and his advisors, including Kennan and Clayton. Coal also constituted more than half the tonnage of supplies flown into Berlin during the Airlift, outpacing even food in terms of Airlift priority. That coal seems to have been the most important item in both the Marshall Plan and the Airlift seems to have been due to the fact that in addition to being used for heat, coal was vital to getting steel and other European industries back on their feet. Whenever possible during the Airlift, mainly toward the end of the Berlin blockade when the Airlift was working quite smoothly, manufacturing firms which had begun to operate again in Berlin after the war were supplied with enough coal to keep on producing finished goods.[69]

---

[67] Collier, *Bridge Across the Sky*, 108–109, 123–124.

[68] Collier, *Bridge Across the Sky*, 108–109, 136, 145–146, 182. The first flights to and from Tegel took place on November 5, 1948.

[69] Pogue, *Statesman*, 206. Collier, *Bridge Across the Sky*, 162.

General Marshall's biographer explains the seeming obsession with coal that was apparent whenever Marshall spoke of European recovery thus:

> Coal was needed for factories, utilities, railroads, homes. Damaged mines must be reopened, and that in turn required steel, and steel depended on even more coal. Less coal meant less production. The coal shortage had become critical to France, to Britain, and to the Soviet Union. They all needed increased German production in their zones to produce goods to pay for needed imports, and yet [Marshall] knew that with any buildup of heavy industry in Germany would rise fears of future aggression.[70]

Indeed, it is interesting to note that the Airlift was not an entirely one-way affair. According to Richard Collier; "[t]oward the lift's end, for every 260 tons of raw material flown in daily, 100 tons of manufactured goods were flown out."[71] Thus, during the Airlift Berlin was not only being kept alive, but the city's economy was continuing to recover and develop, albeit not as quickly as it would have recovered without the blockade.

General Clay traveled to Washington in October 1948 to brief President Truman on the Airlift, which was then at its height. Clay was able to tell the president and the National Security Council that the Airlift was doing more to teach Germans the great merits of the democratic form of government than any traditional education program could have done and that, because of the Airlift, the German people were becoming staunchly anti-communist in their outlook.[72]

Meanwhile, the letters from the children of Berlin to Gail Halvorsen, their new Santa Claus, continued to pour in. A letter dated November 13, 1948 was typical:

> Angel from the Heavens,
> You have given us a great joy; today my father watched a Skymaster, which a small parachute of pocket-handkerchief with

---

[70] Pogue, *Statesman*, 198.

[71] Collier, *Bridge Across the Sky*, 162.

[72] Cherny, *The Candy Bombers*, 437.

a piece of chocolate cast down. He picked it up and brought it to us. We were very joyful because we have eaten long time no chocolate.

We think always of this, that the American pilots bring a great offering for our town and our life.

The best respects and thanks to all the men of the Skymaster. from Uta Ryll, thirteen years old.[73]

"Skymaster" was indeed becoming one of the most common words in the vocabulary of Berlin's children. It cannot have hurt that the C-54 Skymaster was a very elegant looking airplane. Reading the letters Halvorsen received from the children of Berlin is a poignant reminder of the simple pleasure that could, and can, be derived from eating a bar of chocolate.

Even though the Marshall Plan quickly became quite popular in the United States once the aid began to flow and it became apparent almost immediately that that aid was having highly positive effects, it took some doing to get funding for the plan through Congress, the financial committees of which were still digesting a tremendously expensive war.[74] The "citizen-soldier" Secretary of State Marshall was much more comfortable dealing with Congress than was George Kennan. Marshall had many admirers on Capitol Hill whose trust he had earned during the war when, as Army Chief of Staff, his necessarily large budget requests for an army fighting a world war had always seemed sensible and fair, and were never, ever, laden with what would today be called "pork." On January 12, 1948, Marshall told the House Foreign Affairs Committee that "If the United States refused to aid in the reconstruction of Europe . . . we must accept the consequences of the collapse into the dictatorship of police states."[75] Kennan himself could not have put it better (in fact Kennan himself may even have drafted those words for Marshall). Secretary Marshall felt that an economically revitalized Europe would make the world safer and that the United States would thus eventually be able to spend less money on national security. Marshall was fully convinced by this time that the

---

[73] Cherny, *The Candy Bombers*, 476–477.

[74] Pogue, *Statesman*, 230–231.

[75] Pogue, *Statesman*, 242.

Russians would be the main beneficiaries if the Marshall Plan should fail to be enacted.[76] The communist coup in Prague in February and March, 1948 seemed to bring the fears of Marshall and Kennan to reality.[77]

Ironically, Marshall's most powerful ally in Congress was Republican Senator Arthur Vandenberg of Michigan; Chairman of the Senate Foreign Relations Committee. A diehard isolationist until the closing months of World War II, Vandenberg had then done a complete about face, realizing that the United States could not afford another retreat into isolationism, and was now doing everything he could to get congressional approval for the ERP. Senator Vandenberg was a key player in the success of the Marshall Plan. By the time the full program went to Congress for approval on December 19, 1947, Truman was calling it the Marshall Plan. Ever the practical politician, of Truman, Pogue notes that "[r]ealistically, he told his supporters, 'Can you imagine its chances of passage in an election year in a Republican congress if it is named for Truman and not Marshall?'"[78]

During the Airlift, American and British air crews delivered some 2,300,000 tons of supplies to Berlin.[79] As for a cost-benefit analysis, the Airlift was clearly a major win for western Europe and the United States and a big loss for Moscow. John Lewis Gaddis sums up the situation at the end of the Airlift thus:

> The events in Prague, together with the Berlin blockade, convinced the European recipients of American economic assistance that they needed military protection as well. . . . By the time Stalin grudgingly lifted the Berlin blockade in May, 1949, the North Atlantic Treaty had been signed in Washington and the Federal Republic of Germany had been proclaimed in Bonn—another result that Stalin had not wanted.[80]

---

[76] Pogue, *Statesman*, 243.

[77] Pogue, *Statesman*, 248.

[78] Truman, as noted in Pogue, *Statesman*, 236.

[79] MacGillis, "Uncle Wigglywings to take to skies again: Candy Dropper to help mark Berlin airlift," A2.

[80] Gaddis, *The Cold War*, 34.

Kennan summed up what American foreign policy should be in the "X" article by writing that "[t]o avoid destruction the United States need only measure up to its own best traditions and prove itself worthy of preservation as a great nation."[81] The Marshall Plan, the Berlin Airlift, and all that candy that was rained down on the children of Berlin by Gail Halvorsen and his fellow "Chocolate Bombers" were tangible evidence that, in the late 1940s, American foreign policy was following Kennan's good advice to the letter.

---

[81] George F. Kennan. "The Sources of Soviet Conduct", in *Foreign Affairs*. Vol. 25, No. 4, July 1947, 582.

CHAPTER 3

HAVE CLEAR AND CONSISTENT WAR AIMS

A rticulating and then achieving clear and consistent war aims is one of the most important hallmarks of successful military strategy. The United States has a mixed record in this area, but America's greatest successes in warfare have almost always occurred in those conflicts in which American war aims were most coherent and consistent. The Spanish-American War of 1898, which was ad hoc from start to finish, is a rare exception to this fact. Indeed, in the wildly successful war against Spain, President William McKinley was barely even consulted about the decision to wrest control of the Philippines from Spain. That decision originated instead from war plans made at the Navy Department that were eagerly activated immediately upon the outbreak of war in April 1898 by an impetuous force of nature named Theodore Roosevelt, then serving as Assistant Secretary of the Navy.[1]

It is no accident that the highly successful American contribution to Allied victory in World War II was accompanied by crystal clear American war aims. Those aims never wavered in any substantial manner from the time of American entry into the war in December 1941 until

---

[1] Kathleen Dalton. *Theodore Roosevelt: A Strenuous Life*. (New York: Alfred A. Knopf, 2002): 169–171. H.W. Brands. *TR: The Last Romantic*. (New York: Basic-Books, 1997): 315, 325–327, 340.

the surrender of Germany and Japan in May and August of 1945, respectively. Namely, the Americans were determined to see the complete destruction of the armed forces of Germany and Japan, the evacuation of German and Japanese forces from all territories the Axis nations had conquered early in the war, and the replacement of the governing regimes in Germany and Japan, respectively, with governments that would be willing to live at peace with the rest of the world.

For the Allies, World War II was very much a coalition war. It was essential to the United States to have Great Britain and the Soviet Union as allies. All three nations understood that this would be a total war in which the resources of the United States, Britain, and Russia would be geared entirely towards winning the war. Anything else was of secondary importance. Total Allied mobilization stands in stark contrast with the great irony that the leaders in Germany and Japan, having started the Second World War, did not see the need to mobilize for total war until it was too late. Total mobilization is one of the reasons why the Allies were victorious.

Total mobilization was for the Allies a manifestation of the fact that Allied war aims were far more clear and rational than were those of the Axis nations. Even though the war aims of the "Big Three" Allied nations did not always coincide, all three of those nations were in complete agreement on the immediate need to inflict complete and total defeat upon the armed forces of Germany and Japan. Because it was the heroic efforts and sacrifices made by Russian armies that destroyed the German Army in World War II, the Russians felt compelled to maintain a truce with Japan until August 7, 1945, just one week before Japan surrendered. Thus, while Stalin's armies did not play a major role in the defeat of Japan, it was definitely in Stalin's interest to see the greed with which Japan had for forty years eyed the prospect of territorial gain in maritime Siberia ended once and for all in the form of the crushing defeat inflicted upon Japan at the hands of the United States.[2]

The late historian Christopher Thorne has correctly and brilliantly identified the chief difference in fundamental war aims for Great Britain and the United States in World War II as being the question of what to

---

[2] Akira Iriye. *Power and Culture: The Japanese-American War 1941–1945*. (Cambridge, Massachusetts: Harvard University Press, 1981): 138–140.

do with the prewar British empire in Asia. In blunt terms, the British empire was a vast overseas network in which relatively small groups of white British administrators ruled over vast populations of non-whites in distant lands. It was a severe blow to British prestige that large chunks of the British empire in Asia, such as Burma, Malaya, Singapore, and Hong Kong had been overrun by Japan, an Asian power, early in World War II. The lesson that European colonial overseers were not in fact invincible was not lost on the Asian residents in those territories. Another blow for the British was finding out that their American allies expressed no sympathy whatsoever for the desire of Winston Churchill and other British policymakers to recover those lost parts of the empire.[3] Similarly, Stalin's determination to set up buffer states in eastern Europe that would be subservient to Moscow after the war created great tension within the Grand Alliance late in the war and led to forty-five years of Cold War after 1945. Despite these far from insignificant differences of opinion between the "Big Three" Allied nations, their common desire to see Germany and Japan completely and thoroughly defeated never wavered.

In the Gulf War of 1991, the United States-led coalition had a very specific and simple war aim: the ejection of Iraqi forces from Kuwait and the restoration of Kuwait's sovereignty as an independent nation. Upon achieving that objective, then President George H.W. Bush ended the war on February 28, 1991. Many at the time felt that the president had been too hasty in ending the war while leaving Saddam Hussein in power in Iraq. However, recent history has shown that the elder Bush was wise to stick with his limited, clear, and consistent war aims during the 1991 Gulf War.

The war with Mexico and the American Civil War are two conflicts that deserve greater recognition as wars in which the American government had very clear war aims. By way of contrast, the Vietnam War is the prime example of how dangerous it can be for the United States to get into a war without clear war aims.

The Mexican War of 1846–1848 provides an example of American forces operating with very clear war aims. President James K. Polk was determined, upon taking office in March 1845, to double the size of the

---

[3] Christopher Thorne. *Allies of a Kind: The United States, Britain and the War Against Japan, 1941–1945.* (New York: Oxford University Press, 1978): *passim.*

United States, and he proceeded to do just that. While the American war with Mexico has been referred to as the largest and most illegal land grab in history, there was nothing obscure about Polk's aims. The joint sovereignty that Britain and the United States exercised over the Oregon territory when Polk took office meant that the United States would have some sort of access to the Pacific Ocean in the Pacific Northwest region, but Polk wanted more than that. He wanted American access to the Pacific in what is now the American southwest. Acquiring the land that would allow that access was Polk's most important goal upon taking office. It went without saying that President Polk's determination to extend the territory of the United States to the Pacific Ocean south of Oregon could only be accomplished at Mexico's expense. The independence Mexico had won from Spain in 1821 proved very convenient for Polk because it meant he could initiate a war with Mexico without running the risk of war with Spain.

As president, James K. Polk was greatly aided by a powerful spirit of westward expansion that had taken hold in the United States by 1840. A few months after Polk was sworn in as president in March 1845, John O'Sullivan, the editor of both the *United States Magazine and Democratic Review* and the *New York Morning News* used the expression "Manifest Destiny" in both publications to describe with missionary zeal what he felt was the duty of white American settlers—to expand the nation westwards to the Pacific Ocean. O'Sullivan's specific motivation for writing in the summer of 1845 was to drum up popular support for the annexation of Texas; but his ultimate dream, shared by many Americans, extended well beyond Texas.[4]

James K. Polk was that rarest of presidents; the president whose campaign speeches were not just rhetoric, but actually represented a plan

---

[4] Robert W. Merry, *A Country of Vast Designs: James K. Polk, The Mexican War and the Conquest of the American Continent.* (New York: Simon & Schuster, 2009): 128. Julius W. Pratt. "The Origin of 'Manifest Destiny'", in *The American Historical Review.* Vol. 32, No. 4, July 1927, 795–798, text and notes. Carol Berkin, Christopher L. Miller, Robert W. Cherny, and James L. Gormly. *Making America: A History of the United States.* Vol. 1. *To 1877.* Sixth Edition. (Boston: Cengage, 2013): 339.

that was thoroughly and completely implemented once he was elected president. In a revealing quote, Henry R. Nau states that:

> James Polk was without question one of the most ambitious and successful presidents in American history. In four short years, he expanded American territory to incorporate Texas, the southwest territories of New Mexico and California, and the northwest territories of Oregon. Remarkably, he announced all of these goals beforehand. And he accomplished them as a lame-duck president . . . because he promised upon his unexpected nomination in 1844 to serve only one term.[5]

Actually, President John Tyler orchestrated the annexation of Texas shortly before Polk's inauguration, although the ratification of annexation by the people of Texas did not take place until July 4, 1845 and it would be February 1846 before Texas was up and running as a fully functioning U.S state.[6] Polk's contribution regarding Texas was to obtain all of the western Texas territory that remained in dispute between the United States and Mexico at the time of Polk's inauguration in March 1845. Also, it was almost certainly *because* Polk never intended to run for re-election that he was able to accomplish so much. A president hoping to serve two terms cannot be too daring in the first term. Polk is probably the only US president who never even hoped to serve two terms. As such, President Polk could afford to be daring. Polk, the quintessential Jacksonian Democrat, could afford to give the major field commands in the war against Mexico to Whig generals like Zachary Taylor and Winfield Scott who would have become his political rivals had Polk intended to remain in politics. He could also instigate a major war without worrying about how that war would impact his political future. Knowing from the outset that he was a one-term president freed Polk to act.

---

[5] Henry R. Nau. *Conservative Internationalism: Armed Diplomacy Under Jefferson, Polk, Truman, and Reagan.* (Princeton, NJ: Princeton University Press, 2013): 110.

[6] Daniel Walker Howe. *What Hath God Wrought: The Transformation of America, 1815–1848.* (New York: Oxford University Press, 2007): 732.

Polk was also determined to settle the Oregon boundary with Great Britain. (It would not be until after 1900 that Canada would gradually gain the right to make its own foreign policy, without the need to seek prior approval from Great Britain.) Polk's rhetoric made much of the American popular demand for a northern boundary for Oregon at latitude 54° 40', much further north than where the actual northern border of Washington state (carved out of the Oregon territory) lies today. In reality, Polk never intended to risk war with Britain on the Oregon boundary issue. He knew that war with Britain would be far more risky than war with Mexico. Also, while the Oregon boundary was important to Polk, it never loomed as large in his mind as did the Mexican territory in the southwest. Thus, Polk gave up his claim against Britain for a far north boundary for the Oregon territory and was content to negotiate a settlement with Britain that set the northern boundary of the Oregon territory at the 49th Parallel, even accommodating a British desire to retain for Canada all of Vancouver Island, the southern tip of which dips slightly below the 49th Parallel.[7]

John C. Calhoun, then serving as a Democratic senator from South Carolina, advised Polk to pursue a peaceful and moderate course in the Oregon boundary dispute. Describing a discussion he had had with Calhoun on the Oregon boundary, Polk wrote in his diary in late March 1846: "[Calhoun] insisted that the two governments ought to settle it, and that they could do it on the basis of 49°. He said that a question of etiquette ought not to prevent either from reopening the negotiation by a new proposition. I told him I could make no proposition."[8] The shrewd Polk refrained from enlightening Calhoun about his (Polk's) true feelings on the Oregon question. Calhoun had had experience trying to resolve the Oregon question when he had served as President Tyler's Secretary of State, but had been replaced in the Cabinet by James Buchanan after

---

[7] Howe, *What Hath God Wrought*, 715–722.

[8] James K. Polk. *The Diary of James K. Polk During His Presidency, 1845 to 1849* (Hereinafter *Polk Diary*, Vol. 1). Edited and Annototated by Milo Milton Quaife. Vol. 1. (Chicago: A.C. Mclurg & Co. on behalf of the Chicago Historical Society, 1910): entry for March 30, 1846, 313.

Polk's election. Calhoun had taken the loss of his position as Secretary of State somewhat personally, especially since Polk was a fellow Democrat.[9] Relations between Calhoun and Polk were undoubtedly a bit tense. For his part, President Polk probably never quite trusted Calhoun, for whom Polk's patron and mentor Andrew Jackson had developed a cordial hatred due to Calhoun's fondness for the doctrine of "nullification," by which a state could supposedly ignore a Federal law if it so chose.[10] A few weeks after taking that seemingly intransigent position with Calhoun, Polk confided to Calhoun's fellow South Carolina Senator George McDuffie, whom Polk seems to have found more congenial than Calhoun, "that if G[reat] B[ritain] made an offer of 49° or what was equivalent to it, or with slight modifications, I would feel it to be my duty to submit such proposition to the Senate for their previous advice before I took any action on it."[11] The Oregon Treaty was duly ratified by the Senate on June 18, 1846. By submitting an Oregon treaty that contained a bit less than what he wanted to the Senate, Polk displayed that he knew how to pick his battles.

Contrasting with his wise approach to the Oregon issue, President Polk had personal characteristics that should have prevented him from getting things done, but that somehow did not have that effect. He was a micromanager of the first order, and he seemed to feel it was his duty to speak with anyone who desired to see him; whatever their reason. Despite the resultant constant distractions and despite his obsession with detail and his discomfort at delegating responsibility to anyone, Polk was always able to maintain his focus. Polk felt it his duty to hold public office hours every weekday, even though he knew that that meant he would be besieged by office-seekers. The Pendleton Civil Service Act, which would finally get office seekers out of a president's hair, was still some forty years in the future. Polk confided to his diary in late 1845: "Had more office seekers to-day [*sic*] than for many days past, but appointed

---

[9] Howe, *What Hath God Wrought*, 764.

[10] Merry, *A Country of Vast Designs*, 6.

[11] *Polk Diary*, Vol. 1, April 24, 1846, 349.

none of them."[12] Early in his presidency, Polk seems to have had open office hours in the morning when office seekers and others could see him without an appointment. He would then work on official business in private in the afternoon and evening; taking a break for dinner at 4:00 p.m.[13] Later in his Presidency he changed his schedule a bit. In the summer of 1847, Polk was still fending off hordes of office seekers, but he seems to have then been working in private in the morning and then seeing visitors in the early afternoon.[14] The pressure from office seekers never abated during his Presidency. For a man who hated to waste time, President Polk seems to have felt it was his duty to at least listen to the pitches of various office seekers.[15] As late as March 1848, Polk was still fulminating in his diary that:

> It would seem that the annoyance to which I am subjected by the importunities of office seekers is never to cease. To-day [sic] an unusual number of them crowded my office, and among them several females, seeking places for their sons, brothers, or husbands. At one time to-day [sic] two ladies of respectability, whom I know, were addressing me at the same time in behalf of their brother, whom I have undersood is a drunkard & wholly unworthy of any public trust. They desired to have him pensioned on the Government.[16]

Curiously, Polk never simply told his staff to keep office seekers away from him. Reading Polk's diary and his correspondence takes one back to a very different time. In addition to the constant complaints about office seekers found in his diary, Polk's published correspondence shows that

---

[12] *Polk Diary,* Vol. 1, October 13, 1845, 56.

[13] *Polk Diary,* Vol. 1, April 27, 1846, 360.

[14] James K. Polk. *The Diary of James K. Polk During His Presidency, 1845 to 1849* (Hereinafter *Polk Diary*, Vol. 3). Edited and Annototated by Milo Milton Quaife. Vol. 3. (Chicago: A.C. Mclurg & Co. on behalf of the Chicago Historical Society, 1910): See for instance, the entries for July 19 and July 23, 1847, respectively, 93, 96.

[15] *Polk Diary*, Vol. 3, May 3, 1847, 9.

[16] *Polk Diary*, Vol. 3, March 16, 1848, 386.

while president he sometimes became actively involved in negotiations for the purchase of slaves for his Mississippi plantation.[17]

Polk was a very good Democrat. The office seekers wasted his time, but the micromanager in Polk did like to keep track of who was working where. The president castigated the Secretary of the Treasury, Robert J. Walker, in April 1846 because Walker was failing to exercise the Jacksonian prerogative of utilizing the spoils system to pack the Federal bureaucracy with functionaries from one's own party. In Polk's view, there were still far too many "obnoxious Whig clerks" in the Treasury Department and not enough good Democrats. Polk instructed Walker to get busy and start firing Whigs and hiring Democrats. Polk was armed on this occasion with a list that showed the names of each and every Whig currently employed in the Treasury department.[18] The creation of an Independent Treasury department in July 1846 fulfilled one of Polk's most cherished domestic policy goals. Thus, the dressing down that Walker received a few months prior to that date about the political affiliation of Treasury clerks was not entirely a simple feature of Polk's well deserved reputation as a micromanager. Polk wanted reliable Party men in the transformed and enhanced Treasury department.

President Polk's lifelong propensity for working very long hours was undoubtedly a major factor in his early death shortly after leaving office at age fifty-three—by which time he looked twenty years older. As president, however, Polk made more time for leisure activities than is sometimes realized. He did take exercise while in the White House, riding horseback and usually taking a walk each morning and again each evening, the weather and his delicate health permitting.[19] The president and his beloved wife, Sarah, entertained regularly at the White House.

---

[17] For a slave purchase, see Polk's letter to Robert Campbell, Jr. April 20, 1846. Wayne Cutler, ed., James L. Rogers II; Benjamin H. Severance, Assoc. Eds. Cynthia J. Rogers; Trevor A. Smith, and William K. Bolt, Assist. Eds. *Correspondence of James K. Polk*. Volume XI: 1846. (Knoxville: The University of Tennessee Press, 2009): 130–131. For the location, see Howe, *What Hath God Wrought*, 702.

[18] *Polk Diary*, Vol. 1, April 22, 1846, 345–346. The quote is on 345.

[19] *Polk Diary*, Vol. 1, April 27, 1846, April 9, 1846, 361, 322–323.

The instigation for entertaining undoubtedly came from the graceful Sarah rather than from the abstemious president.

A White House reception on Tuesday, April 14, 1846 was a typical gathering. The president and First Lady had more than one hundred guests in the "parlour" on the first floor of the White House that evening. (Polk's office was on the second floor.)[20] Polk wrote of these receptions:

> I find these informal evenings of reception twice a week pleasant. They afford all strangers who desire to do so an opportunity [to] call in an informal way. By setting apart two evenings in the week, too, to receive company, I am enabled to devote the other evenings of the week to my public duties.[21]

Polk seems to have seen his social guests sort of the way he saw office seekers, as items that needed to be processed.

Office seekers were far from the only distraction for Polk. Even though he was very driven and determined, he did tolerate insubordination from those who worked for him, such as Secretary of State James Buchanan. One reason for his tolerance is that Polk disliked personal confrontation. He did not mind delivering written ultimatums to the Mexican government, but he did not like to deliver a dressing down to someone who was in the room with him.[22]

The Mexican War was surrounded by moral ambiguity right from the moment it began because President Polk clearly provoked Mexico into declaring war on April 22, 1846 after he had sent American troops to the Rio Grande river, well into the area of Texas still in dispute between Mexico and the United States. An additional provocation for Mexico was that Polk had by that time also sent separate detachments of American troops under Brigadier General Stephen Kearny and Lieutenant Colonel John C. Frémont, respectively, to seize New Mexico

---

[20] *Polk Diary,* Vol. 1, April 14 and April 24, 1846, respectively; 331, 348.

[21] *Polk Diary,* Vol. 1, April 14, 1846, 331. Brackets in original.

[22] Merry, *A Country of Vast Designs,* 266, 269–270. Nau, *Conservative Internationalism,* 118. As micromanager—Walter R. Borneman, *Polk: The Man Who Transformed the Presidency and America.* (New York: Random House, 2008): 354–355.

and California—territories which Polk was determined to detach from Mexico. After a skirmish between Mexican and American troops in Texas on the Rio Grande, Polk persuaded the US Congress to declare war on Mexico on May 13, 1846.[23]

Working with General-in-Chief of the Army Major General Winfield Scott would prove to be a major challenge for Polk. While undoubtedly highly intelligent and talented, Scott would also prove to be insubordinate. Scott did appear to have mellowed a bit with age by the time he was advising President Lincoln during the first months of the Civil War in 1861. However, during the Mexican War, Scott was a vain prima donna who, in his contempt for presidential authority over the armed forces, was very much in the mold of George B. McClellan and Douglas MacArthur.[24] Immediately upon the outbreak of war, Polk offered General Scott the supreme command of American forces in the field. When Polk and Secretary of War William Marcy subsequently enquired why Scott was slow to leave Washington for the front, they got more of an answer than they bargained for. Scott answered with a level of candor unusual for one who should have developed sharper political antennae during his long service in Washington. In late May 1846, Scott made it clear that he felt that meddling politicians in Washington, particularly Democrats, were going to cause him at least as much trouble in this war as was the Mexican Army and said so in a notorious letter to Marcy that includes what is perhaps the most well-known quote to come out of the Mexican War.[25] The quote and Polk's reaction to it are perhaps best described by Polk himself as recorded in his diary: "He [Scott] uses language not only exceptionable but unbecoming an officer. After making false insinuations against the administration, he concludes by using the following language, *viz.*: 'My explicit meaning is, that I do not desire to place myself in the most perilous of all positions, a fire upon my rear from

---

23 Borneman, *Polk,* 186–188. Berkin, et al., *Making America*, Vol. 1, Sixth Ed., 346–348.

24 Merry, *A Country of Vast Designs*, 253–263. Howe, *What Hath God Wrought*, 752–753.

25 *Polk Diary*, Vol. 1, May 23, 1846, 419–420. Merry, *A Country of Vast Designs*, 258.

Washington and the fire in front from the Mexicans.'"[26] More than a few generals in American history have undoubtedly felt the same way but had the good sense to keep such thoughts to themselves. President Polk was not amused at General Scott's clear contempt for civilian control of the military.

For all his micromanaging, Polk does seem to have had some gifts as a strategist. He could see that holding the northern Mexican provinces (which at that time included California) was not enough. It was apparently Polk himself who came up with the idea of the landing at Vera Cruz, which would result in General Scott's successful advance on Mexico City itself.[27] In addition to the American incursion into California which he had authorized, Polk's strategy was to have Major General Zachary Taylor's army grab a chunk of Mexican territory to the west and southwest of the Rio Grande for bargaining purposes.

The California expedition would result in one of the many headaches for Polk caused by the inflated egos of his subordinates in the field. In California, Kearny, Frémont, and US Navy Captain Robert F. Stockton would become embroiled in an administrative turf battle of epic proportions that would result in Frémont being court-martialed for insubordination.[28]

The very slow communications of the 1840s forced Polk to delegate far more authority than he would have liked to his two top field commanders, Generals Scott and Taylor. The situation was exacerbated by the fact that Polk never quite trusted either man. The difficulties of communicating over long distances had much to do with the misunderstanding between the president and his generals. It took at least six weeks for any two way communication to occur between President Polk and his generals in Mexico; that is three weeks for a dispatch from the president to reach Scott or Taylor in the field in Mexico and another three weeks for an answer to arrive back at the White House.[29] The nation's rail network was then in its infancy. Telegraph service south of Richmond, Virginia

---

[26] *Polk Diary*, Vol. 1, May 23, 1846, 419–420.

[27] Merry, *A Country of Vast Designs*, 318–320.

[28] Borneman, *Polk*, 269–285.

[29] Borneman, *Polk*, 246.

was nonexistent.[30] Some of the mail was carried by oceangoing ships from Vera Cruz, through the Gulf of Mexico, around the tip of Florida, and up the east coast of the United States into Chesapeake Bay—and the same route in reverse. While oceangoing steamships were beginning to appear on the North Atlantic route between New York and Liverpool in the 1840s, sailing vessels were still the norm for coastal shipping. The mail that went by sea the entire way between Washington and Vera Cruz was undoubtedly carried in sailing ships and was no faster than overland mail; the latter being the most common mode of mail transport. The couriers carrying dispatches from Polk to the commanders at the front would travel by a combination of rail, stage coach, river steamboat, and finally horseback. Polk tried to speed up communications after he became aware that the *Baltimore Sun* newspaper was getting war news a day earlier than he was by improvising its own private transportation system.[31] In an apparent reference to getting more steamboats running on the Mobile and Alabama rivers, respectively, he wrote in his diary in May 1847 that

> I brought also before the Cabinet the importance of running an express from Mobile to Montgomery, in Alabama, so as to gain a day upon the regular mail time, and thereby receive at Washington despatches from the army as early as the express of the Baltimore *Sun* newspaper obtains the latest news from the seat of War.[32]

Such difficulties in communication seem almost quaint in the twenty-first century when an American president can communicate instantaneously with any military commander anywhere in the world. During the Mexican War, events at the front and diplomatic activity in Washington and Mexico City often meant that written communications were very much out of date by the time they arrived. For instance, after his brilliant victory over a Mexican Army at the battle of Monterrey, some one hundred miles southwest of the Rio Grande in September 1846, General

---

[30] Howe, *What Hath God Wrought*, 696. See also *Polk Diary*, Vol. 3, August 28, 1847, 152. Polk received war news by telegraph from Richmond on that day.

[31] *Polk Diary*, Vol. 3, May 25, 1847, 36.

[32] *Polk Diary*, Vol. 3, May 25, 1847, 35.

Taylor felt justified in offering generous surrender terms, including an eight week-long regional truce, to the Mexicans. Taylor did this in part because he was aware that President Polk's initial goal was to gain control of Mexico's northern provinces via negotiation and cash payments rather than war, if possible. According to Henry R. Nau, "Polk wanted to acquire New Mexico and California by purchase, not by conquest. His efforts involved four distinct strategic forays that tightly linked the dispatch of diplomatic envoys with the incremental escalation of force."[33] Generous terms of surrender were Taylor's way of ensuring that it would never be too late to hold out an olive branch to the Mexicans. However, during the summer of 1846, and unbeknownst to Taylor, Polk had gradually become convinced that the Mexican government was stalling for time rather than negotiating in good faith. Thus, by the time of Taylor's victory at Monterrey, Polk wanted the Mexicans to be taught a lesson about American resolve, not to be treated with kid gloves.[34] Of the president's changed attitude, one of Polk's biographers has noted that "Taylor, half a continent and three weeks away, could hardly be blamed for not knowing it."[35] Polk was (somewhat unjustifiably) outraged when he found out that Taylor had not destroyed the Mexican Army he had beaten at Monterrey.[36] Polk would confide to his diary in May 1847 that "Gen'l Taylor is a good fighter, but I do not consider him a great General."[37]

Such misunderstandings would continue to bedevil Polk's relationships with his generals in the field. There were other reasons for friction in addition to lengthy and slow lines of communication. Both Taylor and Scott were talented generals but, like their commander-in-chief, each was an ambitious man jealous of his respective prerogatives. As such, General Scott was incensed in the summer of 1847 to find, while marching an American Army from Vera Cruz toward Mexico City, that he had suddenly been saddled with a State Department representative,

---

[33] Nau, *Conservative Internationalism*, 123.

[34] Borneman, *Polk*, 244–245.

[35] Borneman, *Polk*, 245.

[36] Borneman, *Polk*, 245–246.

[37] *Polk Diary*, Vol. 3, May 6, 1847, 15.

Nicholas P. Trist, who was empowered to negotiate with the Mexican government as President Polk's personal representative. While Trist and Scott would eventually and somewhat surprisingly become good friends, during Trist's first weeks in Mexico the two men refused to cooperate with each other at all—with unfortunate results. In July 1847, Polk was again enraged when he learned that Scott had failed to pass on to the Mexican government a peace treaty that Trist had brought with him from Washington.[38] A disgusted Polk wrote that as a result of the feud between Trist and Scott, "the danger has become imminent that because of the personal controversy between these self important personages, the golden moment for concluding a peace with Mexico may have passed."[39]

A hostage to poor communications networks and surrounded by insubordinate lieutenants, it must have seemed to Polk that he was trying to push a wheelbarrow full of cats. That he somehow got his wheelbarrow across the finish line with the Treaty of Guadalupe Hidalgo, which was signed on February 2, 1848, was proof that Polk was focused to a degree unique amongst American politicians. Once the Treaty of Guadalupe Hidalgo was ratified by the US Senate on March 10, 1848, only the small slice of territory acquired in the Gadsden Purchase of 1853 would remain to be added before the territory of the lower forty-eight states would be filled out in its present outline form.

Polk had a clear set of priorities from which he never wavered. Unlike many recent presidents, Polk never tried to be all things to all people. Having a limited number of objectives enabled Polk to focus on achieving those goals to the exclusion of all else, despite the distractions he seemed unable to escape, such as office seekers.[40]

How much of Mexico to take was not entirely clear to everyone, but it was to Polk. Many Americans wanted to take all of Mexico. As late as December 1847, Polk felt compelled to write in his State of the Union report to Congress that he was not contemplating taking all of Mexico.[41]

---

[38] Borneman, *Polk*, 261–265.

[39] *Polk Diary*, Vol. 3, July 9, 1847, 76–77.

[40] Nau, *Conservative Internationalism*, 117. Howe, *What Hath God Wrought*, 708.

[41] Borneman, *Polk*, 306–307.

It is well known that Polk was not entirely satisfied with the Treaty of Guadalupe Hidalgo, which finally ended the war. It took "only" eighteen days for the Treaty to be sent to Washington, which qualifies as rapid mail service during the Mexican War. Polk had the treaty in his hands on February 20, 1848. He wrote in his diary that by that time he wished he had taken more Mexican territory, but that the treaty as written did conform generally to the instructions Polk had given Nicholas Trist prior to Trist's departure for Mexico in April 1847. As for the extra territory he wished he had demanded from Mexico, Polk wrote in his diary that "if the treaty was now to be made, I should demand more territory, perhaps to make the Sierra Madra the line."[42] It is difficult to know exactly what Polk meant by this remark since the Sierra Madre mountains run in three separate spurs; two of which run on a north-south axis. The third and southernmost spur runs on a northwest-southeast axis. Most likely, the "more territory" Polk wished he had demanded would have been a relatively modest addition to what the treaty already gave to the United States. Polk may have meant that he wished he had told Trist to push the border of Texas out to the scene of Scott's victory at Monterrey, which lies at the eastern base of one of the Sierra Madre spurs. Since the treaty as written was generally in line with Polk's objectives and gave the United States vast territory including the future states of California, New Mexico, and Arizona, he was wise enough to not overreach by rejecting it. According to Nau: "Like all great negotiators, Polk also had an exquisite sense of timing. The Democratic Party had lost the House elections of fall 1847. The American people were growing weary of war. He knew a long occupation of Mexico would be costly."[43]

James K. Polk is seen as a president who greatly expanded the power of the Executive Branch. However, he always had great respect for the separation of powers enshrined in the US Constitution. President Polk was well aware that Congress has a Constitutional right to be involved in foreign policy and in military affairs.[44] Polk kept Congress well informed of what he was doing at all times. By way of contrast, in the 1960s Lyndon

---

[42] *Polk Diary*, Vol. 3, February 21, 1848, 347.

[43] Nau, *Conservative Internationalism*, 134.

[44] Nau, *Conservative Internationalism*, 118.

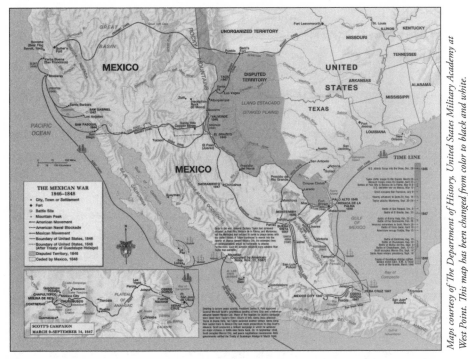

Maps courtesy of The Department of History, United States Military Academy at West Point. This map has been changed from color to black and white.

This map shows the vast distances involved in the Mexican War and the enormous amount of territory the United States gained in 1848 via the Treaty of Guadalupe Hidalgo.

Johnson as president used his intimate knowledge of the workings of Congress, learned from Johnson's years in the House of Representatives and later as Senate Majority leader to hide what he was doing in Vietnam from Congressional scrutiny and from the public.[45]

At first glance, it seems that President Abraham Lincoln altered Union war aims dramatically in the Civil War when he issued the Emancipation Proclamation on January 1, 1863. In reality, there was far more continuity than change in Lincoln's war aims throughout the Civil War. It has traditionally been understood that President Lincoln issued the

---

[45] H.R. McMaster. *Dereliction of Duty: Lyndon Johnson, Robert McNamara, The Joint Chiefs of Staff, and the Lies that Led to Vietnam*. (New York: HarperPerennial, 1997): 312–313. John Lewis Gaddis. *Strategies of Containment: A Critical Appraisal of American National Security Policy During the Cold War*. (New York: Oxford University Press, 1982, 2005): 268–269.

Emancipation Proclamation on January 1, 1863 because it was necessary to broaden the original war aim of reuniting the nation politically by also placing the American Civil War on a moral footing. The moral aspect was more than a reflection of Lincoln's distaste for slavery. Focusing on the repugnance of slavery as an institution was necessary to prevent Great Britain from extending diplomatic recognition to the Confederacy or worse yet, entering the war on the side of the Confederacy. In this regard, the Emancipation Proclamation clarified Union war aims brilliantly. As a result of the proclamation and Union victories at Gettysburg and Vicksburg, Great Britain, which had outlawed slavery throughout the British Empire in 1833, had by the end of 1863 ceased to engage in the very non-neutral activity of building warships for the Confederacy in British shipyards. That activity had created a real threat of war between the United States and Great Britain. The British government could not withstand the public relations fallout from being publicly "outed" as a fervent supporter of a budding nation-state that was built on slave labor. The precise, limited, legalistic language of the Emancipation Proclamation, the tone of which is so very different from the universalist and timeless tone of the Gettysburg Address, shows that President Lincoln thought long and hard before making the decision to alter Union war aims in the midst of the war. The Emancipation Proclamation had much to do with keeping Britain out of the war.

The extent of the bitterness felt by Lincoln and his advisors over Confederate warships being built in British yards is borne out in an exchange of letters between Thomas H. Dudley, the American consul in Liverpool (home of the Confederate Navy's favorite shipyard—Laird) and J. Price Edwards, the British Collector of Customs at Liverpool. Dudley was unable to get Edwards to detain a mysterious vessel known as "Hull Number 290," that was nearing completion at the Laird shipyard in the spring of 1862. The "290" would in fact go on to become the Confederate commerce raider *Alabama*, a formidable warship which would destroy more than fifty Union merchant ships during the war.[46]

---

[46] Dudley–Edwards Correspondence, July 1862, as reprinted in Stephen W. Sears, ed. *The Civil War: The Second Year Told by Those Who Lived It.* (New York: Library of America, 2012): 309–313.

The Lincoln administration was appalled that the British government would blithely allow agents of the Confederacy to place orders for warships to be built in British shipyards. Union officials in Great Britain, such as Dudley in Liverpool and American ambassador Charles Francis Adams in London protested this policy vigorously. Until mid-1863, the British government stonewalled all Union enquiries into the construction of a Confederate Navy in British yards. In the case of the *Alabama*, the first tactic tried by the shipyard managers to allay Union suspicions was to say that the vessel was being built as a merchantman. Dudley was not fooled, and informed Edwards in July 1862 that

> Everything about the vessel shows her to be a war vessel; she has well-constructed magazines; she has a number of canisters of a peculiar and expensive construction, for containing powder; she has already platforms screwed to her decks for the reception of swivel guns.[47]

The shipyard managers then concocted a story that the vessel was indeed a warship, but that it was being built for the navy of Spain, not for the Confederacy. Dudley quickly ascertained, via the American embassy in London, that the government of Spain had no warships under construction in Liverpool at that time.[48] The British government was completely apathetic to Dudley's pleas that the ship be seized and prevented from leaving British waters. The reply of Edwards to Dudley's request in this regard is a masterpiece of diplomatic dodging:

> I have to acquaint you, that I am directed by the commissioners of her Majesty's customs to apprise you that their solicitor informs them that the details given by you in regard to the said vessel are not sufficient, in a legal point of view, to justify me in taking upon myself the responsibility of the detention of this ship.[49]

---

[47] Dudley to Edwards, July 9, 1862, as reprinted in Sears, ed., *The Civil War: The Second Year Told by Those Who Lived It*, 311–312.

[48] Dudley to Edwards, July 9, 1862, as reprinted in Sears, ed., *The Civil War: The Second Year Told by Those Who Lived It*, 312.

[49] Edwards to Dudley, July 16, 1862, as reprinted in Sears, ed., *The Civil War: The Second Year Told by Those Who Lived It*, 313.

Edwards then closes with that classic Victorian flourish issued only when one is holding all the cards and has no intention of giving an inch—

> I have the honor to be, sir, your most obedient servant,
> J. PRICE EDWARDS, *Collector.*[50]

Not only was the construction of warships for the Confederacy in British yards a violation of Britain's neutrality, it was also a violation of domestic British law. The Foreign Enlistment Act, enacted by the British Parliament in 1819, specifically forbade the construction of warships in British shipyards for any foreign power that was at war. The Confederacy's naval agent in Britain, Captain James D. Bulloch, was completely unfazed by the existence of the Foreign Enlistment Act. He simply arranged for the *Alabama*, and two other Confederate warships, to sail from Britain without armament. The guns and ammunition were added later. In the case of the *Alabama*, the new ship left Liverpool in July 1862 unarmed and under the innocuous sounding and very temporary name *Enrica*. Upon reaching Terceira in the Azores, Confederate officers took command of the vessel, its guns and ammunition were transferred from another ship that had sailed out from England for that express purpose, and Confederate naval captain Raphael Semmes persuaded almost all of the rank and file (and mostly British) sailors who had brought the ship from Liverpool to enlist as crew for the ship's war patrol. That the ship was built in England with the express purpose of destroying Union merchant shipping on the high seas and that the vast majority of its enlisted personnel, and even one of its officers, were Britons explains why an enraged Ambassador to Great Britain Charles Francis Adams was unable to restrain himself from using the word "pirate" whenever he spoke of the *Alabama*.[51]

---

[50] Edwards to Dudley, July 16, 1862, as reprinted in Sears, ed., *The Civil War: The Second Year Told by Those Who Lived It*, 313.

[51] David Rigby. *The C.S.S.* Alabama *and British Neutrality During the American Civil War*. (Unpublished paper, 1991): *passim*. Brooks D. Simpson, ed., *The Civil War: The Third Year Told by Those Who Lived It*. (New York: Library of America, 2013): 502.

According to Eric Foner, Secretary of State William Seward, and many other State Department personnel had been lobbying hard throughout the year 1862 in order to convince President Lincoln of the view then prevalent in the State Department "that emancipation [must] be made an explicit war aim in order to forestall foreign recognition of the Confederacy or some kind of international mediation proposal."[52]

However, even the pressing need to keep Great Britain and other European nations out of the Civil War does not fully explain why a man like Abraham Lincoln, so conservative and cautious by nature, would abandon his antislavery stance of the 1850s to become the greatest abolitionist of all time by issuing the Emancipation Proclamation. Being "antislavery" in the 1850s was a very different matter from being an abolitionist. The antislavery viewpoint, which became the founding plank of the Republican party in the 1850s, was that slavery should be kept out of the territories owned by the United States, but not yet incorporated as states. These areas (greatly expanded thanks to the activities of James K. Polk) included what are now the states of Kansas, Nebraska, Nevada, New Mexico, Arizona, Utah, the Dakotas, and Montana.

In the 1850s, Lincoln felt that slavery would gradually be extinguished if it could be prevented from growing, which contrasts with abolitionists such as William Lloyd Garrison and Harriett Beecher Stowe who favored immediate emancipation with no compensation for slave owners. "Gradual" is the key word in describing Lincoln's views on emancipation in the 1850s. How then, could such a man issue the Emancipation Proclamation on January 1, 1863, a document that promised immediate emancipation for any slaves found by advancing Union armies in such Confederate territory where white residents were deemed to be still in rebellion as of January 1, 1863 without any financial compensation whatsoever to the owners of said slaves?

The answer is that by late 1862, Lincoln realized that the Civil War was no longer a matter of simply putting down a rebellion and restoring the status quo. The Emancipation Proclamation grew out of Lincoln's growing belief that his ultimate aim, preserving the Union, could be

---

[52] Eric Foner. *The Fiery Trial: Abraham Lincoln and American Slavery.* (New York: Norton, 2010): 219.

attained only if it were accompanied by the complete destruction of slavery. Therefore, the Emancipation Proclamation was not as radical a change of policy by Lincoln as it is sometimes thought to be. Indeed, Lincoln seems to have had an inkling as far back as 1858 that American society would be transformed completely and permanently should the nation descend into civil war. Lincoln's "House Divided" speech at the Republican State Convention in Springfield, Illinois on June 16, 1858 includes the famous phrases:

> A house divided against itself cannot stand.
> I believe this government cannot endure, permanently half *slave* and half *free*.
> I do not expect the Union to be *dissolved*—I do not expect the house to *fall*—but I *do* expect it will cease to be divided.
> It will become *all* one thing, or *all* the other.[53]

Lincoln's other writings, including the remainder of that speech, make it clear that he never expected the "all one thing" to be slavery everywhere. Therefore, the Emancipation Proclamation was more of a necessity to ensure the future integrity of the Union rather than a change in policy.

By August 1862, some Union generals, following the lead of Major General Benjamin F. Butler, were treating slaves who fell into their hands as "contraband" of war—that is, as laborers who could be put to work for wages (or perhaps just for room and board) as free men and women who could build fortifications, work as teamsters hauling supplies, and perform cooking and laundry duties for Union troops in camp. By that time the first and second Confiscation Acts had been passed by Congress and signed into law by President Lincoln. These gave Union forces the right to seize the property of rebels; although Lincoln retained fears that Congress might have overreached, in legal terms, in drafting the Confiscation Acts and it was with more than a little trepidation that Lincoln had signed these acts into law in July 1861 and

---

[53] Abraham Lincoln to the Republican State Convention, Springfield, Illinois, June 16, 1858, as reprinted in Abraham Lincoln. *The Gettysburg Address and Other Writings.* (New York: Fall River Press, 2013): 21.

July 1862, respectively.[54] Horace Greeley, the influential editor of the *New-York Daily Tribune* and a diehard abolitionist, was convinced that Lincoln's tacit acceptance of contraband status for former slaves laboring in non-combat roles for the Union Army and his somewhat more explicit acceptance of the Confiscation Acts were nowhere near enough. Greeley was convinced that the president was dragging his feet on the issue of slavery and wrote to tell him so. The letter Greeley wrote to Lincoln at that time, and particularly the president's response (both of which were published in contemporary newspapers) contain some of the most frequently quoted lines ever written about slavery. Lincoln stated in his response to Greeley that:

> My paramount object in this struggle *is* to save the Union, and is *not* either to save or destroy slavery. If I could save the Union without freeing *any* slave I would do it, and if I could save it by freeing *all* the slaves I would do it; and if I could save it by freeing some and leaving others alone I would also do that. What I do about slavery, and the colored race, I do because I believe it helps to save the Union; and what I forbear, I forbear because I do *not* believe it would help to save the Union.[55]

Historians are quick to point out that Lincoln then tips his hand when he closes this letter by telling Greeley that despite his pragmatic views on the issue, "I intend no modification of my oft-expressed *personal* wish that all men every where could be free."[56]

Eric Foner has written that even had he not put his thumb on the scale in the concluding sentence, Lincoln's letter responding to Greeley was not nearly as neutral a document as it appears to be on first glance.

---

[54] Brookes D. Simpson, Stephen W. Sears, and Aaron Sheehan-Dean, eds. *The Civil War: The First Year Told by Those Who Lived It.* (New York: Library of America, 2011): 364. Allen C. Guelzo. *Fateful Lightning: A New History of the Civil War & Reconstruction.* (New York: Oxford University Press, 2012): 176–177.

[55] Lincoln to Greeley, August 22, 1862, as reprinted in Sears, ed., *The Civil War: The Second Year Told by Those Who Lived It*, 372–373.

[56] Lincoln to Greeley, August 22, 1862, as reprinted in Sears, ed., *The Civil War: The Second Year Told by Those Who Lived It*, 373.

In fact, says Foner, the response to Greeley was a sort of trial balloon, gently and rather indirectly setting forth the idea that the president had already made up his mind to issue an emancipation proclamation but that he needed to test the waters of northern public opinion first to see if northerners would accept such a proclamation. Lincoln had grown as a war leader, and by mid-1862 he realized that the war had become far more complex than it had been at the time of the outbreak of hostilities in April 1861. It was no longer a straightforward question of putting down a rebellion and restoring the old Union, but rather the time had come to build an entirely new Union.[57] Foner writes that Lincoln's response to Greeley was "a way of preparing northern public opinion for a change in policy on which he [Lincoln] had already decided. Certainly, it suggested that freeing all the slaves was now a real option, something that had not been the case a year or even six months earlier."[58] This would mean that while emancipation was a change of course in Union war aims, it was an evolutionary, *not* a revolutionary, alteration.

Henry Adams, son of Union Minister to Great Britain Charles Francis Adams, wrote from London to his brother Charles (then serving in the Union Army of the Potomac as a cavalry officer), in January 1863, telling Charles that the Emancipation Proclamation had gone over big with the British public. "The Emancipation Proclamation has done more for us here than all our former victories and all our diplomacy. It is creating an almost convulsive reaction in our favor all over this country."[59] Young Henry went on to inform his brother that the *The London Times* had leveled scathing criticism at the Emancipation Proclamation, but added that he thought that that was only because the *Times* was then the tool of the British aristocracy who did not like to see stirrings of "republicanism." The upper classes in Britain, wrote Henry, were worried that the Emancipation Proclamation might have a sort of trickle down

---

[57] Foner, *The Fiery Trial*, 229.

[58] Foner, *The Fiery Trial*, 229.

[59] Henry Adams to Charles Francis Adams, Jr. January 23, 1863, as reprinted in Simpson, ed., *The Civil War: The Third Year*, 9.

effect; forcing the British government to do something to improve the lives of the British working class, whose members were then commonly living in Dickensian squalor. Ordinary Britons on the other hand, felt Adams, were quite enthusiastic about the proclamation.[60] He concludes by informing his brother, who was serving in an army that had not yet quite turned the corner in the war (disaster at Chancellorsville was then still four months in the future) that "If only you at home don't have disasters, we will give such a checkmate to the foreign hopes of the rebels as they never yet have had."[61]

President Lincoln's masterful skills as a politician; particularly his ability to know himself, to know when it was time to abandon his generally cautious approach to problem-solving in order to take bold action, coupled with his keen sense of timing, allowed him to issue the Emancipation Proclamation at a time when northerners were ready to believe that what all northerners agreed was the great crime of the Confederacy—secession—was caused by the slave owning class, or "slaveocracy." Northerners were far more divided upon the issue of slavery than they were on the issue of secession. In the second half of the war, with the Emancipation Proclamation published and in force, Lincoln was gradually able to convince his soldiers to keep fighting, not to help blacks, but by successfully inculcating the idea that the slave owning class in the South were responsible for starting the war. They had to go.

Bringing northern public opinion around to where he needed it to be was quite a feat for Lincoln. The vast majority of the northern boys who enlisted in the Union Army in 1861 and 1862 had absolutely no interest in freeing slaves.[62] They had enlisted instead for adventure and out of a sincere belief that secession was treason and thus could not be tolerated. Northern racism was quite strong. Lincoln himself never saw blacks

---

[60] Henry Adams to Charles Francis Adams, Jr. January 23, 1863, as reprinted in Brooks D. Simpson, ed. *The Civil War: The Third Year Told by Those Who Lived It*, 9.

[61] Henry Adams to Charles Francis Adams, Jr. January 23, 1863, as reprinted in Brooks D. Simpson, ed. *The Civil War: The Third Year Told by Those Who Lived It*, 10.

[62] Foner, *The Fiery Trial*, 252.

as biologically equal to whites. The president felt that, if emancipated, former slaves should voluntarily emigrate to a distant colony. Colombia was the destination Lincoln discussed most often in regard to his "colonization" scheme for former slaves.[63] Harriett Beecher Stowe, a northern white middle class abolitionist, was motivated to write *Uncle Tom's Cabin* because she was enraged that the tough new Fugitive Slave Law that was part of the Compromise of 1850 stipulated that law enforcement personnel in northern states must actively assist southern slave catchers who were pursuing escaped slaves in northern states. Outrage that after 1850, escaped slaves could not really be safe unless and until they could make it to Canada, and not just into the northern United States, is a strong theme in the novel. While Stowe was an abolitionist who wanted to see slaves freed immediately, she too did not regard blacks as equal to whites (unless they looked white; the best educated and most attractive slaves in the novel are those with the lightest skin) and she would have been horrified if one of her sisters had decided to marry a black man. In the novel, Stowe's often patronizing descriptions of slaves as lazy and childlike make the book seem dated. However, one of the main reasons why *Uncle Tom's Cabin* has endured as a literary classic is that Harriett Beecher Stowe was well aware of the pernicious, subtle, and widespread phenomena of northern racism, although she may not have been aware that she herself was a prime example of that sentiment. In the novel, the character of Miss Ophelia is a transplanted Vermonter who represents northern apathy, if not quite northern racism. Persuaded by her cousin, the kindly slave owner with a guilty conscience, Augustine St. Clare, to come south to New Orleans to care for St. Clare's young daughter Eva, Miss Ophelia understands the cruelty of slavery, but is not initially sufficiently motivated to do anything about it. During one of several discussions between the cousins on the subject, St. Clare asks Miss Ophelia a rhetorical question as to whether or not blacks would be welcomed with open arms in northern states if slave owners were to suddenly emancipate all of their slaves.

---

[63] James M. McPherson. *Tried by War: Abraham Lincoln as Commander-in-Chief.* (New York: Penguin, 2008): 128–129. Berkin, et al., *Making America.* Vol. 1., 366.

Is there enough Christian philanthropy, among your northern states, to bear with the process of their education and elevation? . . . If we emancipate, are you willing to educate? How many families, in your town, would take in a negro man and woman, teach them, bear with them, and seek to make them Christians? . . . You see, Cousin, I want justice done us. We are in a bad position. We are the more *obvious* oppressors of the negro; but the unchristian prejudice of the north is an oppressor almost equally severe.[64]

It was precisely this northern prejudice that Lincoln needed to overcome. He got help when Union soldiers who saw action in the South also became acquainted with the brutality of slavery and were moved by what they saw. Many high ranking Union Army officers despised abolitionists as radical extremists. For example, Major General George Gordon Meade, the Union hero of Gettysburg, had joined this war to put down a rebellion, not to free slaves. Of Meade, Bruce Catton writes: "A professional soldier, he was inclined to distrust volunteers, and he had no use whatever for abolitionists."[65] It seems that there was more sympathy for emancipation amongst the rank and file infantry of the Union Army than amongst their officers.[66] However, even Union officers began to come around after the Emancipation Proclamation was issued. Major General Ulysses S. Grant wrote his friend and patron, Illinois Congressman Elihu B. Washburne, in August 1863 that:

I never was an Abolitionest [*sic*], not even what could be called anti slavery, but I try to judge farely [*sic*] & honestly and it become [*sic*] patent to my mind early in the rebellion that the North & South could never live at peace with each other except as one nation, and that without Slavery. As anxious as I am to see peace reestablished I would not therefore be willing to see any settlement until this question is forever settled.[67]

---

[64] Harriett Beecher Stowe. *Uncle Tom's Cabin: Or Life Among the Lowly.* (Garden City, NY: International Collector's Library, 1958): 333–334.

[65] Bruce Catton, *Glory Road: The Bloody Route from Fredericksburg to Gettysburg.* (Garden City, NY: Doubleday, 1956): 278.

[66] Foner, *The Fiery Trial*, 208–210.

[67] Grant to Washburne, August 30, 1863, as reprinted in Simpson, ed., *The Civil War: The Third Year Told by Those Who Lived It*, 501.

Grant wrote those lines to Washburne shortly after Grant had captured Vicksburg, which is interesting because in one of the many ironies of the Civil War, Grant's wife Julia visited him at his Mississippi headquarters at both Corinth and Vicksburg and when she did, she brought one of her father's slaves to wait on her.[68]

One way in which the Emancipation Proclamation showed Lincoln the pragmatist is the blunt fact that he needed black troops in the Union armies. True, far more young white men of military age resided in the North than in the South in 1861, and that meant that the Union was always able to field larger armies than the Confederacy. Nevertheless, this war was so destructive of human life, due primarily to the vast improvement in weapons, such as standard infantry rifles on both sides that could kill at a range of half a mile, coupled with a stubborn insistence by commanders on both sides to continue using outdated Napoleonic era tactics such as frontal assaults, meant that Lincoln needed more men—black men. Grant agreed, writing Lincoln in August 1863 that:

> I have given the subject of arming the negro my hearty support. This, with the emancipation of the negro, is the heavyest [sic] blow yet given the Confederacy. The South rave a greatdeel [sic] about it and profess to be very angry. But they were united in their action before and with the negro under subjection could spare their entire white population for the field [of battle]. Now they complain that nothing can be got out of their negroes.[69]

The Emancipation Proclamation was limited in its immediate effects. It did not apply to slaves in Tennessee, Kentucky, Maryland, Delaware, Missouri, and the area soon to become the new state of West Virginia. However, the Emancipation Proclamation was the essential first step on the path to the Thirteenth Amendment of 1865, which abolished slavery completely and forever in the United States. The Emancipation Proclamation was also an indication that President Lincoln had realized

---

[68] H.W. Brands. *The Man Who Saved the Union: Ulysses Grant in War and Peace.* (New York: Doubleday, 2012): 195–196, 283–284.

[69] Grant to Lincoln, August 23, 1863, as reprinted in Simpson, ed., *The Civil War: The Third Year Told By Those Who Lived It,* 488–489.

that by late 1862 the Civil War had become a total war. Before he could rebuild the Union, Lincoln would have to win a complete and total military victory over the Confederacy. In that sense, the Emancipation Proclamation can be seen as even more of a point of no return than was the bombardment of Fort Sumter, which act had initiated hostilities in April 1861.[70] The border slave states of Delaware, Kentucky, Missouri, and Maryland, which had remained loyal to the Union, were not enthusiastic about Lincoln's early attempts in 1861 and 1862 to persuade them to adopt gradual emancipation of their slaves with financial compensation from the Federal government.[71] With the failure of his border state emancipation initiative, Lincoln decided to take a different tack; namely to leave the border states as is for the time being and go for the jugular of slavery instead. Lincoln's decision to issue an executive order emancipating slaves in the Confederacy seems to have been made during the summer of 1862. He was motivated by the need for black troops in the Union armies; his determination to keep Great Britain out of the war; the seeming inability of Union forces in the crucial eastern theater to win a decisive victory; and the unwillingness of the border slave states to adopt voluntary emancipation. Union Navy Secretary Gideon Welles wrote that "Lincoln had concluded that emancipation in rebel areas must precede that in the border, not the other way around."[72]

With the proclamation, Lincoln essentially also gave up his hitherto persistent desire to send freed slaves somewhere else to live—i.e., his ideas about "colonization" in places like Colombia. By 1863, President Lincoln had become reconciled to free blacks remaining in this country.[73]

In contrast to Polk in the Mexican War, Lincoln in the Civil War, and FDR in World War II, Presidents John F. Kennedy, Lyndon Johnson, and Richard Nixon never had clear, consistent, and coherent war aims in the Vietnam conflict. H.R. McMaster, in his critique of the manner in which the Vietnam War became "Americanized" in 1964 and 1965, finds

---

[70] Foner, *The Fiery Trial*, 245.

[71] McPherson, *Tried by War*, 85–88. Foner, *The Fiery Trial*, 245.

[72] As quoted in Foner, *The Fiery Trial*, 217.

[73] Foner, *The Fiery Trial*, 258.

plenty of blame to go around amongst President Lyndon Johnson, the Joint Chiefs of Staff, and the president's civilian foreign policy advisors. McMaster is particularly unsparing when describing the arrogance and naiveté of Defense Secretary Robert McNamara. McMaster writes in *Dereliction of Duty*:

> In McNamara's concept of 'graduated pressure,' the aim of force was not to impose one's will on the enemy but to communicate with him. Gradually intensifying military action would convey American resolve and thereby convince an adversary to alter his behavior.[74]

The contrast between Robert McNamara and James K. Polk could not be more striking. For Polk, war had absolutely nothing to do with "communication," but was instead about taking land—lots of it. Robert McNamara explains in his 1995 memoir why he came to agree with President Johnson in January 1966 that the so-called Christmas bombing pause had to end and targets in North Vietnam be bombed again: "We had to start bombing again to blunt criticism that the pause was leading to even higher levels of infiltration, and to avoid sending the wrong signal to Hanoi, Beijing, and our own people." He goes on to relate that he and Secretary of State Dean Rusk "urged that the bombing program be kept under tight control—and more limited than the [US Joint] chiefs wished—to minimize the risk of Chinese intervention."[75] It would appear that H.R. McMaster is correct in asserting that Robert McNamara did in fact cling to the bizarre idea that armed conflict could be communication, not war. It is fascinating that as late as 1995 when drafting his memoirs, Robert McNamara showed in the quotes listed above that even in his old age he still thought it was acceptable that none of his reasons for ending the 1965 Christmas bombing pause had anything to do with concrete military strategy and military objectives, but were instead all about sending "signals," and that he maintained his belief that it was perfectly acceptable for him to sideline the Joint Chiefs

---

[74] McMaster, *Dereliction of Duty*, 62.

[75] Robert McNamara, with Brian VanDeMark. *In Retrospect: The Tragedy and Lessons of Vietnam.* (New York: Times Books/Random House, 1995): 229.

of Staff—the organization that was and is supposed to be the president's principal military advisory body.

McNamara believed that the Vietnam War could be won with statistics and with systems analysis. On McNamara and statistics, H.R. McMaster writes that: "His notebook full of statistics, McNamara reassured one persistent reporter that 'every quantitative measurement we have shows that we're winning this war.'"[76] Unfortunately, of all human activity, warfare is probably least amenable to quantification. Indeed, had Admiral Chester W. Nimitz engaged in quantitative measurement prior to the Battle of Midway in June 1942, he would undoubtedly have concluded that with three aircraft carriers, a handful of cruisers, and a dozen destroyers, he could not hope to defeat the vast Japanese fleet that was bearing down on his modest forces, and that therefore the upcoming Battle of Midway was unwinnable for the United States. Fortunately, unlike Robert McNamara, Admiral Nimitz was well aware of the many intangibles in war.

In contrast to the ruthlessness and simplicity of Polk's war aims, Lyndon Johnson never seemed able to explain to himself or to anyone else exactly why American ground troops were in Vietnam. Historians have long noted that the Johnson administration had felt it necessary to preserve American credibility, an idea that actually dates back to the acceptance by President Truman in 1950 of the conclusions found in NSC-68, a document that was, as John Lewis Gaddis states, an attempt at "reducing the strategy [of containment] to writing" in one document.[77] NSC-68 was drafted by a committee headed by Paul Nitze, George Kennan's successor as head of the State Department's Policy Planning Staff, and including personnel from the State and Defense Departments, respectively. In retrospect, it seems clear that the United States, and the world, would have been better off had NSC-68 never been written. The document coupled aggressive provisions such as the supposed need for the United States to build a hydrogen bomb and the idea that all threats were equally relevant with the surprisingly passive idea that the United States

---

[76] McMaster, *Dereliction of Duty*, photo caption facing pg. 256.

[77] Gaddis, *Strategies of Containment*, 88.

should not take the initiative, as it had for instance when implementing the Marshall Plan, but should instead *react* to Soviet moves. Perhaps the gravest flaw in NSC-68, however, was the idea that the basic tenets of containment could be written out as a set of rules that would be as easy to understand by policymakers as say, the sexual harassment definitions and policies of a large corporation in the twenty-first century United States. In reality, containment was not formulaic and proved instead to be an intensely personal strategy that relied on personal relationships for its success. Containment worked best when it was seen as a set of guiding principles that still left American officials the latitude to follow unwritten rules that allowed for spontaneity. Unfortunately, the word "containment" has a sort of negative connotation hinting at the use of force to keep something unpleasant, like a disease, from spreading. In reality, Kennan meant for containment to be a strategy of hope for a bright (or at least brighter) future. Gail Halvorsen's impulsive decision to begin dropping candy to German children during the Berlin Airlift in 1948; Richard Nixon bypassing the State and Defense departments entirely and sending his National Security Advisor, Henry Kissinger, to negotiate with the Chinese, the Russians, and the North Vietnamese in 1971 and 1972; and the genuine friendship that developed between Ronald Reagan and Mikhail Gorbachev in the 1980s were occasions when containment as a strategy was able to produce real results. Containment at its nadir in Vietnam was containment blithely following a badly written and completely inflexible script. The 1960s American strategy of "Flexible Response" proved in reality to be the most *inflexible* of strategies because it left no room for the human element. Ronald Reagan never expected to actually become friends with a Soviet leader, but when he realized that he and Gorbachev actually liked each other, Reagan was wise enough to take advantage of the opportunities that such a friendship could offer.[78]

By contrast, the badly written script followed in Vietnam began with NSC-68, with its emphasis on appearances and on reacting to Soviet moves; doing only what was necessary to counter those moves and no more (which provided the basis for the McNamara-Kennedy doctrine of "Flexible Response"); and the idea that the United States supposedly had

---

[78] Gaddis, *Strategies of Containment*, 297, 299–305, 331–334, 373–377.

unlimited resources with which to pursue these foreign policy objectives. John Lewis Gaddis states that "NSC-68 was not intended as a repudiation of Kennan."[79] In fact, however, that is exactly what its authors did in making such radical departures from the original features of containment as a policy.

H.R. McMaster expresses amazement and outrage that

> [Lyndon] Johnson and McNamara succeeded in creating the illusion that the decisions to attack North Vietnam were alternatives to war rather than war itself. Graduated pressure defined military action as a form of communication, the object of which was to affect the enemy's calculation of interests and dissuade him from a particular activity.[80]

McMaster goes on to explain that such a philosophy was and is wholly unsuited to an activity as violent and unpredictable as warfare. Killing people never puts the friends and family of those killed in a mood to have a friendly chat with the party doing the killing in order to settle differences.[81] In short, war is not something that can be turned on and off at will, as if by a switch. Henry Kissinger seems to have realized this, but in the context of ending the war rather than in finding ways of fighting it. Gaddis mentions Kissinger's view that "Great nations had to preserve their dignity, even while cutting their losses. 'We could not simply walk away from [Vietnam] as if we were switching a television channel.' Kissinger later wrote."[82]

American strategy, or lack thereof, in the Vietnam War was predicated on the idea that the enemy would behave exactly as President Johnson and Robert McNamara expected him to behave; i.e., that the North Vietnamese would "understand" the Johnson administration's strange idea that war was not really war, but rather a form of "communication." The manner in which Johnson and McNamara deluded themselves is similar to the way in which, prior to the Battle of Midway in June 1942,

---

[79] Gaddis, *Strategies of Containment*, 88.

[80] McMaster, *Dereliction of Duty*, 326.

[81] McMaster, *Dereliction of Duty*, 327.

[82] Gaddis, *Strategies of Containment*, 286.

the Japanese believed that in the upcoming battle, the US Navy would behave exactly as the Japanese expected it to behave.[83] In the Vietnam War, Robert McNamara seemed surprised that the Hanoi regime did not understand the message the United States was trying to send via the Rolling Thunder bombing campaign. He expressed his dismay in summer 1965, as related by Gaddis, that

> 'There are no signs that we have throttled the inflow of supplies for the VC,' McNamara acknowledged after five months of bombing. 'Nor have our air attacks on North Vietnam produced tangible evidence of willingness on the part of Hanoi to come to the conference table in a reasonable mood.'[84]

Why McNamara felt that dropping bombs on North Vietnam would put the North Vietnamese in a "reasonable mood" for negotiations has never been explained. Even the operational code name "Rolling Thunder" is redolent of graduated pressure and calibration. The much more aggressive "Linebacker" bombing campaigns undertaken by Richard Nixon in 1972 had a correspondingly aggressive code name. Why did McNamara and President Johnson think bombing North Vietnam would create a favorable environment for negotiations? Why did they enter this war willingly when they knew that there could be no ground invasion of North Vietnam?[85] By January 1968, there were over 500,000 American troops in Vietnam, but they were all in the south. Not one of them ever set foot in North Vietnam. If the erroneous decisions of President Johnson and Robert McNamara can themselves be quantified, perhaps the most egregious error was the failure to realize that if you cannot conduct a ground invasion of the enemy's homeland; i.e., North Vietnam, for fear of bringing in the Chinese, you should not go into that war at all.

The Japanese found themselves with a similar problem when Japanese naval planners in World War II felt that a few very sharp attacks, such as at Pearl Harbor and Midway, would bring the Americans to the conference

---

[83] Jonathan Parshall and Anthony Tully. *Shattered Sword: The Untold Story of the Battle of Midway*. Washington, DC: Potomac Books, 2005): 61–63, 67–68, 410.

[84] McNamara, as quoted in Gaddis, *Strategies of Containment*, 256.

[85] McNamara, *In Retrospect*, 211.

table in a mood to negotiate a peace that was favorable to Japan. Such a strategy had worked for the Japanese in the Russo-Japanese war of 1904–1905. It would not work in World War II against the Americans. The Pearl Harbor attack blew the cork out of a bottle of resentment that had been building toward Japan in the United States for ten years owing to Japan's invasion of China in the 1930s; the naval arms race between the two countries in the interwar years that the Washington Naval Treaty of 1922 had been able to slow but not to stop; and Japan's incursions into French Indochina in 1940–1941.[86] After Pearl Harbor, the American people would be satisfied with nothing less than the complete destruction of the Japanese military machine.[87] Jonathan Parshall and Anthony Tully state that between Pearl Harbor and Midway

> the Americans were still willing to fight and had declared that nothing short of total victory would satisfy their war aims against Japan. Herein lay the fundamental strategic conundrum that now faced the Japanese—how to force to the negotiating table an enemy who, although wounded, was both vastly more powerful in the long term, and in the short term had demonstrated a furious disinclination to bargain?[88]

During the Vietnam War, the American refusal to even consider a ground invasion of North Vietnam seemed understandable on the one hand because it could have brought in the Chinese, who share a common border with North Vietnam. Nobody wanted another Korea, especially since by 1964 the Chinese possessed nuclear weapons. But, nobody seems to have asked the question, if you cannot even consider a ground invasion of the enemy's homeland, should you get into a war in the first place? Polk had no such qualms when he authorized General Scott to occupy Mexico

---

[86] Akira Iriye. *The Origins of the Second World War in Asia and the Pacific.* (New York: Longman, 1987): 7–13, 17, 18, 23–24, 27–28, 45–47, 49–50, 65–66, 69–70, 78–79, 148–150. John T. Kuehn. *Agents of Innovation: The General Board and the Design of the Fleet that Defeated the Japanese Navy.* (Annapolis, MD: Naval Institute Press, 2008): 28–30, 57–59.

[87] Parshall and Tully, *Shattered Sword*, 53–54, 403–404.

[88] Parshall and Tully, *Shattered Sword*, 32–33.

City during the Mexican War. Regarding the "Flexible Response" strategy as an article of faith, Johnson and his advisors were quite willing to wade into the Vietnam thicket. Key to the "Flexible Response" strategy was the strange idea that war was something that could be turned on and off, like a faucet; thus allowing the United States to apply increasing levels of military pressure with (wholly unjustified) confidence that those levels of pressure could be changed, or even turned off altogether, at any time. Carefully measured applications of American military force in Vietnam were supposed to allow the Johnson administration to have total control over events. That must have seemed very appealing to a lifelong micro-manager like Lyndon Johnson. However, when a person, or a group of persons, attempts to maintain complete control of a given situation, they usually end up facing the unpleasant fact that they have in reality *lost* control of events completely and utterly.[89] According to H.R. McMaster,

> McNamara . . . viewed the [Vietnam] war as another business management problem that, he assumed, would ultimately succumb to his reasoned judgment and others' rational calculations. He and his assistants thought that they could predict with great precision what amount of force applied in Vietnam would achieve the results they desired and they believed that they could control that force with great precision from halfway around the world.[90]

Other Johnson advisors, such as National Security Advisor McGeorge Bundy, were in complete agreement with McNamara's ideas about limited war, carefully measured, as a form of "communication."[91] Gaddis notes that in fighting the Vietnam War, the Johnson administration had "a curiously myopic preoccupation with process—a disproportionate fascination with means at the expense of ends."[92] A perfect example of this is an image that would be humorous were it not tragic: that of Robert

---

[89] Gaddis, *Strategies of Containment*, 241.

[90] McMaster, *Dereliction of Duty*, 327.

[91] McGeorge Bundy to Lyndon Johnson, May 22, 1964, as reprinted in Gaddis, *Strategies of Containment*, 249.

[92] Gaddis, *Strategies of Containment*, 236.

McNamara, the business and statistical genius, who was determined when he arrived in Washington in 1961 to cut the fat from the Pentagon budget, grimly traveling to Saigon for one of his numerous inspection tours in the cargo hold of a "McNamara Special," a stripped-down, no frills Air Force KC-135 tanker aircraft. There would be no comfortable VIP-configured airplanes for this man, or for anyone in his entourage. All the while, the same McNamara, via a systems analysis bloody installment plan, was causing the United States and the Vietnamese to expend a King's ransom in blood and treasure to fight a war that he could not quite bring himself to admit was really a war and not "communication." The parallel is striking between McNamara traveling to Vietnam on the cheap while bleeding two countries white and the well-known restrictions McNamara and Johnson placed on American military activity in Vietnam. Gaddis writes that:

> The bombing campaign against North Vietnam was intended to be the most carefully calibrated military operation in recent history. . . . Extraordinary precision was demanded of pilots—one 1966 order specified that piers at Haiphong could be hit only if no tankers were berthed at them, that vessels firing on American planes could be struck only if they were 'clearly North Vietnamese,' and that no attacks were to be launched on Sunday.[93]

The senselessness of bombing Haiphong harbor only when no valuable targets were actually present fits in perfectly with the McNamara-Johnson idea of the Vietnam conflict as the "communication" of American resolve rather than war itself. Bombing empty piers showed what the United States *could* do if it decided to get serious. McNamara and Johnson were interested in issuing threats, but never carried through on those threats. The Emancipation Proclamation of 1863 was also a threat directed at portions of the South that were in rebellion during the Civil War. Historians have long noted that in the legalistic, carefully measured language of the Emancipation Proclamation, President Lincoln was issuing an Executive Order that only applied to areas in which it could not be enforced immediately because those were precisely the areas that

---

[93] Gaddis, *Strategies of Containment*, 245.

were still in rebel hands. What Lincoln was saying in the Emancipation Proclamation was that as Union armies continue to invade Confederate territory, any slaves found in that territory will be freed. One of the many differences between Abraham Lincoln and Lyndon Johnson is that Lincoln did follow through on his threat. Slaves *were* freed as Union armies advanced into Confederate territory after January 1, 1863.

The clarity of President James K. Polk's war aims in the Mexican War stands in marked contrast to the incoherence of American war aims in the Vietnam War. Without disputing that Lyndon Johnson was forced to play out a very bad hand vis-á-vis Vietnam that had been dealt to him as far back as President Eisenhower's decision to sabotage the Geneva Accords in 1954, it is hard to deny that Johnson did not have a strategy for Vietnam, much less any clear and consistent war aims. By way of contrast, as soon as the Mexican War began, President Polk laid out his basic strategy to his Secretary of War William Marcy and to General Winfield Scott: "I gave it as my opinion that the first movement should be to march a competent force into the Northern Provinces and seize and hold them until peace was made. In this they concurred."[94] Although the Mexican War did not unfold exactly as Polk wished and dragged on far longer than he had hoped, he did stick with his basic strategy. Selling his war aims to himself does seem to have required Polk to delude himself into thinking that the United States was embarking on some sort of humanitarian crusade in Mexico instead of a naked land grab. On May 13, 1846, Polk laid out his war aims for Secretary of State James Buchanan:

> I told him [Buchanan] that though we had not gone to war for conquest, yet it was clear that in making peace we would if practicable obtain California and such other portion of the Mexican territory as would be sufficient to indemnify our claimants on Mexico, and to defray the expenses of the war which that power by her long continued wrongs and injuries had forced us to wage.[95]

---

[94] *Polk Diary*, Vol. 1, May 14, 1846, 400.

[95] *Polk Diary*, Vol. 1, May 13, 1846, 397.

This sounds eerily similar to the excuses Adolf Hitler would make ninety-five years later to attempt to justify why Germany supposedly had no choice but to invade the Soviet Union on June 22, 1941.

Of President Polk during the Mexican War, Henry R. Nau writes that Polk "coupled force and diplomacy so adroitly that his approach remains a model for contemporary statesmanship. He took military risks to achieve ambitious objectives but was always flexible with a diplomatic plan to compromise military gains for peace at any time."[96] Lyndon Johnson and Robert McNamara on the other hand never coupled diplomacy with their military actions. For instance, they failed to realize that despite China's successful test of its own nuclear weapon in 1964, the Sino-Soviet split and the failure of a Chinese-backed Communist coup in Indonesia in the fall of 1965 meant that China was actually much less of a player in international affairs than policy makers in Washington realized.[97]

A group of high ranking Johnson administration foreign policy advisors (including General Maxwell Taylor and McNamara's deputy John McNaughton) known as the "Thompson Group," prepared a report on the Vietnam War in the fall of 1965, in which the authors felt the need to remind McNamara and Johnson that "North Vietnam seemed less willing to negotiate while under attack."[98] It was a bad sign that the president and the Secretary of Defense needed to be reminded of such an elementary fact. In 1966 and 1967, emissaries from Canada, Italy, Great Britain, Poland, and even the Soviet Union tried to broker peace talks between Washington and Hanoi. However, on each occasion, without fail, the Johnson administration managed literally to blow up the deal by either ending a bombing pause or by greatly escalating the bombing of North Vietnam already underway.[99] Even McNamara admits that "we failed miserably to integrate and coordinate our diplomatic and military actions as we searched for an end to the war."[100]

---

[96] Nau, *Conservative Internationalism*, 113.

[97] McNamara, *In Retrospect*, 214–215.

[98] McNamara, *In Retrospect*, 214.

[99] McNamara, *In Retrospect*, 223, 247–252.

[100] McNamara, *In Retrospect*, 252.

CHAPTER 4

TAKE ADVANTAGE OF ENEMY MISTAKES

American military forces have benefited from the mistakes made by enemy forces in several different wars. In World War II, for instance, the German troops involved in Hitler's Ardennes offensive, the Battle of the Bulge, made considerable progress for a week after the battle began on December 16, 1944. Ultimately, however, the Battle of the Bulge ended as a major Allied victory that greatly reduced what was left of Hitler's already rapidly dwindling military strength. Hitler's biggest mistake in this instance was to undertake that offensive at all, especially since by December 1944 the German Air Force had been almost completely destroyed and could provide little in the way of air cover. Thus, German troops in the Ardennes offensive could only advance while the weather was bad. Once the skies cleared on December 23, 1944, the overwhelming air power that the Americans and the British were able to bring to bear changed the course of the battle almost immediately. German supply lines were highly vulnerable to low level Allied air attack; a situation of which Allied pilots took full advantage. The Allies also used their vast fleet of cargo aircraft to drop supplies to the beleaguered American infantry within and facing "the Bulge."

It does not seem to have occurred to Hitler that the Allies in 1944 would not behave as had the French when Hitler's forces broke through the French lines in almost the same area in 1940. Namely, historians such as Omer Bartov have pointed out that the German victory over France in 1940 was not inevitable. The ground forces on each side were quite evenly matched in that campaign. What made the difference in 1940 was the German willingness to utilize new tactics: keeping all of their tanks together in armored divisions which could achieve a quick breakthrough—ably assisted by strong tactical air strikes furnished by the *Luftwaffe*.[1] Along with these new "Blitzkrieg" tactics, the Germans held a psychological advantage in 1940. Young German soldiers in 1940 had been so heavily indoctrinated with Nazi ideology while they were in the Hitler Youth before the war that according to Bartov "conscription was not experienced as a move to a fundamentally different environment."[2] It is true that the German people as a whole were not delighted to find themselves at war in 1939, in stark contrast to the cheering crowds that had celebrated the outbreak of war in 1914.[3] Nevertheless, young German soldiers in 1940 were deeply affected by having spent their teenage years reading about, and listening to, Hitler's glorification of struggle.[4] This Nazi idea that war and struggle were supposedly "good" things was a very different message from what young French and British soldiers were being taught in the late 1930s.

On a more specific note in terms of psychology, the French and the British were still "fighting the last war" in 1940. Thinking in terms of World War I, the French and British commanders on the scene during Hitler's offensive in the west in 1940 still thought that the best and only way to avoid defeat in battle was to form a defensive line and prevent a breakthrough by enemy forces—a very passive strategy. The First World War had involved four years of bloody stalemate on the western front because neither side was ever able to achieve and maintain a significant breakthrough along the lines of trenches in France and Belgium. The power of the defense had reigned supreme in the Great War. French

---

[1] Omer Bartov. *Hitler's Army: Soldiers, Nazis, and War in the Third Reich.* (New York: Oxford University Press, 1992): 12–14.

[2] Bartov, *Hitler's Army*, 117.

[3] David Rigby. *Allied Master Strategists: The Combined Chiefs of Staff in World War II.* (Annapolis, MD: Naval Institute Press, 2012): 102.

[4] Bartov, *Hitler's Army*, 109–118.

and British military leaders learned all the wrong lessons from the First World War. They failed to understand that new weapons, particularly tanks and aircraft, could by 1940 achieve a major breakthrough when attacking against the sort of static defensive positions that had proved to be so invulnerable during the First World War. The French and the British also failed to realize in 1940 that such a breakthrough need not mean disaster for the defenders; that in fact such a breakthrough could instead present excellent opportunities for the defenders. If an enemy's armored spearheads are allowed to get way out ahead of his supporting infantry, the latter in the case of Germany marching on foot, the two can be separated via a pincer counterattack. Bartov points out that an armored division whose commanders are foolish enough to let the enemy get behind them and cut their supply lines is an armored division that will quickly run out of fuel. A tank without fuel is just a useless hunk of metal. The French and the British failed to realize this critical fact as Hitler's tanks dashed across northern France toward the English Channel in the spring of 1940.[5]

To his credit, Winston Churchill does seem to have had an inkling that the German armored spearheads were vulnerable, and he was beginning to ask the right questions as the German invasion of France unfolded. Two weeks after the German offensive in the west began in May 1940, Churchill advised French Premier M. Paul Reynaud:

> The [German] tank columns in the open must be hunted down in the open country by numbers of small mobile columns with a few cannon. Their tracks must be wearing out, and their energy must abate. This is the one way to deal with the armoured intruders. As for the main body, which does not seem to be coming on very quickly, the only method is to drive in upon the flanks. The confusion of this battle can only be cleared by being aggravated, so that it becomes a *mêlée*.[6]

---

[5] Bartov, *Hitler's Army*, 12–14.

[6] Churchill to Reynaud, May 21, 1940, reprinted in Winston S. Churchill. *The Second World War*. Vol. 2. *Their Finest Hour*. (Boston: Houghton Mifflin Company, 1949): 54.

That was just the trouble. For reasons that still puzzle historians, the German invasion of France in 1940 never did turn into a mêlée. One reason for this had to have been the simple fact that Blitzkrieg tactics were so new that an army using such tactics must have seemed invincible. The audacity of the Germans in driving tanks through the wooded Ardennes region, north of the Maginot line, but south of the bulk of the British and French armies was a shock from which the defenders never really recovered. Once the initial breakthrough was achieved in May 1940, the Germans encountered very little resistance. Everything had hinged on preventing a breakthrough. The French lacked a contingency plan. Churchill noticed a distinct sense of paralysis and panic in the French leadership during the 1940 German invasion. Reynaud telephoned Churchill on May 15th, just five days after the German attack began, and led off the conversation by saying "We have been defeated."[7] When Churchill flew to Paris that afternoon to confer with French leaders he was shocked to find French civil servants already burning sensitive documents on the grounds of the Quai d'Orsay.[8] There was little Churchill could do at the time. He himself was still settling in as Britain's new prime minister. It is difficult to escape the conclusion that the French leadership had lost hope almost before the battle began in 1940. Indeed, the tactics used by the French and the British in 1940 were purely defensive in both a micro and a macro sense. In addition to the "prevent a breakthrough at all costs" mentality described above, the British and the French made no attempt to invade Germany from the west in late 1939 or early 1940. Hitler was thus free to devour and digest Poland without having to worry about an attack from the west.

The situation was very different four years later. By late 1944, the great Russian victories at Moscow, Stalingrad, Kursk, and in the Bagration offensive in the center of the Russian front had quite destroyed the myth of German invincibility. In December 1944, General Eisenhower and his field commanders realized immediately the inherent vulnerability of the German forces that had broken through the Allied lines in what would be Hitler's last major offensive in the west. Churchill explains that

---

[7] Quoted in Churchill, *Their Finest Hour*, 38.

[8] Churchill, *Their Finest Hour*, 42.

the Allied high command experienced surprise, but not panic, when the Battle of the Bulge began on December 16, 1944:

> Although the time and weight of the attack surprised the Allied High Command its importance and purpose were quickly recognised. They resolved to strengthen the 'shoulders' of the breakthrough, hold the Meuse crossing both east and south of Namur, and mass mobile troops to crush the salient from north to south.[9]

What Churchill is saying is that in 1944 the Allies were no longer fighting the "last war" and were not plagued by the kind of defeatism that had proved so fatal to the French in 1940. As they scrambled to respond to the new German offensive in the west in December 1944, the western Allies, instead of panicking, actively worked to solve a problem. They did not lose hope and give up, as the French high command had given up in despair in May and June 1940. Hitler should have realized that the vast American force he was facing in the west in late 1944 was an army that had crossed 3,000 miles of ocean to undertake, with its British and Canadian allies, the liberation of western Europe. The Americans were never going to simply pack up and go home should the Germans launch a counterattack. In contrast to the British and the French waiting for Hitler to attack in the west in 1940, the American, British, and Canadian forces in France and Belgium in 1944 were actively engaged in an offensive campaign to liberate western Europe and to invade Germany itself from the west. The German Ardennes offensive of December 1944 was a temporary setback to the Allied offensive. It could not reverse the overall tide of that offensive.

The western Allies of 1944 were far more powerful and well equipped than was the British-French coalition of 1940. In addition to the critical role played by Allied air power in beating back the 1944 German Ardennes offensive, General Eisenhower greatly reinforced the Allied ground troops in that sector to counter the threat. Allied troops were thus able to contain the German forward advance and then pinch off the salient by attacking from each side of it. The mostly American forces that

---

[9] Winston S. Churchill. *The Second World War*. Vol. 6. *Triumph and Tragedy*. (Boston: Houghton Mifflin Company, 1953): 274.

confronted the Germans in the Ardennes in December 1944 and January 1945 were greatly aided by the fact that the US Army was mechanized to an extent far in excess of that of any other nation in the world during the Second World War. The abundance of motorized transport meant that American troops in Europe spent far less time walking than did their German opponents. Thus, the Americans could move fast to counter an emergency situation.[10]

Lieutenant General George Patton, commanding the US Third Army, succinctly and accurately described the opportunity presented to the Allies by the German Ardennes offensive. On December 19, 1944, as he prepared to swing three of his divisions to the north and head toward Bastogne to relieve the beleaguered American forces there, Patton laconically informed Eisenhower and other senior American generals that "The Kraut has stuck his head in a meat grinder and I've got the handle."[11] Patton's daring and successful maneuver is the type of aggressive counterattack that never even would have occurred to the members of the French and British high commands during Hitler's invasion of France in 1940.

Japan shared with Germany the two most costly mistakes of the Axis in World War II: failing to work together with one's allies and going to war without adopting anything even close to an adequate level of economic mobilization.[12] Other mistakes on the part of Japan included the failure to use its excellent submarine force to raid American merchant shipping in the Pacific. The Japanese Navy clung to the idea that its submarines should be used to sink American warships, not cargo vessels. While Japanese I-boats did score some notable successes in this area, such as sinking the American aircraft carrier USS *Wasp* in September

---

[10] Richard Overy. *Why the Allies Won*. (New York: W.W. Norton & Company, 1995): 224–225. William T. Goolrick and Ogden Tanner, and the Editors of Time-Life Books. *The Battle of the Bulge*. (Alexandria, Virginia: Time-Life Books, 1979): 186–188.

[11] George Patton, as quoted in Terry Brighton. *Patton, Montgomery, Rommel: Masters of War*. (New York: Crown Publishers, 2008): 357. See also Goolrick, et al, *The Battle of the Bulge*, 110–111, for the details of this conference and Patton's boast.

[12] Rigby, *Allied Master Strategists*, 92–115.

1942 and the heavy cruiser USS *Indianapolis* in July 1945, Japanese submarines never reached anything like their full potential during the war. By failing to target the huge numbers of American merchant ships that were required to support the American offensives in the Pacific, the Japanese allowed the Americans to gradually forego the use of convoys in the Pacific, which in turn freed up American destroyers for fleet work.[13]

As the war turned against Japan, its submarines were often pressed into service in a role described by Samuel Eliot Morison "as seagoing packmules"[14] to transport supplies to Japanese troops on islands in the central and south Pacific that had been cut off by the advancing Americans. While American submarines did bag a fair number of Japanese warships, such as the battleship *Kongo* and the aircraft carrier *Taiho*, it was against Japanese merchant shipping that American submarines scored their greatest successes. Attacking Japanese merchant ships may have lacked the glamour of engaging the enemy battle fleet, but the Americans correctly perceived that this was the area in which American submarines could make a genuinely war-winning contribution; and they did, sending to the bottom of the ocean well over half of the Japanese merchant shipping destroyed during the war. Denuded of surface transport, the Japanese were forced to use their submarines for supply missions that should have been handled by surface ships. American submarines routinely operated in Japanese coastal waters even early in the war. By way of contrast, the area between the west coast of the United States and Hawaii should have become "the graveyard of the Pacific" for American merchant shipping, but it never did, due to the failure of the Japanese to concentrate their long range submarines in that area.[15]

In the Spanish-American War of 1898, the United States greatly benefited from the incomplete understanding on the part of the Spanish

---

[13] Samuel Eliot Morison. *History of United States Naval Operations in World War II.* Vol. 4. *Coral Sea, Midway and Submarine Actions May 1942–August 1942.* (Edison, NJ: Castle Books—by arrangement with Little, Brown and Company, Inc., 1949, 2001): 188, 195–198.

[14] Morison, *Coral Sea, Midway and Submarine Actions,* 198.

[15] Morison, *Coral Sea, Midway and Submarine Actions,* 195–204.

government of the way in which modern communications equipment could be used very effectively as a weapon of war. Specifically, the world had become much smaller in the second half of the nineteenth century with the laying down of thousands of miles of trans-oceanic submarine cables that by 1900 crisscrossed the world's ocean floors. The telegraph had already proved itself as a weapon of war on one continent during the American Civil War. By the 1890s, submarine cables meant that the telegraph was now a major factor in diplomacy and in far flung military operations. American Commodore George Dewey's crushing victory over the Spanish fleet in the Battle of Manila Bay on May 1, 1898 would not have been possible without telegraphic communication. Dewey was able to achieve complete surprise, catching the Spanish warships at anchor, because the Spanish never expected that the Americans would be able to act so quickly. The war was only a week old at that point but in that one short week, Dewey, waiting at Hong Kong, had been notified immediately by telegraph of the American declaration of war on April 25, 1898 and had hastened to carry out his orders to neutralize the Spanish fleet in the Philippines. In the weeks leading up to the outbreak of hostilities, Dewey had been ordered (also by telegraph) to keep his ships fully provisioned and ready to steam from Hong Kong to Manila at a moment's notice. He did not disappoint. Spanish authorities in the Philippines were likewise quickly made aware of the outbreak of war via a Spanish-controlled cable running from Manila to Hong Kong. However, the Spanish did not expect Americans to arrive in Manila so quickly. The American ships under Dewey were far more modern and more heavily gunned than were those in the Spanish fleet, but rapid response and surprise were Dewey's greatest weapons. The rapidity of communication ushered in by the telegraph and by deepwater cables enabled Dewey to use those weapons with great success.[16]

---

[16] US Navy Department. Selected Naval Documents: Spanish-American War. "Naval Battle of Manila Bay, May 1, 1898. Communications Before the Battle," from *Appendix to the Report of the Chief of the Bureau of Navigation, Annual Reports of the Navy Department for the Year 1898*. Washington: Government Printing Office, 1898. Online source: http://www.history.navy.mil/docs/spanam/manila1.htm. Accessed January 20, 2014.

The telegraph and the submarine cables that carried its messages enabled the United States to project its power thousands of miles from home not just quickly, but also quite efficiently. Communications between Dewey at Hong Kong and his superiors in Washington, DC, suffered none of the maddening delays and misunderstandings that had plagued President Polk during the Mexican War when Polk tried to project American military power over a much shorter distance. Hong Kong, then a British possession, was the most important cable communications hub in the Far East in 1898. As a neutral power in the Spanish-American War, Great Britain did attempt to impose some restrictions on the war messages being sent and received by both sides during that war. However, these efforts were half-hearted at best. British censorship did not even begin until after the Spanish fleet had been sent to the bottom of Manila Bay by the guns of Commodore Dewey's ships on May 1, 1898.[17] Dewey was able to send and receive from the British cable station in Hong Kong right up until the moment his ships departed Hong Kong for Manila on April 27, 1898. Because long range radio transmission was still a few years in the future, Dewey remained completely dependent on Hong Kong for his cable communications to Washington even when he was in Manila. From Manila, Dewey was compelled to write out his dispatches to the Navy Department on paper and then detach one of his ships to carry those messages back to Hong Kong. Thus, his report of the victory did not reach Washington until May 7, 1898—a week after the battle. By then, the authorities in Washington had already heard the news from other sources. When Dewey's dispatch vessel arrived in Hong Kong on May 7, its crew found waiting there a dispatch from Navy Secretary John D. Long that had been sent on May 3 congratulating Dewey on the victory.[18] Thus, while transoceanic telegraph cables did revolutionize

---

[17] Daniel R. Headrick. *The Invisible Weapon: Telecommunications and International Politics 1851–1945.* (New York: Oxford University Press, 1991): 83–84.

[18] Dewey to Long, April 27, 1898, from US Navy Department. Selected Naval Documents: Spanish-American War. "Naval Battle of Manila Bay, May 1, 1898. Communications Before the Battle," from *Appendix to the Report of the Chief of the Bureau of Navigation, Annual Reports of the Navy Department for the Year 1898.* Washington: Government Printing Office, 1898. Online source:

communications in the late nineteenth century, there was still room for improvement, which is why long range radio was so quickly installed in ships after 1900.

The Battle of Saratoga during the American Revolution is arguably the foremost example of enemy mistakes working to the advantage of American military forces. Indeed, the British made so many mistakes in the Saratoga campaign at both the strategic and tactical levels that they practically defeated themselves. Rather than a single battle, Saratoga was actually a campaign involving several minor skirmishes and four major battles in the summer and fall of 1777. It began when British Lieutenant General John "Gentleman Johnny" Burgoyne's Army of the North, comprising some 9,000 troops, began moving south from Montreal in May 1777. Their immediate destination was a forward base at St. Johns at the northern tip of Lake Champlain. The expedition really got underway on June 20th, when Burgoyne's army departed St. Johns by boat and small sailing ship for the trip south down the 125-mile length of Lake Champlain.[19] The campaign reached its climax in the battles of Freeman's Farm and Bemis Heights, which were fought out between Burgoyne's army and an American army of regulars and militia commanded by Major General Horatio Gates roughly twenty miles north of Albany on high ground overlooking the west bank of the Hudson River on September 19 and October 7, 1777, respectively. After the Bemis

---

http://www.history.navy.mil/docs/spanam/manila1.htm. Accessed February 24, 2014. See also Dewey to Long, written May 1, 1898—sent May 8th; and Long to Dewey, sent May 3, 1898. US Navy Department. Selected Naval Documents: Spanish-American War. "Naval Battle of Manila Bay, May 1, 1898. Miscellaneous Documents," from *Appendix to the Report of the Chief of the Bureau of Navigation, Annual Reports of the Navy Department for the Year 1898*. Washington: Government Printing Office, 1898. Online source. http://www.history.navy.mil/docs/spanam/manila2.htm. Accessed February 24, 2014.

[19] Robert Middlekauff. *The Glorious Cause: The American Revolution, 1763–1789*. (New York: Oxford University Press, 1982, 2005): 377–380. John Ferling. *A Leap in the Dark: The Struggle to Create the American Republic*. (New York: Oxford University Press, 2003): 200. Richard M. Ketchum. *Saratoga: Turning Point of America's Revolutionary War*. (New York: Henry Holt, 1997): 137.

Heights battle, the British Army retreated approximately ten miles north to Schuylerville, New York, where Burgoyne surrendered on October 17, 1777. The events that led up to the unprecedented surrender of an entire British Army to American forces were accompanied by some bold tactical moves by the Americans. Mainly, however, the American victory at Saratoga was the result of the Americans capitalizing on an almost unbroken series of disastrous British mistakes.

The American cause was sorely in need of the boost provided by the victory at Saratoga. General Washington's victories at Trenton and Princeton in December 1776 and January 1777, respectively, prevented the rebellion from being snuffed out before it really had a chance to get going. What the Americans accomplished with their victory in the Saratoga campaign was to force the British to see that they were not engaged in a minor police action to discipline a few unruly colonists, but were instead fighting a major war; one that would in fact soon become a world war for Britain. In addition to the immediate tactical gain for the rebels, the victory at Saratoga convinced the French government that the Americans were in this fight for the long haul and that they could win. American delegates in Paris under the skillful direction of Benjamin Franklin were thus able to conclude an American alliance with France in February 1778. The French alliance, although not without its problems, was critical to American victory in the War of the Revolution. That alliance would have been impossible without the American victory at Saratoga.

In the Saratoga campaign the British high command committed almost every major mistake that can be made in warfare. They underestimated their enemy; scattered their forces; allowed the outsized egos of commanders in the field to impact strategy in a negative manner; failed to attain unity of command; paid little attention to logistical problems; were appallingly ignorant of geography and terrain; antagonized the local civilian population; and allowed a major military operation to go forward with only the most cursory of communications networks existing between the British principals.

The basic British outline plan for the Saratoga campaign, as it was understood by General Burgoyne, the commander of the British Army of the North, was not a bad plan. The trouble lay in the fact that the

Devil was in the details, and those details were never properly worked out. The British plan for operations in North America for 1777 called for Burgoyne's army to move south from Montreal through the Lake Champlain and Hudson River Valleys and to seize Albany. What exactly was supposed to happen after that has been disputed by historians ever since 1777. It seems that British Secretary of State for the Colonies Lord George Germain's intention was to create a line of fortifications eventually extending all the way from Montreal to Manhattan in order to cordon off the New England colonies as a first step in stamping out the rebellion.[20] Whether this entire line was to be completed in 1777, or just the segment reaching from Montreal to Albany, is not entirely clear to this day.[21] It was definitely expected that Burgoyne would reach Albany and that he would be assisted in capturing that city by at the very least a modest force of British regulars, American loyalists (Tories), and Indian allies under the command of Lieutenant Colonel Barry St. Leger, who was to sail up the St. Lawrence River into Lake Ontario. From there, St. Leger was to march east from Fort Oswego through the Mohawk River Valley to attack Albany from the west.[22]

Lieutenant General Sir William Howe, the Commander-in-Chief of British land forces in North America, was the wild card in the events at the time and has continued in that role in the historical debate since. Many accounts of the Saratoga campaign state that General Howe was supposed to move his army up the Hudson River Valley from Manhattan to meet Burgoyne and St. Leger at Albany and that Howe's failure to do this was to blame for the disaster that befell Burgoyne's army. Furthermore, the traditional argument has it that by taking his army in exactly the opposite direction and heading for Philadelphia, Howe became one of history's most notorious examples of an incompetent commander "fiddling while Rome burns." What General Howe's exact role was supposed to be during the Saratoga campaign is the most controversial aspect of

---

[20] Troyer Steele Anderson. *The Command of the Howe Brothers During the American Revolution.* (New York: Oxford University Press, 1936): 253, 272–273.

[21] Rupert Furneaux. *The Battle of Saratoga.* (New York: Stein and Day, 1971): 27.

[22] Ketchum, *Saratoga,* 332.

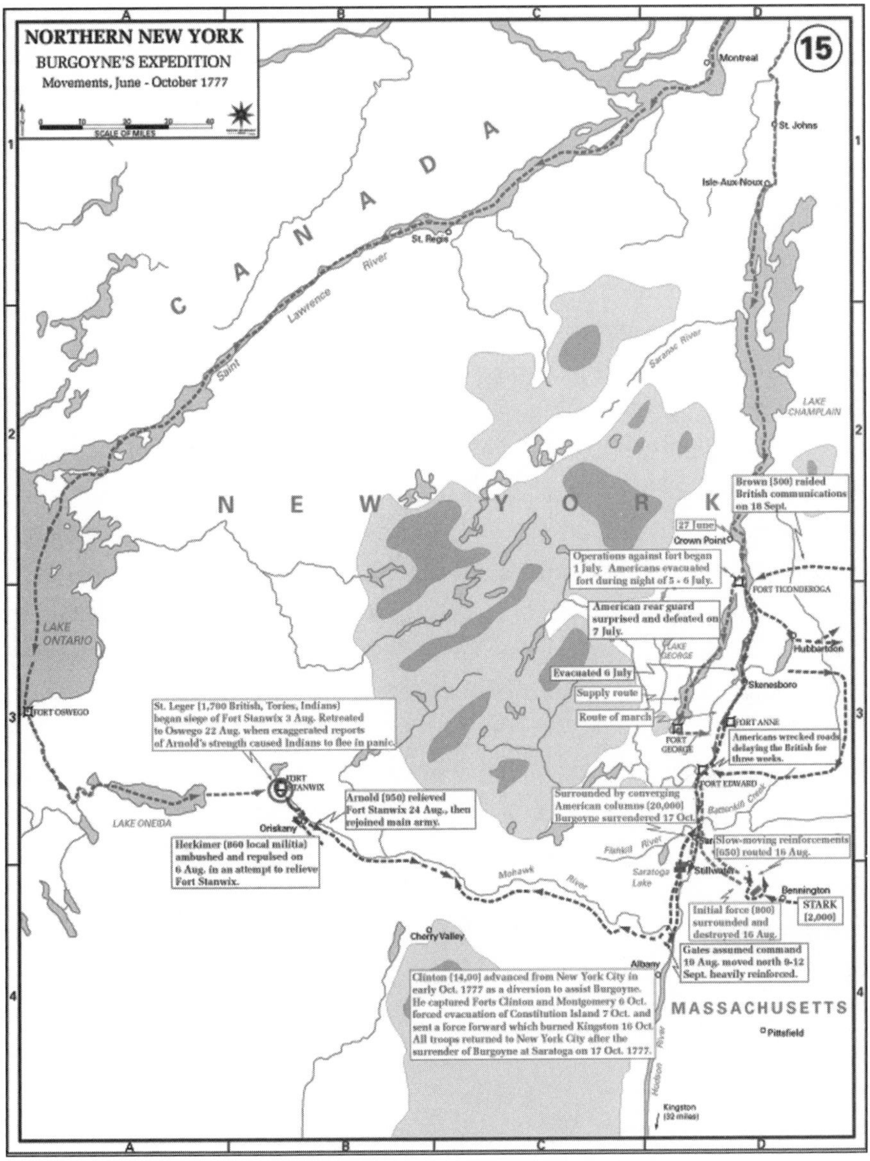
NORTHERN NEW YORK
BURGOYNE'S EXPEDITION
Movements, June - October 1777
SCALE OF MILES
15
CANADA
NEW YORK
MASSACHUSETTS
Montreal
St. Johns
Isle-Aux-Noux
St. Regis
Saint Lawrence River
Saranac River
LAKE CHAMPLAIN
LAKE ONTARIO
FORT OSWEGO
LAKE ONEIDA
FORT STANWIX
Oriskany
Brown (500) raided British communications on 18 Sept.
27 June
Crown Point
Operations against fort began 1 July. Americans evacuated fort during night of 5 - 6 July.
FORT TICONDEROGA
American rear guard surprised and defeated on 7 July.
Hubbardton
LAKE GEORGE
Evacuated 6 July
Supply route
Route of march
Skenesboro
FORT ANNE
FORT GEORGE
Americans wrecked roads delaying the British for three weeks.
FORT EDWARD
Batten Kill Creek
St. Leger (1,700 British, Tories, Indians) began siege of Fort Stanwix 3 Aug. Retreated to Oswego 22 Aug. when exaggerated reports of Arnold's strength caused Indians to flee in panic.
Arnold (950) relieved Fort Stanwix 24 Aug., then rejoined main army.
Herkimer (860 local militia) ambushed and repulsed on 6 Aug. in an attempt to relieve Fort Stanwix.
Surrounded by converging American columns (20,000) Burgoyne surrendered 17 Oct.
Fishkill River
Slow-moving reinforcements (650) routed 16 Aug.
Saratoga Lake
Stillwater
Mohawk River
Bennington
STARK (2,000)
Initial force (800) surrounded and destroyed 16 Aug.
Cherry Valley
Albany
Gates assumed command 19 Aug. moved north 9-12 Sept. heavily reinforced.
Clinton (14,00) advanced from New York City in early Oct. 1777 as a diversion to assist Burgoyne. He captured Forts Clinton and Montgomery 6 Oct. forced evacuation of Constitution Island 7 Oct. and sent a force forward which burned Kingston 16 Oct. All troops returned to New York City after the surrender of Burgoyne at Saratoga on 17 Oct. 1777.
Pittsfield
Hudson River
Kingston (32 miles)

Maps courtesy of The Department of History, United States Military Academy at West Point. This map has been changed from color to black and white.

The Saratoga campaign, 1777. Lakes and rivers were critical for transportation. Burgoyne's Army of the North sailed southward the entire length of Lake Champlain. Barry St. Leger's composite force sailed down the St. Lawrence River and across Lake Ontario before beginning an abortive march through the Mohawk River Valley.

the historical debate over the British defeat at Saratoga. While historians continue to argue the point of Howe's exact level of culpability for the disaster that befell British forces, the evidence suggests that until he received definite word to the contrary in early August 1777, General Burgoyne had indeed expected General Howe's army to meet him at Albany.[23]

As usual, getting at the truth of what happened and why requires dispensing with simplistic answers. What is clear is that the British defeat at Saratoga was due far more to mistakes made by the British than to any kind of strategically brilliant plan executed by their American adversaries. Perhaps the wisest act of the Americans in the Saratoga campaign was simply to not interfere unduly as the British Army of the North engaged in an act of self-destruction. Amongst British military and civilian policy makers, there is plenty of blame to go around for the Saratoga fiasco. Four men in particular, Howe, Burgoyne, Germain, and British Prime Minister Lord Frederick North deserve the bulk of the blame, but in differing degrees. The failure of General Howe to head north to Albany was utterly disastrous for the British, but Howe had received conflicting and vague orders from London in early 1777.[24] Also, neither Lord Germain nor Lord North forced Howe to be specific and clear when he was reporting his plans to London. Howe and Burgoyne both underestimated the fighting abilities of the Americans, but Howe's contempt for Americans as soldiers ran deeper than did Burgoyne's. All four men had a surprisingly poor grasp of the geography of North America, particularly of the difficulties of moving an army through heavily wooded terrain. For this, Howe and Burgoyne had no excuse because they had seen the territory with their own eyes.

---

[23] Michael Stephenson. *Patriot Battles: How the War of Independence Was Fought.* (New York: HarperCollins, 2007): 290. Don Cook. *The Long Fuse: How England Lost the American Colonies, 1760–1785.* (New York: The Atlantic Monthly Press, 1995): 273.

[24] Sir John Fortescue. *The War of Independence: The British Army in North America, 1775–1783.* (London: Greenhill Books, 1911. Mechanicsburg, PA: Stackpole Books, 2001): 60.

Exceedingly poor communications between the four men was one of the biggest British mistakes. North and Germain failed to impress upon Howe the necessity for ending the rebellion in 1777. Howe's move on Philadelphia might have made some sense if it had been prompted by some urgent strategic necessity; but all Howe did when he got to Philadelphia was to go immediately into winter quarters.

British mistakes in the Saratoga campaign occurred at both the strategic level of grand strategy and also locally at the tactical level. While he has many defenders, it can be argued that Sir William Howe deserves most of the blame for the British disaster at Saratoga. Howe's strategic blunder in moving his army south to Philadelphia instead of north to Albany was the most devastating single British mistake, and the one that doomed the Saratoga campaign for the British. The enormity of Howe's error is summed up by Don Cook:

> When General Howe reached Philadelphia on September 25 [1777], he received from [Major General Sir Henry] Clinton a copy of a dispatch from Burgoyne already blaming Howe for his precarious predicament. On the eve of capturing Philadelphia, Howe had to face the fact that he had gone to an enormous effort to bring his army to the wrong place at the wrong time. The decision virtually to ignore Burgoyne's advance had been Howe's, regardless of Germain's and the king's approval.[25]

Howe belatedly realized his responsibility for the disaster and offered to resign in late October after he learned of the defeat and capture of Burgoyne's army at Saratoga.[26]

General Burgoye also made critical mistakes. Burgoyne actually made more mistakes than did Howe, but Burgoyne's errors were mostly at the tactical level and might not have led to disaster had General Howe held up his end. Both Howe and Burgoyne were well aware that getting a letter to London and receiving an answer in the age of sailing ships required a minimum of eight weeks. They should have made more of an effort to communicate directly with each other and to cooperate. Knowing that

---

[25] Cook, *The Long Fuse*, 279–280.

[26] Cook, *The Long Fuse*, 280.

London was so far away, Howe and Burgoyne both should have been better at improvising a coherent plan in the absence of clear and timely dispatches from London. The two generals were certainly aided and abetted in their mistakes by conflicting instructions from London, but that is all the more reason why they should have worked together to forge an effective strategy on their own. It is always dangerous to try to ascertain the thought processes of long dead historical figures. Nevertheless, it is difficult to avoid the conclusion that Howe and Burgoyne were each angry that there were large British forces in North America that were under someone else's command. Petty jealousy had much to do with the British defeat at Saratoga. For the British, all of these mistakes resulted in the situation described earlier in Chapter One, namely, the failure to concentrate one's forces at the decisive place at the decisive time.

Despite the disastrous mistakes made by the British, Saratoga was not an easy campaign for the Americans. The American officer who accepted Burgoyne's surrender on October 17, 1777, Major General Horatio Gates, was a mediocrity at best. According to Richard Ketchum, Gates "was cautious, unimaginative, at his best as an administrator and organizer rather than a field commander."[27] Gates was also an inveterate schemer who drove George Washington crazy. The two were rivals, or at least Gates thought of Washington as a rival. Gates was constantly angling for Washington's job as Commander-in-Chief of the Continental Army. While he never managed to displace General Washington in the top job, Gates did succeed to the command of the Northern Department effective August 19, 1777 when the Continental Congress relieved his immediate superior, Major General Philip Schuyler. Bad feelings between Schuyler and Gates had been simmering for a year, but the real reasons for Schuyler's removal were that he had enemies in Congress and he was unfairly blamed for the British capture of Fort Ticonderoga—one of the few episodes in the Saratoga campaign that had gone Burgoyne's way.[28] Schuyler was a better general than Gates, and changing horses midstream

---

[27] Ketchum, *Saratoga*, 355.

[28] James Thomas Flexner. *George Washington in the American Revolution (1775–1783)*. (Boston: Little, Brown and Company, 1967, 1968): 100. Ketchum, *Saratoga*, 335–337.

when the climax of the campaign was fast approaching was a foolish move on the part of Congress.[29] Somehow, however, in this campaign the mistakes made by the Americans never turned out to be as disastrous as were British mistakes. Luck seemed to be on the side of the Americans during the Saratoga campaign.

Gates went out of his way to be disrespectful to General Washington. For instance, Gates delayed sending a personal report on the Saratoga battle directly to Washington for so long that Washington had to learn the details from others. Congress inadvertently made it easy for Gates to snub Washington in that Congress had grown accustomed to treating Schuyler's Northern Department as if it was a completely independent command. George Washington was, of course, the senior general, but after the British evacuated Boston in March 1776, Washington was preoccupied with the middle-Atlantic states. He did not have time to closely monitor what was going on in New England and in the Hudson River Valley.[30]

Gates was lucky during the Saratoga campaign. His own very real limitations as a strategist and a fighter were offset by his good fortune in having talented subordinates such as Benedict Arnold and John Stark at his disposal. Gates also benefited greatly from the sound decisions of his predecessor General Schuyler, such as to reinforce Fort Stanwix on the Mohawk River and to see that that outpost was defended vigorously. Gates got the credit for the Saratoga victory, but Schuyler had done much, probably more than Gates, to bring that victory about.[31]

That Burgoyne became stranded in the wilderness of upstate New York at the end of the very long and tenuous supply line presented Schuyler and then Gates with an extremely rare opportunity. The Americans took full advantage of this opportunity, unlike the French in 1940 who had failed to separate Hitler's tanks from their supporting infantry. As stated previously, General Howe made the most disastrous mistake of

---

[29] Fortescue, *The War of Independence*, 85.

[30] Ketchum, *Saratoga*, 52–55.

[31] Ketchum, *Saratoga*, 332–337. Jack Rakove. *Revolutionaries: A New History of the Invention of America.* (Boston: Houghton Mifflin Harcourt, 2010): 139.

the Saratoga campaign by failing to support Burgoyne. However, one mistake Howe himself avoided making with his own army was getting too far ahead of his own supplies. General Howe was careful to always remain close to the eastern ports such as New York and Philadelphia from whence he drew his supplies. Thus, George Washington was never presented with an opportunity to cut off and capture Howe's entire army. Also, New York and New Jersey were full of Tories. There was never a chance that Washington would enjoy the services of a large force of local militia such as would be of great assistance to Gates.

The difference in mood between civilians in Pennsylvania and those in New York and New England is demonstrated by the fact that Howe's army had a fine time in Philadelphia, receiving a warm welcome, while Washington's army froze and starved twenty miles away at Valley Forge. The northern colonies were the heart of the rebellion while Washington at Valley Forge was confronted with apathy and profiteering amongst the local populace.[32] Washington always tried to remain above petty vanity, but he must have felt some chagrin that a mediocrity like Gates was receiving all the accolades in the months after Saratoga—at the same time that Washington was settling his army in for its miserable winter at Valley Forge.

American generals Schuyler and Gates were served by energetic subordinates who injected an urgency into the American effort at Saratoga that was completely lacking amongst the British high command in 1777. Generals Howe and Burgoyne could have learned much from the energy and ability to improvise shown by Benedict Arnold, then a major general in the Continental Army. One reason Arnold's betrayal of the Patriot cause in 1780 was so devastating to the Americans is that, in terms of strategic grasp and energy, Benedict Arnold was probably the most brilliant American general of the Revolution. It had been Arnold who in August 1777 had traveled ninety miles west along the Mohawk River Valley to take command of the American forces that were under siege by St. Leger's force at Fort Stanwix in central New York State. After St. Leger was turned back, Arnold returned to Saratoga in time to play a critical

---

[32] Ron Chernow. *Washington: A Life.* (New York: Peguin, 2010): 312–315, 323, 328–329. Rakove, *Revolutionaries*, 139, 143–144.

role in the fighting both at Freeman's Farm and at Bemis Heights. He and Gates had had a falling out in late summer. Gates decided to punish his former friend by keeping Arnold away from what Arnold loved most—namely, action. Thus, during the fighting at Bemis Heights on October 7, Arnold disobeyed a direct order from Gates that he, Arnold, should avoid the action and remain in camp that day. Instead, Arnold rode out to the front lines and provided the vigorous battlefield leadership that Gates, back in his headquarters behind the lines, seemed incapable of furnishing.[33]

One area in which the Continental Army may have had an institutional advantage over the British Army during the Revolutionary War was that its officer corps was more of a merit-based system than was the officer corps of the British Army. In the eighteenth and early nineteenth centuries, wealthy British men could purchase commissions and then promotions in the British Army. A young man of humble origins in the American ranks like Alexander Hamilton, despite his brilliance, never would have been able to attain the rank of Lieutenant Colonel at the tender age of twenty-one had he been in the British Army because he would have lacked the money to purchase promotions—and probably even his initial commission. Likewise, American Brigadier General John Stark, who would defeat Burgoyne's German mercenaries at the Battle of Bennington during the Saratoga campaign, had also been raised in modest circumstances that would have made it very difficult for him to obtain an important command in the British Army. The British purchase system made the British officer corps heavily weighted toward wealth, regardless of talent. This is not to say that wealth was absent from the high command of the American army. George Washington and Philip Schuyler were two of the wealthiest men in North America, but each had also learned the trade of soldiering by commanding troops in the Seven Years War.

Even if a talented young Briton of modest means could scrape together the money for an entry-level commission as an ensign, he would

---

[33] Ketchum, *Saratoga*, 350–353, 359–369, 394–400. Robert Leckie. *George Washington's War: The Saga of the American Revolution.* (New York: HarperCollins, 1992): 408–414.

probably remain trapped in the lower ranks of the British Army due to an inability to purchase promotions. The British system was open to other abuses as well. The activities of Mary Anne Clarke—mistress of Frederick, the Duke of York, and ancestor of George du Maurier, the celebrated Victorian era *Punch* illustrator—and of du Maurier's granddaughter, the novelist Daphne du Maurier, became the subject of a major scandal in Parliament when it was discovered that Mary Anne had financed the lavish lifestyle for herself and the Duke, who was also Commander-in-Chief of the army, by selling commissions and promotions—monies that never made it into the British treasury. Mary Anne Clark, a courtesan, thus became for a time the de facto personnel manager of the British Army. When the scandal broke in 1809, the Duke of York was forced to temporarily relinquish his army post and no less a personage than the Duke of Wellington felt compelled to testify before Parliament to reassure members of the House of Commons that Mary Anne Clarke's machinations had not harmed the fighting effectiveness of the British Army.[34]

That commissions could be purchased, regardless of merit, produced a very mixed bag of talent in the British Army. Fine officers like Sir Jeffrey Amherst, Sir James Wolfe, and the Duke of Wellington rose through the ranks under the purchase system. However, the practice also allowed dead wood such as Sir William Howe, John Burgoyne, and Sir Charles Cornwallis to rise in the officer corps of the British Army. (It should be noted that even a merit-based system is not an absolute guarantee that the best officers will rise to the high command. For instance, Sir

---

[34] Daphne du Maurier. *The Du Mauriers.* (New York: The Literary Guild of America, Inc., 1937): *passim.* Ketchum, *Saratoga,* 72–73. Chernow, *Washington,* 239. Elizabeth Longford. *Wellington: the Years of the Sword.* (New York: Harper & Row, 1969): 169–171. William Hazlitt and John Gurwood, eds. *The Speeches of the Duke of Wellington in Parliament: Collected and Arranged by the Late Colonel Gurwood.* (London: J. Murray, 1854): 47–49, 54, 65–67. Hathi Trust Digital Library. http://babel.hathitrust.org/cgi/pt?id=mdp.39015027329815;view=1up;seq=76. Accessed February 2, 2014. Background on the purchasing of commissions can be found in C. Woodham-Smith. *The Reason Why.* (New York: McGraw-Hill, 1953, 1954): 30–34.

Douglas Haig, arguably Great Britain's worst general of all time, entered the British Army after the practice of allowing commissions to be purchased had been abolished in 1870.[35])

Even a merit-based system for promotions would not have rectified a critical deficiency in the British military system; namely, the absence of a true General Staff. During World War II, the British Chiefs of Staff Committee (COS) would prove invaluable for formulating and coordinating British strategy. The British Army fighting the American Revolution lacked such an organization. Thus, in that war instead of receiving their instructions from a command staff in London that had sifted through the various strategic options away from the distractions of the front lines, British commanders in the field, in this case Generals Howe and Burgoyne, made individual pitches of their respective ideas to Lord Germain. This meant that Britain lacked a unified command structure. The fact that George Washington was saddled with insubordinate lieutenants such as Horatio Gates shows that the American command structure in the War of the Revolution was equally rickety and equally lacking in unity. However, the vast distances that Great Britain had to overcome in this war made the lack of both a General Staff and of any kind of unity of command critical factors in the British defeat at Saratoga and later in the entire war.

An example of this command disunity is that General Howe had received permission from Lord Germain, in a letter dated March 3, 1777, to head for Philadelphia.[36] That Germain would grant such permission was quite strange since he and the British Cabinet had just a few weeks earlier approved Burgoyne's plan to move south from Montreal.[37] This contradiction was a major mistake on the part of Germain; a mistake that motivated Sir John Fortescue to write some of the most often quoted lines regarding the Saratoga campaign: "Howe was left with directions to attack Philadelphia, and Burgoyne with positive and unconditional commands to advance on Albany and there place himself under Howe's orders. . . .

---

[35] Woodham-Smith, *The Reason Why*, 30–34.

[36] Cook, *The Long Fuse*, 266.

[37] Cook, *The Long Fuse*, 268.

Never was there a finer example of the art of organizing disaster."[38] Fortescue is correct in that these two contradictory sets of instructions certainly set the stage for the coming disaster, but Howe and Burgoyne as career army officers still could have and should have worked out a coherent plan between themselves. Germain's ignorance of the geography of the Americas is nowhere more evident than in these contradictory orders to his commanders in the field. Germain seems to have thought that Philadelphia and Albany were located quite close to one another and that they were connected by good roads.[39] In fact, the two cities are approximately 230 miles apart, and two-thirds of the route would have been through the wooded Hudson River Valley, where the only good road in 1777 was the river itself. One huge advantage the colonists had during the war was simply that they lived in the theater and knew its geography quite well.

Although some historians would argue the point, and despite the contradictory instructions he issued, it does seem that Germain fully intended for Howe and Burgoyne to coordinate their efforts. Germain knew that his generals in North America were chronically short of troops and that there could be only one major campaign for 1777. His ignorance of the vast distances and the poor roads in North America seems to have convinced Germain that capturing Philadelphia and Albany could in fact be encompassed in one major operation.[40] According to Richard Ketchum, "As the events of 1777 were to reveal, Germain had no real comprehension or appreciation of the distances and natural obstacles an army would encounter in America."[41]

---

[38] Fortescue, as reprinted in Cook, *The Long Fuse*, 268; also reprinted in James Lunt. *John Burgoyne of Saratoga*. (New York: Harcourt Brace Jovanovich, 1975): 134.

[39] Lunt, *John Burgoyne of Saratoga*, 130, 133–134.

[40] Lunt, *John Burgoyne of Saratoga*, 126. Rakove, *Revolutionaries*, 132. Middlekauff, *The Glorious Cause*, 373–374, 377. Jane Clark. "Responsibility for the Failure of the Burgoyne Campaign," in *American Historical Review*. Vol. 35, No. 3, April 1930, 547.

[41] Ketchum, *Saratoga*, 69.

The personalities of Sir William Howe and of General Burgoyne are critical factors to consider when trying to make sense of the British disaster at Saratoga. General Howe and his brother, Admiral Lord Richard Howe, seemed to see the war as a regrettable but necessary step in the advancement of their respective careers. They shared a vision of a benevolent empire, not of an empire based on military dictatorship. Sir William Howe even had doubts as to whether Britain had any legal right to compel the colonies back into the fold using force. He was lazy, preferring liquor, gambling, and the company of his mistress to fighting. The Howe brothers were quite ambivalent about the war. They liked Americans and would have preferred to see the rebellion resolved through negotiation rather than fighting. They were not cowards, but they lacked the killer instinct.[42] Although Sir William Howe and General Burgoyne are usually described as rivals, Burgoyne's attitude in this regard was actually quite similar to that of the Howe brothers. Back in London in December 1776, Burgoyne had lobbied hard for Britain's northern command with Germain,[43] but he had lobbied out of ambition, not conviction. Burgoyne was like Generals Howe and Sir Henry Clinton in not wanting to fight Americans. In fact, many high ranking British commanders did not like this war, including General Sir Jeffrey Amherst who declined to get involved in the American war at all.[44]

Germain compounded his ignorance of geography by giving only vague instructions to Howe and by accepting vague replies from Howe. Germain's ignorance of the distance between Philadelphia and Albany meant he did not know how impossible it would be in a pre-industrial era without railroads, or even good roads for wagons, for a British Army to march on Philadelphia, take that city, then wheel about and move on Albany in one campaigning season. To even attempt it, Howe would have needed explicit instructions as to the urgency of the situation from Germain. Such instructions were never forthcoming. It was uncommon

---

[42] Chernow, *Washington*, 239. Ketchum, *Saratoga*, 56–58, 76–77. Middlekauff. *The Glorious Cause*, 344.

[43] Ketchum, *Saratoga*, 72–73.

[44] Ketchum, *Saratoga*, 56–58, 76–77. Chernow, *Washington*, 239.

for Howe and Burgoyne to even communicate directly. The petty jealousy between the two men was nowhere more evident than in that each man preferred to communicate his respective plans in writing to Germain, who was three thousand miles, and at least four weeks by sailing ship, away in London. Using Germain as the conduit for communications they should have been sending directly to each other was a critical error for which Generals Howe and Burgoyne were equally to blame.[45]

In fact, it had to have been more than an error; most likely it was an example of Howe and Burgoyne each deliberately doing the barest minimum to keep their superior, Germain, informed of what they each intended to do. Each could then say afterwards that they had made their respective intentions known. Perhaps having done so, Howe and Burgoyne each expected to have his particular campaign chosen by Germain as the main effort to which everything and everyone else would be subordinated. Unfortunately for both generals, Germain lacked the fortitude to make such a tough, but necessary, call. Germain also lacked a General Staff in London that could have pointed out the discrepancies between the two plans to Germain and advised him on how to reconcile them.

Since Burgoyne needed Howe far more than Howe needed Burgoyne, "Gentleman Johnny" was a fool in failing to understand that clear communications between himself and General Howe would be as important as ammunition in the coming campaign. The two generals did make some attempts to communicate directly, but they never made the establishment and maintenance of a permanent and regular courier service between their two armies a priority. That was especially unfortunate for the British since several of the couriers who were dispatched with correspondence were captured by the Americans and the letters thus never delivered.[46] Incidentally, being a courier was a dangerous job. Tories dressed in civilian clothes captured by the Continental Army while carrying British dispatches were considered to be spies and traitors and were often hanged—a grim reminder that this was a civil war as well as a war of rebellion against British rule.[47]

---

[45] Ketchum, *Saratoga*, 103–105. Middlekauff, *The Glorious Cause*, 373–374, 377.

[46] Ketchum, *Saratoga*, 282.

[47] Ketchum, *Saratoga*, 330, 384.

One letter that Burgoyne did receive directly from Howe arrived by courier on August 3, 1777, having been written in mid-July. By the time he received this letter, Burgoyne's army was already south of Lake Champlain, deep in New York State. Here, Burgoyne finally got definite word of Howe's intentions. The news was not good. Howe laconically informed Burgoyne that "My intention is for Pennsylvania, where I expect to meet Washington, but if he goes to the northward contrary to my expectations, and you can keep him at bay, be assured that I shall soon be after him to relieve you."[48] Washington did not head north. It did not even occur to Howe (or to his superiors in London) that if Washington remained in New Jersey or Pennsylvania, the rebels might be capable of assembling a separate army to operate against Burgoyne in the northern theater independently of Washington's force. It was at about the time that he wrote this letter in mid-July that Howe got the news that Burgoyne was now in possession of Fort Ticonderoga.[49] That means that Howe knew Burgoyne was deep in enemy territory; he should have hastened to Burgoyne's aid. This kind of lackadaisical, incomplete, nonsensical behavior and lack of clarity represents a failure of command on the part of the British all the way up the line from Burgoyne and Howe in America to Germain, Lord North, and even the King in London. Such a muddled situation never would have been tolerated by William Pitt, the Elder and his field commanders, such as General Sir James Wolfe, during the French and Indian War. It came as quite a shock to Burgoyne that the entire southern half of the pincer he had envisioned as closing on the rebels at Albany no longer existed. On the vague messages between Germain and Howe, Michael Stephenson writes:

> Whatever the niceties of language, there is no doubt that Burgoyne and his army expected a rendezvous with a British force at Albany. On 6 May (1777), for example, Burgoyne repeated the objective laid out in his February plan. He wrote to General Simon Fraser, 'The military operations, all directed to make a junction with Howe, are committed to me.'[50]

---

[48] Howe to Burgoyne, as quoted in Ketchum, *Saratoga*, 283.

[49] Rakove, *Revolutionaries*, 133. Ferling, *A Leap in the Dark*, 198.

[50] Stephenson, *Patriot Battles*, 290.

Historians who have defended Howe's decision to *not* move north toward Albany have challenged the view that Howe, either deliberately or due to gross incompetence, left Burgoyne in the lurch.[51] The letter Stephenson quotes from seems to indicate that Burgoyne was indeed depending on Howe, but there is also evidence that Burgoyne felt that he would need Howe's aid only *after* he had reached Albany. Again, the personalities of the two generals must be taken into account. Howe was irritated that Burgoyne had been given an independent command. Germain probably sensed this and that perhaps is the reason why Germain was reluctant to give explicit instructions to Howe and tolerated vague responses from Howe. Burgoyne was a romantic. When he struck off into the forests, Burgoyne's well-known propensity for living large became a tremendous handicap. According to Don Cook:

> Gentleman Johnny lived and traveled in style, and he loved the glamour of eighteenth-century soldiering. Twenty-six wagons were allocated for the baggage belonging to Burgoyne and his senior staff: tents, camp beds, blankets, cooking stoves, dinner china, silver and crystal, wines, personal supplies, and of course, uniforms. Gentleman Johnny was immaculately uniformed.[52]

Burgoyne also had a mistress traveling with him.[53] Indeed, Burgoyne seemed to see campaigning as something of a family affair. Several of his officers and enlisted men had their wives and even their children with them.[54] As a romantic warrior, it seems that Burgoyne hoped to go down in history as the dashing general who had fought his way through to Albany against heavy odds. The key point is that Burgoyne expected aid from Howe *after* he had reached Albany. Burgoyne did not expect, and probably did not want, Howe's aid in *getting to* Albany. Burgoyne wanted Howe to meet him *at* Albany. Because he had more respect for

---

[51] Mark Mayo Boatner III. *Encyclopedia of the American Revolution.* (New York: David McKay Company, 1966): 134–135.

[52] Cook, *The Long Fuse*, 275.

[53] Cook, *The Long Fuse*, 275.

[54] Ketchum, *Saratoga*, 410–411, 416–417.

the fighting abilities of the Americans than did General Howe, Burgoyne apparently did expect a tough fight to get through to Albany, but he thought he could carry the day unaided as far as Albany. If he could do that, he would be a hero, and that would have meant everything to Burgoyne. However, his army would then be a spent force and would dearly need the rest and replenishment it could get only if Howe was waiting for him in Albany.[55] Burgoyne knew that if Howe was not waiting for him in Albany, the northern army would be in real trouble. James Lunt writes that "The one thing certain is that Burgoyne reckoned on Howe's assistance and support, once Albany had been taken."[56] Howe's defenders are thus only partly correct. General Howe was not expected to help Burgoyne get to Albany, but he was supposed to meet Burgoyne once "Gentleman Johnny" arrived in Albany.

Even before he headed south from Montreal in May 1777, Burgoyne seems to have perceived his drive toward Albany as a one-way trip, but not one that would end in disaster. He knew his forces would be exhausted by the time he reached Albany, but all would be set right if General Howe were waiting to meet him in Albany. Burgoyne saw his departure from Montreal as permanent. He wanted Albany or perhaps Manhattan to become his new base of operations. It was unthinkable to Burgoyne that Howe would fail to meet him in Albany. It was of course a major mistake on the part of Burgoyne to never even consider that General Howe would head south instead of north—but then again the idiocy of Howe's decision to head south would have been difficult for any rational person to predict. Burgoyne probably thought that the worst that could happen would be that Howe would remain in Manhattan for the time being. In light of the many variables such as sporadic and vague instructions, clashing egos, trekking through dense wilderness, and the presence of a rebel army facing him, it was reckless and naïve of Burgoyne to stake

---

[55] William Digby Journal, July 24–October 13, 1777; reprinted in John Rhode-hamel, ed. *The American Revolution: Writings from the War of Independence.* (New York: The Library of America, 2001): 313–314. Furneaux, *The Battle of Saratoga*, 28. Lunt, *John Burgoyne of Saratoga*, 122–123. Anderson, *The Command of the Howe Brothers During the American Revolution*, 248.

[56] Lunt, *John Burgoyne of Saratoga*, 129.

everything on a meeting with Howe's army in Albany and then to continue trying to get through to Albany even after learning in early August that Howe had no intention of meeting him.[57]

While he sometimes truly deserved the label of "fool," Burgoyne was not all frivolity and stupidity. He had experienced grief in his life. Burgoyne's wife Charlotte had died in 1776, and he was utterly devastated at his loss and that he had been unable to get home from Canada in time for her funeral. Their only child, a girl, had died fifteen years earlier. Burgoyne was also far more willing than was his opponent, General Gates, to accept the danger of commanding from the front lines instead of hunkering down in a headquarters tent behind the lines.[58] Even his critics agree that "Gentleman Johnny" was never afraid to expose himself to enemy fire.

Burgoyne's original intention may have been to conduct an operation similar in concept to the shuttle bombing missions that would be undertaken in World War II by the Americans and the Japanese, respectively. The attacking force in a shuttle operation "shuttles" between two bases, fighting a battle or series of battles while en route between the two bases. In an air battle, the use of shuttle tactics can increase the range at which attacking aircraft can strike. In a ground battle, shuttle tactics can enable an army to abandon its lines of supply—to worry only about what is ahead, not behind. Military shuttle operations offer great potential rewards, but they are risky. In World War II, Operation Frantic in the summer of 1944 saw American heavy bombers conducting shuttle bombing raids against cities in eastern Germany in which the Americans took off from bases in Britain or Italy and after dropping their bombs flew on to air bases in the Soviet Union, where they would refuel and rearm. This tactic enabled the Americans to bomb targets beyond their normal range and it confused German fighter pilots who were looking for targets to attack along the return route to Italy or Britain. Japanese naval pilots employed shuttle bombing tactics against American ships during the Battle of the Philippine Sea in July 1944. Then, Japanese

---

[57] Ketchum, *Saratoga*, 65–66, 404.

[58] Ketchum, *Saratoga*, 65–66, 404.

naval aircraft launched from carriers at extreme range attacked American aircraft carriers that were covering the landing of American troops in the Mariana Islands. Some of the Japanese pilots who managed to survive the onslaught of American fighter aircraft and anti-aircraft fire were then able to land on Japanese-held islands such as Guam; where they could take on more bombs and fuel in preparation for making another attack on the return trip. Japanese success in this maneuver was limited, however, since American naval aircraft vigorously attacked those landing fields in the Marianas. Likewise, the Allied Frantic shuttle bombing missions had to be curtailed after a great many American bombers were destroyed in June 1944 when the German Air Force bombed the airfields in the Ukraine that the American aircrews were using for their turnarounds.[59]

The difficulties encountered by the Americans and the Japanese, respectively, in those World War II shuttle bombing missions help explain why General Burgoyne's plan for a shuttle-type ground campaign ended so disastrously at Saratoga. The attacking forces in a shuttle operation, be it Burgoyne's army moving south from Montreal in 1777 or the Japanese pilots in the Philippine Sea or the American pilots in the Frantic campaigns of 1944, usually only have complete control over the base or bases from which they depart. Control over the base on the other end of a shuttle operation tends to be tenuous at best since such a base is usually quite close to the enemy, and therefore readily subject to counterattack. In Burgoyne's case, his objective was a city, Albany, that he knew to be in enemy hands. Either he or Howe would have had to capture the city before it could become Burgoyne's new base of operations. Burgoyne would not be the last ground force commander to attempt a shuttle-type operation. The best and most successful example of such a campaign is Major General William T. Sherman's march from Atlanta to Savannah in the fall of 1864 during the American Civil War. Sherman abandoned his supply line completely and had his army live off the land. He did not

---

[59] Edward P. Stafford. *The Big E: The Story of the U.S.S. Enterprise.* (Annapolis, MD: Naval Institute Press/Bluejacket Books, 1962): 388, 394–399. Donald L. Miller. *Masters of the Air: America's Bomber Boys Who Fought the Air War Against Nazi Germany.* (New York: Simon & Schuster, 2006): 323–324. Rigby, *Allied Master Strategists*, 113.

have any control over his destination, Savannah, until his army actually arrived there and took the city in December 1864. Sherman's march was risky, but it does show that a ground shuttle operation does not have to end in disaster.

Amongst the many unanswered questions regarding the Saratoga campaign is why Burgoyne continued on toward Albany even after he learned on August 3, 1777 that General Howe was nowhere near. Even after the Freeman's Farm battle in September Burgoyne could have fallen back on Fort Ticonderoga from which his supply line to Canada would have been relatively secure—at least until Lake Champlain froze over, and maybe even after that if sledges could have been obtained. He deliberately chose not to seek the safety Ticonderoga could offer him.[60] Repeated failures to make tactical withdrawals were Burgoyne's most egregious errors in the campaign.

General Sir Henry Clinton was the British officer who probably had the clearest grasp of the strategic situation in the summer of 1777. Clinton had joined Howe as second in command in July just before Howe departed New York for Philadelphia. Having just come from London, Clinton knew what Germain was thinking but he lacked the documentation to back it up. According to Don Cook, "Clinton was aware that having the armies join up at Albany was a priority for Germain, even if this had not been spelled out precisely in orders."[61] Germain should have abandoned the exceedingly slow method of writing individually to Howe and to Burgoyne. He should have insisted that the two generals communicate directly with each other. Dispatching Clinton to serve with Howe was the time for Germain to transmit to Howe, via Clinton, a crystal clear plan of action. That did not happen, however. Knowing Germain's intentions, and perhaps being blessed with a better strategic brain than General Howe, Clinton was opposed to the move on Philadelphia and sensed that better cooperation between Burgoyne and Howe was desperately needed. Clinton could see that the key to victory was to focus everything on the northern operation. Clinton's instincts

---

[60] Ketchum, *Saratoga*, 388.

[61] Cook, *The Long Fuse*, 273.

were sound but unfortunately he did *not* have a letter from Germain specifically ordering Howe to forget about Philadelphia and head north. All Clinton could do was try to persuade Howe to move north, not south. Howe was unmoved, literally and figuratively, by Clinton's entreaties.[62] It did not help that Clinton and Howe did not get along well together. According to Ketchum:

> No matter what his motives were, Clinton was addressing the central question that should have been decided unequivocally by Germain before the campaign was launched. If the government truly wanted to end the war this year, a leisurely advance on Philadelphia was no way to do it. And for all Clinton's small-minded, oversensitive quibbling with Howe and his obsession with imagined slights and insults, he was right, and Howe might have seen it if only he had been less pigheaded, more willing to strain every nerve to win.[63]

That is just it; except for Clinton, the British commanders on the ground in North America seemed to be in no hurry. They did not realize that time was on the side of the colonists.

One man who did understand that time was not on the side of Great Britain was the old lion, William Pitt, the Elder; now 1st Earl of Chatham. During the Saratoga campaign, Pitt in London was advocating an immediate grant of independence and an end to the war. He considered the colonies to be unconquerable and in the right to desire their freedom. He also presciently feared French intervention. Pitt was in a position to know how vast a territory the North American colonies encompassed and how angry the French were after their humiliating defeat in the French and Indian War, having served as Secretary of State for War during that earlier conflict.[64] Unfortunately, Chatham's ability to influence British policy was quite limited by 1777 because he was then out of office, in poor health, and a member of the House of Lords. Then as now, the House of Lords had great prestige, but far less practical influ-

---

[62] Ketchum, *Saratoga*, 256–261. Middlekauff, *The Glorious Cause*, 373–374, 377. Clark, "Responsibility for the Failure of the Burgoyne Campaign," 551–552.

[63] Ketchum, *Saratoga*, 260.

[64] Cook, *The Long Fuse*, 271, 280

ence than did the House of Commons.[65] It had been from the Commons that Pitt had orchestrated British grand strategy during the French and Indian War.

General Burgoyne compounded Howe's strategic error with a series of tactical mistakes. The whole point of invading south through the valleys of Lake Champlain and Lake George, respectively, was to take advantage of water transportation. The lakes and rivers of America were its highways in the eighteenth century when roads were scarce and where they existed were narrow, bumpy, and unpaved. Transporting his army primarily in sturdy, shallow draft boats known as bateaux and in a few small sailing ships southwards on Lake Champlain, Burgoyne initially made good time down its 125-mile length and was able to capture Fort Ticonderoga at the southern end of the lake on July 5, 1777. However, after arriving at the southern end of Lake Champlain (often referred to as the "head" of the lake since Lake Champlain and Lake George both drain to the north), Burgoyne unwisely chose to halt. He settled down at Skenesborough, now known as Whitehall, New York, for over two weeks to rest himself and his troops. That was his first mistake. It allowed the American army to continue to fall back from Ticonderoga unmolested and to regroup.

Burgoyne's second mistake was to decide that his troops would then march overland to Fort Edward on the upper Hudson River instead of having them travel south by boat on Lake George, which like Champlain is long and narrow—tailor made for north-south waterborne transportation. The latter course still would have necessitated a twelve-mile overland trek from the southern end of Lake George to Fort Edward, but perhaps if Burgoyne had acted quickly his troops could have been landed at the southern tip (technically the "head") of Lake George before the Continental troops could get that far south; a strategy that during World War II would become known as bypassing an enemy strong point. By delaying, and then marching overland southward and parallel to Lake George through a heavily forested area rife with muddy swamps,

---

[65] Cook, *The Long Fuse*, 271, 280. *Encyopaedia Britannica Online*, s.v. "William Pitt, the Elder. http://www.britannica.com/EBchecked/topic/462131/William-Pitt-the-Elder. Accessed January 16, 2014.

Burgoyne gave the colonials the chance to fell trees across the roads in his path and to block tiny Wood Creek, a nearby stream that Burgoyne had hoped to use for the hauling of some of his supplies; canal-style.

American troops under Gates's predecessor in command of the Northern Department, Major General Philip Schuyler, took to the work of creating natural obstacles in Burgoyne's path with great gusto. Cutting down trees became for a while the main activity of the American troops. Historian Mark Boatner has testified to the effectiveness of these tactics in slowing Burgoyne's advance from Skenesboro to Fort Edward thus: "It took the British 20 days to cover the 22 miles. They had to bridge at least 40 deep ravines, and in one place constructed a two-mile causeway."[66] Burgoyne also separated his men from the bulk of their supplies after deciding that most of the supplies, but not the men, would in fact travel via bateaux on Lake George.[67] Burgoyne's decision not to send his troops by water the thirty-mile length of Lake George was a critical error, especially since he had just seen how a speedy advance down Lake Champlain had enabled him to capture Fort Ticonderoga.

While Burgoyne failed to take full advantage of the opportunities for transportation by water that were available to him, General Howe placed too much emphasis on water transportation. To move his army from New York to Philadelphia, General Howe elected to have his troops travel by sea in a fleet of oceangoing ships. That flotilla, under the command of his brother, Admiral Lord Richard Howe, left New York Harbor on July 23, 1777. This was a foolish move that seems to have been motivated primarily by Sir William Howe's desire to find employment for his brother's ships. An overland march would have been much faster. Philadelphia is only one hundred miles from New York and the roads between the two most important cities in the colonies were far better than what Burgoyne was contending with in the wilds of the Adirondack mountains up north. The ships carrying Howe's army were becalmed for eighteen days in New York Harbor before a favorable wind even enabled them to leave port. They had a slow time of it even after they sailed,

---

[66] Boatner, *Encyclopedia of the American Revolution*, 138.

[67] Robert K. Wright, Jr. *The Continental Army*. (Washington, DC: Center of Military History, 1986): 116. Ketchum, *Saratoga*, 246–249.

again due mainly to contrary or nonexistent winds. Indeed, it was not until August 25, 1777 that Howe's army went ashore at the northern end of Chesapeake Bay and prepared to march on Philadelphia. Even then, the British had a lengthy overland trek ahead of them before they could reach Philadelphia.[68] This "cruise to nowhere" undertaken by General Howe was a grave tactical error (second only to his decision to head for Philadelphia at all in its senselessness) that wasted precious weeks of the 1777 campaigning season and would have made it all but impossible for Howe to have marched his army to Albany in time to help Burgoyne even if Howe had had the good sense to see the wisdom of such a course of action.[69] Sir William Howe's behavior is difficult for even his supporters to explain. For instance, Troyer Steele Anderson, a sympathetic biographer, writing in the 1930s in regard to the cool, vague, condescending tone of Howe's July letter to Burgoyne quoted previously concedes that:

> It must be confessed that there was something a little inadequate about Howe's attitude, technically correct though it may have been. . . . Sir William wrote a little like a man with an unwelcome servant forced upon him, whom he was obliged to keep busy but for whose services he felt no enthusiasm.[70]

For his part, Burgoyne committed a tactical blunder just as his campaign began on June 20, 1777 when he issued a bombastic threatening letter to the colonists in the Champlain and Hudson River Valleys in which he said he was going to unleash his Indian allies to terrorize Americans in rebel areas; whether they be soldiers or women and children. This was not a wise move. The wording was very pompous. Nobody was really frightened by the letter. They either laughed at Burgoyne or they got mad.[71] Of the rebels who insisted on remaining unrepentant, Burgoyne

---

[68] Ketchum, *Saratoga*, 256–261.

[69] Ketchum, *Saratoga*, 259.

[70] Anderson, *The Command of the Howe Brothers During the American Revolution*, 259–260.

[71] Ketchum, *Saratoga*, 141–142. Boatner, *Encyclopedia of the American Revolution*, 142–143.

concluded his warning by writing that "The Messengers of Justice and of Wrath await them in the Field, and Devastation, Famine, and every concomitant Horror that a reluctant but indispensable Prosecution of Military Duty must occasion, will bar the Way to their Return."[72]

The first real pitched battle of the campaign took place at Hubbardton, Vermont on July 7, 1777 when a group of British infantry and German mercenaries who were pursuing the retreating American garrison from Fort Ticonderoga clashed with a small composite force of American infantry, local militia, and guerrillas. The guerrilla force was part of an outfit known as the Green Mountain Boys that had initially been formed by a Vermont farmer named Ethan Allen. Allen himself had been captured by the British in September 1775. In his absence, the Green Mountain Boys were commanded by an American colonel named Seth Warner. By the end of the day the Americans at Hubbardton had been forced to retreat, but it was a tough fight and the first indication Burgoyne had that this might not be an easy campaign after all.[73]

The next major battle took place at Bennington, in what is now south-western Vermont, on August 16–20, 1777. The Battle of Bennington was a disastrous defeat for Burgoyne and a prime example of the Americans taking full advantage of Burgoyne's limitations as a strategist. For this operation, Burgoyne detached approximately 900 regulars, mostly German mercenaries from the principality of Brunswick under the command of Lieutenant Colonel Friedrich Baum. Several hundred loyalists joined Baum's ranks, as did some Mohawk Indians. They were faced by a group of New Hampshire militia under the command of the highly capable Brigadier General John Stark. Throughout the war, the British would find that loyalists, or Tories, often did not make the best soldiers and were difficult to recruit. Similarly, George Washington and other American generals greatly preferred using their own regulars, or "Continentals" as opposed to militia. However, Stark was a very popular

---

[72] Burgoyne Proclamation; "The Vengeance of the State," June 1777, reprinted in Rhodehamel, ed., *The American Revolution*, 305.

[73] Ketchum, *Saratoga*, 162, 166, 185–206. *Encyclopedia Britannic Online*, s.v. "Ethan Allen." http://www.britannica.com/EBchecked/topic/16166/Ethan-Allen. Accessed January 30, 2014.

general and his militia unit showed an especially high level of devotion—no doubt in part because at Bennington they were protecting their own farms and families from an invading army.[74]

Burgoyne's purpose in the Bennington diversion seems to have been a combination of a desire to guard his left flank and a drastic need to forage for supplies, food, and fresh horses. By August 1777, Burgoyne was belatedly becoming aware of just how tenuous was his supply line back to Montreal, which was almost 200 miles away when Burgoyne reached Fort Edward.[75] However, the Bennington battle amply demonstrated that Burgoyne was a fool to divide his forces; forces which were too small to begin with for the task at hand. Bennington displayed in microcosm a truism of the entire campaign—Burgoyne had overreached.

Freeman's Farm and Bemis Heights were the two largest pitched battles of the campaign. The Freeman's farm battle took place on September 19, 1777. Both sides fought well and took heavy losses, but the Saratoga campaign had by now become a popular cause for the rebels.[76] As Richard Ketchum states, "the rebels smelled victory"[77] and Gates was being reinforced daily by fresh militia troops. In a tactical sense, Burgoyne had won a narrow victory on September 19, but he simply could not afford his losses, which could not be replaced. Burgoyne then squandered a chance to either renew the battle in the days immediately following or to fall back on Fort Ticonderoga because on September 21 he had heard that General Clinton, whom Howe had left in Manhattan with a modest force, might be coming to his aid. Burgoyne's hesitation proved disastrous. Clinton did head north with 3,000 men on October 3 and on October 7 took Fort Montgomery on the Hudson approximately ten miles south of West Point. At this time, Burgoyne was desperately clinging to the hope that Clinton would arrive any day. In fact, however, at Fort Montgomery, Clinton was still more than seventy miles south

---

[74] Ketchum, *Saratoga*, 286–295.

[75] Ketchum, *Saratoga*, 286–295. Boatner, *Encyclopedia of the American Revolution*, 138.

[76] Ketchum, *Saratoga*, 369–370.

[77] Ketchum, *Saratoga*, 381.

of Burgoyne's position. A small advance detachment of Clinton's force, comprising 1,700 men under British Major General John Vaughan did get as far north as what is now Kingston, New York on or about October 15, 1777. This was too little, too late, however. By then Burgoyne was already negotiating the terms of his surrender with Gates, and Vaughan's small force was still forty miles below Saratoga.[78]

Clinton's failure to relieve Burgoyne was really Sir William Howe's failure. In clutching at straws by hoping against hope that Clinton would dramatically appear at the last minute, Burgoyne showed that he was unaware of the difficulties under which Clinton was operating. Burgoyne did not realize that after losing his argument with Sir William Howe over whether Howe's army should move north or south, Sir Henry Clinton no longer had the stomach for a northern campaign. With some justification, Clinton felt that a move north to Albany such as that which he had unsuccessfully implored Howe to undertake in July was simply no longer possible in late September or early October. Much had changed in those few months. General Howe had taken approximately 19,000 troops with him to Philadelphia, leaving Clinton with a force of just 7,000 men with which to see to it that Manhattan remained in British hands. New York was and is the finest harbor on the American east coast. Clinton can hardly be blamed for being convinced that protecting that harbor was his first duty and that with Howe's sizeable force now gone, he (Clinton) simply did not have enough troops to both hold Manhattan and march north to aid Burgoyne.[79]

Ironically, the surviving correspondence indicates that in the later stages of the campaign, Burgoyne communicated by letter more often and with far greater ease with his opponent, General Gates, than he did with Sir William Howe. In late August and early September 1777, at least three letters were exchanged under flag of truce between the two adversaries—two from Burgoyne to Gates and one reply from Gates to Burgoyne (these were in addition to the separate series of letters between

---

[78] Boatner, *Encyclopedia of the American Revolution*, 139. Cook, *The Long Fuse*, 278. Digby Journal in Rhodehamel, ed., *The American Revolution*, 322–323. Ketchum, *Saratoga*, 375–376, 385, 422–423, 438.

[79] Ketchum, *Saratoga*, 257 (text and note), 383–385.

the two men by which Burgoyne's surrender was negotiated in October). In the wake of the sharp defeat of his forces in the Battle of Bennington, Burgoyne implored Gates to treat British prisoners with kindness. Gates replied that while he had every intention of doing just that, he was indignant that Burgoyne would even think that he, Gates, might allow British prisoners to be mistreated. To exemplify the irony of Burgoyne's plea for mercy, Gates informed Burgoyne of the outrage felt by Americans over the fate of an attractive young woman named Jane McCrea who had been brutally murdered after falling into the hands of Burgoyne's Indian allies. Jane McCrea was not the only civilian to be murdered by Indians allied with Burgoyne, and the British general's failure to rein in the Indians under his command represents another major error in British strategy during the Saratoga campaign.[80] According to Ketchum,

> Something about Jane McCrea's murder differed from all the other lurid stories so that it fired the imagination of a thoroughly alarmed public. Her demise was one of the first and in some respects the most dramatic of the atrocities now being committed almost daily by Burgoyne's Indians, and coming on the heels of his earlier threats, it made for extremely effective propaganda.[81]

As his troops fell back after their defeat in the Battle of Bemis Heights in October, Burgoyne was forced to leave his wounded behind. With them, he left another letter for Gates again pleading for merciful treatment for his men.[82]

It is an understatement to say that cooperation was lacking between British generals Howe, Burgoyne, and Clinton. There was, of course, plenty of rivalry amongst the American high command as well. As noted previously, Gates was jealous of Washington's appointment as Commander-in-Chief of the Continental Army and was slow to give Washington news of the Saratoga victory. Washington was angered by

---

[80] Burgoyne–Gates correspondence reprinted in Digby Journal in Rhodehamel, ed., *The American Revolution*, 314–317. See also, Ketchum, *Saratoga*, 273–278.

[81] Ketchum, *Saratoga*, 276.

[82] Digby Journal in Rhodehamel, ed., *The American Revolution*, 330.

the behavior of Gates, but the American Commander-in-Chief did write a letter commending Gates on the latter's great victory, while gently chiding Gates for not sending an immediate and direct report of the outcome.[83]

The friction caused by the cavalier manner in which Gates treated the Commander-in-Chief was evident in Washington's next move. He sent his aide de camp, a brilliant young lieutenant colonel named Alexander Hamilton, north to speak with Gates and to convey Washington's wish that the bulk of Gates' now unemployed troops be sent south to strengthen Washington's army. Gates did in fact interpret this as a rebuke (which perhaps it was, in part) and protested. Hamilton did get Gates to release some of his troops, but not as many as Washington had hoped for.[84] Even if there was an element of retribution in Washington's action, Washington's written instructions to Hamilton do make clear that the troop withdrawal was to be made only if the bulk of Gates's troops were in fact unemployed. Washington understood that egos should not get in the way of the war effort, instructing Hamilton that:

> If, upon your meeting with Genl Gates, you should find that he intends in Consequence of his Success to employ the Troops under his Command upon some expedition by the prosecution of which the common cause will be more benefitted than by their being sent down to reinforce this Army, it is not my wish to give any interruption to the plan.[85]

Washington would never deliberately sabotage a subordinate, even a rebellious and difficult one like Gates. The words chosen by the American Commander-in-Chief for this message are revealing of the differences

---

[83] Washington to Gates, October 30, 1777, as reprinted in Frank E. Grizzard, Jr., ed., and David R. Hoth, Assist. Ed. *The Papers of George Washington: Revolutionary War Series*, Vol. 12, *October–December 1777*—hereinafter *Papers of George Washington,* 12. (Charlottesville: University Press of Virginia, 2002): 59–60.

[84] Chernow, *Washington*, 315–316.

[85] Washington to Hamilton, October 30, 1777. *Papers of George Washington,* Vol. 12, 61.

between himself and Howe. Washington refers to "the common cause," an expression that would have been completely foreign to General Howe. Sir William Howe's cavalier note to Burgoyne stating that he, Howe, was heading for Pennsylvania may not have been a deliberate attempt at sabotage on the part of Howe. It was, however, an act of extreme recklessness which showed Howe's contempt for the fighting abilities of the Americans and an extreme apathy towards any difficulties that Burgoyne might encounter. Howe certainly knew that Burgoyne was headed for Albany, but Howe seemed to think that any British operations that he was not personally directing were operations that did not really matter in the grand scheme of things.[86] General Howe showed at Brandywine and Germantown that he could defeat Washington in the field. However, Howe's character flaws proved Washington to be the superior leader.

Saratoga was unique in Revolutionary War battles in that the Americans for once had enough of everything. As Burgoyne's strength ebbed away via combat losses and desertions, Gates grew much stronger. In early October 1777, Burgoyne had approximately 5,000 troops left out of the 9,000 he had departed Montreal with. Gates on the other hand had more than 10,000 men available for the climactic Battle of Bemis Heights on October 7, 1777. The Americans had adequate supplies of food and ammunition. Burgoyne was lacking both.[87] Burgoyne's surrender on October 17, 1777 marked one of the most important military victories in American history. Word of the defeat arrived in London on December 2, 1777. The Battle of Saratoga was a disaster for Britain. It meant that the war would continue and that Chatham's prophecy of French entry into the war on the side of the colonists would almost certainly become a reality. [88]

---

[86] Cook, *The Long Fuse*, 269.

[87] Boatner, *Encyclopedia of the American Revolution*, 139–140. Ferling, *A Leap in the Dark*, 200.

[88] Cook, *The Long Fuse*, 280–281.

CHAPTER 5

STRIVE FOR UNITY OF COMMAND

Historians have noted that the Combined Chiefs of Staff of World War II, and its American component, the US Joint Chiefs of Staff, had their respective roots in the old Joint Army-Navy Board which had dated back to 1903.[1] Actually, one could argue that the roots of the US Joint Chiefs of Staff as it was set up in 1942 go back even further; to the Civil War in fact. March 1864 was a momentous month in American history because it was then that General Ulysses S. Grant became the first American army officer since George Washington to be promoted to the rank of Lieutenant General (three stars). President Abraham Lincoln had grown considerably as a war leader by that time. Lincoln and the Congress could plainly see that the Union could only win if it instituted a truly unified command structure for its army. Grant's promotion was intended to do just that. Being named in March 1864 commander of all the armies of the United States, Grant could now move Union troops around to wherever they were needed. In 1864, Grant began traveling with the Army of the Potomac, but Major General George Gordon Meade, victor of Gettysburg, was never fired as commander of that army. In fact, Meade continued in command of the Army of the Potomac until the end of the war. Grant traveled with Meade and the Army of the Potomac because that was the Union Army that had been the most plagued by political

---

[1] David Rigby. *Allied Master Strategists: The Combined Chiefs of Staff in World War II.* (Annapolis, MD: Naval Institute Press, 2012): 47.

interference, incompetent leadership (prior to Meade's appointment as its commander), and sheer bad luck; and because it was that army that would fight Confederate General Robert E. Lee. General Grant actually developed a very high regard for Meade, even placing General Meade in the same category as Major General William T. Sherman—high praise indeed. During the Battle at Spotsylvania Court House, Virginia in May 1864, Grant wrote to Secretary of War Edwin M. Stanton that:

> General Meade has more than met my most sanguine expectations. He and Sherman are the fittest officers for large commands that I have come in contact with. If their services can be rewarded by promotion to the rank of Maj. Gen. in the regular army the honor would be worthily bestowed and I would feel personally gratified. I would not like to see one of these promotions at this time without seeing both.[2]

Like a modern day Chairman of the Joint Chiefs of Staff, Grant's job was to avoid tunnel vision, and instead to grasp the war picture as a whole. Thus, while from spring 1864 onward, Grant was based in eastern Virginia, he was also constantly monitoring the progress of, and issuing a stream of directives pertaining to, other campaigns he had ordered for 1864 such as Major General Philip Sheridan's campaign to lay waste to the Shenandoah Valley and Sherman's march through Georgia.[3] The Confederacy, by contrast, never developed a unified command structure. For all his fame, Robert E. Lee was only ever really the commander of one Confederate Army—the Army of Northern Virginia. True, General Lee was very belatedly elevated to Commander-in-Chief of all Confederate Armies in February 1865. However, this desperate act by the Confederate government had little meaning because it came too late. The Confederacy was in its death throes by February 1865. By then General

---

[2] Grant to Stanton, May 13, 1864, reprinted in John Y. Simon, ed.; David L. Wilson, Assist. Ed., *The Papers of Ulysses S. Grant*. Vol. 10. *January 1–May 31, 1864*. (Carbondale and Edwardsville, IL: Southern Illinois University Press, 1982—in conjunction with the Ulysses S. Grant Association): 434.

[3] Gary W. Gallagher. *The Union War*. (Cambridge, MA: Harvard University Press, 2011): 136.

Sheridan had secured the Shenandoah Valley; Sherman had reached Savannah and was marching north toward Columbia, South Carolina; Major General George Thomas had destroyed the army of Confederate Lieutenant General John B. Hood near Nashville; and Grant was laying siege to Lee's army at Petersburg in Virginia.[4]

In fact, General Lee had always been a bit of a prima donna who did not like to leave Virginia—the only theater of the war that seemed to interest him. While he was willing to lead two invasions of northern territory, Lee had no interest in leaving Virginia for any great length of time in order to command Confederate troops in battle in other parts of the Confederacy such as Tennessee, Georgia, or Texas. Like all American Army officers, Robert E. Lee had sworn an oath of loyalty to the United States as a young second lieutenant upon his graduation from West Point in 1829. It is possible that Lee tried to justify his abandonment of that oath by deluding himself into believing that his actions in the Civil War did not actually constitute treason; that he was serving his home state of Virginia instead of the Confederacy as a whole. Whatever Lee's motives, the Confederate war effort was greatly hampered by its disjointed command structure. When Confederate armies were strong in the mid-war period in 1862 and 1863, there was no overall commander to coordinate the activities of different rebel armies at a time when such coordination could have made a difference for the South. An example can be found later in the war; in early 1864 when Lee was getting ready to meet the next Union incursion into Virginia, a campaign in which he would now be fighting General Grant. At that critical time Lee could not order General Joseph Johnston to send Confederate reinforcements from Georgia to Virginia. Lee could ask, but Johnston was not obligated to comply. Part of the problem was that Confederate President Jefferson Davis was himself a West Point graduate and a former Secretary of War who had great faith in his own strategic ability and was unwilling to delegate too much responsibility to any one military commander.[5] Thus, in addition to its greater material resources, the unified command struc-

---

[4] H.W. Brands, *The Man Who Saved the Union: Ulysses Grant in War and Peace,* (New York: Doubleday, 2012): 341–345.

[5] Brands, *The Man Who Saved the Union,* 282–283.

ture adopted by the North in early 1864 was definitely a war winning innovation. Grant and his best commanders, Major Generals William T. Sherman, George Thomas, and Philip Sheridan operated during the final year of the Civil War somewhat like the modern day Joint Chiefs of Staff.

The unprecedented unity of command that Britain and the United States achieved during World War II through the creation in January 1942 of the Combined Chiefs of Staff organization in Washington and via Allied theater commands in the field are more recent examples of the great benefits that have accrued to the United States by adopting a unified command structure in time of war. World War II unity of command in the field for British and American forces meant that all military activity in a given theater became centralized under one officer.[6]

During World War II, political factors sometimes made it necessary for a theater commander to be served by lieutenants who were not to his liking. However, a unified command structure is a whole that is greater than the sum of its parts, and is a system which can withstand personality differences much better than can a system of isolated commands.[7] For instance, General Eisenhower did not have anything like complete control over the selection process for the personnel who would constitute his senior staff at Supreme Headquarters Allied Expeditionary Force (SHAEF). While acquiescing to an American supreme commander for the Overlord D-Day campaign, the British insisted that Eisenhower's immediate staff be top-heavy with Britons. That, in and of itself, was not a problem. Eisenhower was quite happy with his British Deputy Supreme Commander for Overlord, the talented and imaginative Air Chief Marshal Sir Arthur Tedder. However, as Air Commander for Overlord, Eisenhower was saddled with a far less talented British Air Chief Marshal—Sir Trafford Leigh-Mallory; an obstinate, opinionated, and extremely pessimistic man who seemed to be intensely disliked even by his British colleagues. There is some evidence that the Chief of the Air Staff, Marshal of the Royal Air Force Sir Charles Portal, may have believed

---

[6] Rigby, *Allied Master Strategists*, 50–51.

[7] Richard Overy. *Why the Allies Won.* (New York: Norton, 1995): 269.

that with Tedder as his deputy, Eisenhower would have all the good air advice he needed, and that the appointment of Leigh-Mallory as SHAEF Air Commander might have been a way of kicking Leigh-Mallory upstairs in order to get him out of everyone's way. Leigh-Mallory's unpleasantness was characterized by a big ego coupled with morbid pessimism. "Can do" was not in Leigh-Mallory's vocabulary.[8]

Eisenhower would have been delighted to have British Admiral of the Fleet Sir Andrew B. Cunningham as the Naval Commander for Overlord. Eisenhower and Cunningham had worked closely together in the Mediterranean Allied campaigns, beginning with Torch in November 1942. Unfortunately, Cunningham was unavailable, having been tapped in October 1943 to succeed Admiral of the Fleet Sir Dudley Pound as First Sea Lord—the uniformed head of the entire Royal Navy. For Overlord, Eisenhower had to settle for the competent but less-than-brilliant Admiral Sir Bertram Ramsay as Naval Commander.[9]

Eisenhower's biggest staff disappointment by far was that he was unable to obtain the services of Field Marshal Sir Harold Alexander as ground force commander and had to settle instead for Field Marshal Sir Bernard Montgomery as ground force commander for the opening stages of Overlord. Sir Harold Alexander was Eisenhower's favorite British general and the two men had formed an excellent rapport while working together during the North African and Sicilian campaigns, respectively. Unfortunately for Eisenhower, "Alex" was also Prime Minister Winston Churchill's favorite general but the Overlord invasion of western Europe was definitely *not* Churchill's favorite campaign. The prime minister was therefore unwilling to remove Alexander from the Mediterranean theater, which as far as Churchill was concerned was the epicenter of the war.[10] Regarding the intensity of Eisenhower's disappointment at having

---

[8] Michael Korda. *Ike: An American Hero.* (New York: HarperCollins, 2007): 435–436. Geoffrey Perret. *Eisenhower.* (New York: Random House, 1999): 263.

[9] Korda, *Ike*, 435–436. Geoffrey Perret. *Eisenhower.* (New York: Random House, 1999): 263.

[10] Korda, *Ike*, 434–435, 488. Perret. *Eisenhower*, 263.

to accept Montgomery in place of Alexander, Geoffrey Perret writes that in effect:

> Eisenhower chose not to have a ground-force commander, because the man he wanted for that assignment, Alexander, had been denied him. Montgomery would serve as ground force commander only for Overlord, but once SHAEF moved to the Continent . . . Eisenhower would become, in effect, his own ground-force commander, directing the operations of Bradley and Montgomery. This was not an arrangement that Monty was ever going to accept without protest.[11]

Eisenhower's disappointment with some of the personnel assigned to him as staff for Overlord spilled over into the strategic debates that ensued at Eisenhower's headquarters in the spring of 1944 as Overlord planning shifted into high gear. Air Chief Marshal Leigh-Mallory's cautious, defensive-minded nature was wholly unsuited to an operation like Overlord which was all about carrying the fight to the enemy with a maximum emphasis on hard-hitting offensive airpower. The proposed use of three airborne divisions in the initial assault filled Leigh-Mallory with horror. In fact, the paratroopers were not an unbridled success, but were also far from being the disaster that the excessively pessimistic Leigh-Mallory had predicted.[12] Leigh-Mallory had feared that the paratroopers would be all but wiped out and had been muttering words like "slaughter" at SHAEF headquarters whenever he discussed the upcoming operations of Allied airborne troops in the weeks leading up to the invasion. In reality, the paratroopers and airborne infantry used in the Normandy assault were considerably more successful than Leigh-Mallory had predicted.[13]

It seems that the most contentious issue grappled with in Eisenhower's headquarters in the months leading up to the invasion was the Transportation Plan. Proposed by Tedder and enthusiastically supported by Eisenhower, the Transportation Plan was a proposal to

---

[11] Perret, *Eisenhower*, 263.

[12] Perret, *Eisenhower*, 264.

[13] Korda, *Ike*, 478.

pulverize the French railway system via intense air attack in the weeks leading up to D-Day using everything in the Allied arsenal that could fly, from fighter planes to long-range heavy bombers. Air Chief Marshal Sir Arthur Harris, Commander-in-Chief, RAF Bomber Command, did not want to do it because it would mean making precision attacks with British heavy bombers (instead of the carpet, or area, bombing Harris preferred) and would temporarily reduce the bomb tonnage being dropped on German industrial cities. Prime Minister Churchill and Foreign Secretary Anthony Eden wanted no part of the plan because it would kill French civilians; Churchill preferring to hit German oil plants, which is ironic because the prime minister, like Harris, had hitherto expressed little interest in precision bombing as opposed to the area bombing both men cherished. Chief of the Air Staff Sir Charles Portal had initially wanted to keep the bombing focus on destroying German aircraft factories and aircraft component plants as did Field Marshal Sir Alan Brooke, British Chief of the Imperial General Staff. American Army Air Forces General Carl Spaatz agreed with Churchill that the Allied bombing focus should be on German oil plants. However, by mid-April, 1944, Portal was supporting Tedder's railway plan, undoubtedly in part because Portal had long doubted the view of the carpet-bombing obsessed Harris that British heavy bombers could not hit precision targets. Admiral Cunningham liked the Transportation Plan. Tedder argued that while bombing German oil plants was an excellent idea in the long run, it would not make a difference in time for D-Day. What was needed was to immediately curtail the ability of the Germans to bring supplies and reinforcements to the beachhead.[14]

Eisenhower insisted; Tedder kept up steady pressure on Churchill, and FDR and eventually Portal and Brooke supported Eisenhower. The Transportation Plan was duly put into effect but the Allies tried hard, and apparently successfully, to keep the number of French citizens killed below 10,000. Tedder's Transportation Plan was cleverly executed, with rail targets hit all over northern France, many outside the invasion area,

---

[14] Lord Tedder. *With Prejudice: The War Memoirs of Marshal of the Royal Air Force Lord Tedder, G.C.B.* (Boston: Little, Brown and Company, 1966): 516–533. See also, Rigby, *Allied Master Strategists*, 155, 156.

and even some in the south of France, so that the Germans would not be tipped off as to Normandy as the intended invasion spot. The wholesale bombing of rail targets in France in the months leading up to Overlord did necessitate shifting Allied heavy bombers away from the bombing of German fighter aircraft factories. However, this was not really a problem because air-to-air dogfights over Germany and France between German fighter pilots and the American long-range fighters serving as escorts for American heavy bombers were destroying the German Air Force in the air quite effectively in the first half of 1944.[15]

The dispute over the fighting effectiveness of the US Army's 27th Infantry Division during the Central Pacific Drive on the other side of the world in World War II is another example of American forces utilizing unity of command to neutralize difficult personalities. The 27th was a hard luck division that had not performed well in the Gilberts and Marshalls campaigns in late 1943 and early 1944. Things came to a boil in June 1944 on Saipan in the Mariana Islands. The catalyst was Marine Lieutenant General Holland M. Smith, the ground force commander, whose quick temper had earned him the nickname "Howling Mad." The Pacific theater was a navy-dominated area. Army troops that served in the Pacific theater fell under the overall command of Admiral Chester W. Nimitz, Commander-in-Chief, Pacific Fleet and commander of the Pacific Ocean Areas theater. As the navy's ground forces, American marines got along fine with naval officers but army-marine relations were always rocky. The quick temper of "Howling Mad" Smith did nothing to endear the tough talking marine general to the army. Admiral Nimitz did have a high-ranking army officer on his staff at Pearl Harbor—Lieutenant General Robert C. Richardson, the commander of army troops in the Pacific theater. Unfortunately, Richardson, like Holland Smith, had a very short fuse, particularly when he felt that army prerogatives were being threatened.

Although he was well aware of the army-navy tension in his theater, Admiral Nimitz at Pearl Harbor was nevertheless stunned to learn on June 23, 1944 during the Marianas campaign that out at Saipan his marine

---

[15] Tedder, *With Prejudice*, 516–533. See also, Rigby, *Allied Master Strategists*, 155, 156.

commander, General Holland Smith, had fired an army general—Major General Ralph Smith who had been the commander of the 27ᵗʰ Division. With this news, Nimitz knew that he had just been handed the hottest of hot potatoes. In the words of Nimitz's biographer E.B. Potter:

> The 27ᵗʰ Division had bogged down on Saipan, as it had on Makin and Eniwetok. This time it was dangerously exposing the flanks of the marine divisions alongside it. General Holland Smith concluded that the main troubles with the division were lack of offensive spirit and poor leadership and that, therefore, its commander had to be relieved. [Army] Major General Sanderford Jarman, commander-designate of Saipan and the senior army officer on the island, agreed and offered to take command of the division until a replacement for Ralph Smith could be sent out.[16]

The situation, though awkward, could have been much worse. The three men who made the decision to fire Ralph Smith, Marine Lieutenant General Holland Smith, Vice Admiral Richmond Kelly Turner (the amphibious force commander), and ultimately Admiral Raymond A. Spruance (the overall commander of the invasion forces) were all in the navy camp. However, they had the wisdom to replace Ralph Smith with another army general (not with a marine); and that army general, Sanderford Jarman, was in complete agreement that his army colleague Ralph Smith had to go. Nevertheless, a marine firing an army officer was highly irregular to say the least.[17]

The change in command failed to immediately improve the performance of the 27ᵗʰ Division, but that outfit did fight much better later at Okinawa.[18] On Saipan, Major General Ralph Smith had accepted his ouster with good grace. General Richardson at Pearl Harbor, however, was not so easily mollified. He was in fact enraged. Richardson

---

[16] E.B. Potter. *Nimitz.* (Annapolis, MD: Naval Institute Press, 1976, 1987): 305.

[17] Potter, *Nimitz*, 305. Thomas B. Buell. *The Quiet Warrior: A Biography of Admiral Raymond A. Spruance.* (Annapolis, MD: Naval Institute Press, 1974, 1987): 306.

[18] Buell, *The Quiet Warrior*, 306–307. James H. Belote and William M. Belote. *Typhoon of Steel: The Battle for Okinawa.* (New York: Harper & Row, 1970): 193–195, 212–213.

immediately headed out to the Marianas and proceeded to act as if he had been appointed mayor of the archipelago. After handing out decorations to men of the 27th Division, who surely knew they had performed poorly and did not deserve such recognition, Richardson met separately with the three senior commanders on the scene, Holland Smith and Admirals Turner and Spruance. All accounts of Richardson's meeting with Holland Smith agree that Richardson literally shouted and ranted at Smith, who for his part honored a promise he had made to Admiral Spruance not to lose his temper. Kelly Turner was a different kettle of fish, however. It was not for nothing that Admiral Turner had earned the nickname "Terrible Turner." When Richardson shouted at Turner, the admiral gave back as good as he got.

The last act of this sordid little episode was played out on Admiral Spruance's flagship, the heavy cruiser *Indianapolis*. Admiral Spruance, who was probably the calmest officer ever to serve in the United States Navy, tried to pour soothing oil on the waters. Spruance told Richardson not to pay too much attention to Kelly Turner's outburst. "'That's just Kelly Turner's way,' [Spruance] said, 'and no one takes him seriously.'"[19]

Although not delighted with General Richardson's behavior, especially his temper tantrums, even US Army Chief of Staff General George C. Marshall felt compelled to weigh in by telling his colleague on the US Joint Chiefs of Staff, Chief of Naval Operations Admiral Ernest J. King, that he (Marshall) felt that Admiral Nimitz could do a better job of preventing such flare-ups from occurring in his theater.[20] Although he had many supporters for his actions in relieving Ralph Smith at the time and has gained more over the years amongst historians, Holland Smith did not escape unscathed. After the Marianas campaign concluded, in what was ostensibly a promotion, Holland Smith was made the Commander of the Fleet Marine Force, Pacific. Historian Donald L. Miller claims that this was an empty promotion that was really punishment handed down to Holland Smith by Admiral Nimitz. The new job put "Howling Mad" Smith behind a desk in a staff position rather than using him in the type

---

[19] Potter, *Nimitz*, 307–308. The quote is on pg. 308.

[20] Potter, *Nimitz*, 309.

of field command he thrived on.[21] E.B. Potter, the official biographer of Admiral Nimitz, is more circumspect, saying that it had been decided even before the Marianas campaign began that Holland Smith should get this new position.[22] Potter is an excellent source who knew the Nimitz family personally. His views are not to be dismissed lightly. However, it does strain credulity to think that Nimitz was already thinking of kicking Smith upstairs even before the dust-up on Saipan. Prior to that, Nimitz had been quite pleased with Holland Smith's aggressive performance as ground force commander in the Gilberts and Marshalls campaigns, respectively. Indeed, Holland Smith commanding on shore, Vice Admiral Richmond Kelly Turner as the amphibious commander who got the troops from ship to shore, and Admiral Spruance commanding everything as Fifth Fleet commander had been a winning team in the Central Pacific Drive up until Saipan.

The eminent maritime historian Samuel Eliot Morison predictably sides with the navy and the marines in this dispute, and states that army tactics were just not suited to the type of fighting on the islands of the Pacific.[23] According to Morison, American marines in World War II were stealthy, flexible in their tactics, and only fired their weapons when they knew what they were shooting at. During nighttime operations, says Morison, marine practice was to "allow the enemy to infiltrate . . . and, when daylight comes, liquidate the infiltrators. Such tactics require good fire discipline of seasoned troops."[24] Army tactics, on the other hand says Morison, were heavy-handed and inflexible. He claims that because army troops always tried to kill Japanese infiltrators immedi-

---

[21] Donald L. Miller. *D-Days in the Pacific.* (New York: Simon & Schuster Paperbacks, 2001, 2005): 145.

[22] Potter, *Nimitz,* 309.

[23] Samuel Eliot Morison. *History of United States Naval Operations in World War II.* Vol. 8. *New Guinea and the Marianas, March 1944–August 1944.* (Boston: Little, Brown and Company, 1953): 332–333.

[24] Samuel Eliot Morison. *History of United States Naval Operations in World War II.* Vol. 7. *Aleutians, Gilberts and Marshalls.* (Boston: Little, Brown and Company, 1951, 1955): 298.

ately, even in the dark of night, they often ended up accidentally firing at American marines instead. Morison writes that this type of deadly misunderstanding was particularly apparent when American marines and infantry (the latter from the 27th Division) operated in close proximity to one another during the invasion of Eniwetok, an atoll in the Marshalls chain, in February 1944.[25]

There was lingering bad blood between the navy and the army dating back to the sluggish performance of the 27th Division during the Gilberts campaign in November 1943. The US Navy, and its marines, never really forgave the army, especially the 27th Division of that army, for the sinking of the escort carrier USS *Liscombe Bay* with heavy loss of life during that campaign. Of the two atolls taken in the Gilberts by the Americans, Tarawa was secured by the 2nd Marine Division after three days of some of the toughest ground fighting in World War II. Approximately 1,000 American marines were killed at Tarawa. While the fighting raged at Tarawa, elements of the 27th Division had required four days to take the much more lightly held Makin atoll in the northern Gilbert Islands. It was at Makin that Holland Smith first became disenchanted with the 27th Division and with Ralph Smith as its commander. The marine Smith visited the army Smith at Makin on November 21, 1943 to try to speed up the operation. Howling Mad Smith got nowhere in these efforts. The marine general's opinion of army troops was not improved when he himself almost became a friendly fire casualty during a very uncomfortable night he spent ashore as nervous American troops of the 27th Division fired in all directions at the slightest sound.[26]

Morison writes that "Makin was a pushover for the ground troops, but cost the Navy heavily."[27] Indeed it did. The delay in taking Makin gave the Japanese submarine *I-175* the time to get close enough to the atoll to torpedo and sink the American escort carrier USS *Liscombe Bay*, part of the covering force, which took 644 members of its crew to the bottom with it. US naval warships could not leave the vicinity of Makin

---

[25] Morison, *Aleutians, Gilberts and Marshalls*, 298.

[26] Morison, *Aleutians, Gilberts and Marshalls*, 133.

[27] Morison, *Aleutians, Gilberts and Marshalls*, 121.

until the atoll was secured, and the navy considered the performance of the army troops on Makin to be dilatory. The *Liscombe Bay* was sunk on November 24, 1943—the fourth day of the operation, by which time the navy felt the army should have long since secured Makin and thus allowed the covering warships to withdraw from the immediate vicinity. No navy captain likes to keep his ship near an island for any length of time. The best defense for any warship is its ability to move; the ability to be in a different place tomorrow from where it is today. Morison describes the carnage after the torpedo struck the *Liscombe Bay*:

> There was a terrible explosion. A column of bright orange flame rose a thousand feet in the air. Within a few seconds the aircraft bombs stowed in the hold detonated, and with a mighty roar the carrier burst apart as though she were one great bomb, tossing men, planes, deck frames and molten fragments so high that the deck of [battleship] *New Mexico* 1500 yards to leeward was showered with fragments of steel, clothing and human flesh. The entire after third of the escort carrier was demolished. . . . [O]nly 23 minutes after being hit, the doomed ship flared up for the last time and sank hissing into a 2000-fathom deep."[28]

The navy blaming the army for the loss of this ship is a bit harsh. The *Liscombe Bay* was one of fifty *Casablanca* class escort carriers (CVE) built by the Kaiser Shipbuilding Company at Vancouver on the Columbia River in southern Washington State. These were not true aircraft carriers, but rather wartime stopgaps. Hurriedly designed and built at breakneck speed, CVEs were short, stubby, ugly little ships. Each *Casablanca* class CVE weighed approximately 8,000 tons and was just over 500 feet in length, which made them much smaller than either the *Essex* class fleet aircraft carriers that began entering service during 1943 or the *Yorktown* class fleet carriers with which the United States had fought the Battle of Midway. CVEs also carried far fewer aircraft than did a fleet carrier. *Casablanca* class CVEs could each accommodate a maximum of only twenty-eight aircraft. Unlike a fleet carrier, the truncated flight deck of the *Liscombe Bay* had been grafted onto the hull of a merchant ship.

---

[28] Morison, *Aleutians, Gilberts and Marshalls*, 140–141.

Amongst other drawbacks, this meant that the ammunition storage rooms belowdecks in the *Liscombe Bay* were not armored magazines as in a purpose-built warship but were just rooms with ordinary quarter-inch steel plate bulkheads. The trouble was that any World War II aircraft carrier had to carry enormous amounts of ordnance—all of the bombs and torpedoes with which the ship's aircraft would be armed—not to mention all of the one hundred octane aviation fuel those aircraft would need. That is why a hit from a single torpedo caused such a catastrophic series of secondary explosions. The ship's hull had not been designed to safely carry such a highly explosive cargo.[29]

The American Civil War also provides many examples of the value of unity of command. During the Civil War the US Navy was not hurt as badly by defections as was the Army. It is true that after eleven southern states seceded from the Union, beginning with South Carolina in December 1860, over 200 American commissioned naval officers took up arms against their country by serving in the Confederate Navy. However, forty other southern naval officers renounced secession and continued to serve in the navy of the United States. Some of those forty were the best officers in the service. Captain John A. Winslow, for example, the commander of the Union frigate USS *Kearsarge* which sank the Confederate commerce raider CSS *Alabama* after a dramatic duel in the waters off Cherbourg on June 19, 1864 had been raised in North Carolina—a Confederate state. Union naval hero Admiral David G. Farragut hailed from Virginia, which like Winslow's North Carolina was a state in rebellion. The defection of Raphael Semmes, the brilliant commander of the *Alabama*, was certainly a harsh blow to the Union Navy. However, with the possible exception of Semmes, the US Navy, unlike the US Army, managed to avoid losing officers who were of the caliber of a Robert E. Lee.[30]

---

[29] Samuel Eliot Morison. *History of United States Naval Operations in World War II*. Vol 15. *Supplement and General Index*. (Boston: Little, Brown and Company, 1962): 32–33. Arthur Herman. *Freedom's Forge: How American Business Produced Victory in World War II*. (New York: Random House, 2012): 268–272.

[30] James M. McPherson. *War on the Waters: The Union & Confederate Navies, 1861–1865*. (Chapel Hill: University of North Carolina Press, 2012): 14.

The United States Navy was able to keep the vast majority of its warships in Union hands when the Civil War began. The Confederacy, therefore, had to build a new navy and could not do it in the South because all of the shipyards capable of building oceangoing vessels at that time were in the Northern states. Thus, Confederate Navy Secretary Stephen Mallory tried to recoup in quality and innovation what he lacked in quantity. To do this he turned to Great Britain, where he hoped to purchase or have built in British yards warships for the Confederacy. In the end he did both—built and purchased in England. The cruisers *Florida* and *Alabama* were each built from the keel up in England as warships for the Confederacy under the watchful eye of Mallory's agent in Great Britain, Confederate Navy Captain James D. Bulloch. Both of these superb ships were state of the art weapons systems. The *Alabama*, for instance, built at the Laird shipyard in Liverpool, was steam powered, well armed, and possessed of a condenser for making fresh drinking water. Bulloch bypassed the side-paddle wheel system then prevalent for steamship propulsion completely and opted for a single screw propeller, which could be hoisted up into the hull to reduce drag when the winds were good and the ship was using its sails.[31] Screw propellers were more efficient and were always submerged, and thus always able to get "purchase" on the water. A sidewheeler, on the other hand, while rolling in a heavy sea, might have one or the other of its paddle wheels break clear of the water temporarily. When this happened, power would be lost and great strain put on the engine with one paddle wheel deep in the water and the other spinning freely with no load on it at all. The drive shafts and engine of a sidewheeler also took up prime cargo- and fuel-stowage areas amidships. The engine driving a screw propeller, on the other hand, could be placed low and aft in the hull.

---

[31] Craig L. Symonds. *The Civil War at Sea*. (Denver: Praeger, 2009): 72. See also, *Encyclopaedia Britannica Online*, s.v. "American Civil War: The Naval War". http://www.britannica.com/EBchecked/topic/19407/American-Civil-War/229878/The-naval-war. Accessed March 10, 2014. See also, David Rigby. *The C.S.S. Alabama and British Neutrality During the American Civil War*. Unpublished paper, 1991, *passim*.

The Confederacy was never able to coordinate its army-navy activities because in addition to a severe shortage of ships, the best warships the Confederacy did possess, such as those British-built cruisers, were largely confined to raiding Union merchant shipping in international waters and rarely, if ever, attempted to enter a Confederate port since doing so would risk capture or destruction by the blockading Union Navy. The Confederate cruiser *Florida* did run the blockade and dock at Mobile, Alabama in September 1862. However, such visits to Confederate ports were exceedingly rare for Confederate warships. The Confederacy did have dedicated blockade runners frequently going in and out of southern ports, but these were smaller cargo-carrying ships whose task was to bring desperately needed weapons and supplies from abroad into Confederate ports. Blockade runners ran away from Union warships rather than stopping to fight. Thus, in the days before long-range radio and with his best warships in exile; roaming the world's oceans, purchasing supplies wherever their captains could while attacking Union merchant shipping in international waters, it was exceedingly difficult for Confederate President Jefferson Davis to exercise any kind of unified control over the activities of his navy. That is not to say that the Confederate cruisers such as the *Alabama* were not effective fighting units. On the contrary, they were formidable weapons, but their activities were confined to commerce raiding as opposed to direct tactical encounters. Craig L. Symonds reports on the effectiveness of the Confederate cruisers as commerce destroyers: "Altogether during the war, eight Confederate commerce raiders captured and destroyed some 284 Union merchant ships valued at more than $25 million. Most of them were sailing ships, and a third of them (97) were taken by either the *Alabama* or the *Florida*."[32] By way of contrast, however, the direct threat posed by these Confederate raiders to Union *warships*, as opposed to Union merchantmen, was negligible. With notable exceptions, such as the *Alabama*'s final battle in June 1864, it was uncommon for the Confederate cruisers to engage in pitched battles with Union warships. The Confederate cruisers never even tried to break the blockade of southern ports that was very effectively enforced by the warships of the Union Navy throughout the war.

---

[32] Symonds, *The Civil War at Sea*, 84.

Many things had changed between the American Revolution and the Civil War, most notably the killing power of rifles and artillery, which had increased greatly. Also, by the time of the Civil War, the North was crisscrossed by thousands of miles of railroad track. One thing that had not changed between the two wars, however, was the need to control the nation's rivers. This was especially true in the South, where most Civil War battles were fought. The vast majority of the nation's railroad track mileage in 1860 was in the northern states. Thus, in the Civil War South, steam-powered riverboats were critical for moving supplies and troops. Thus, just like British General John Burgoyne in the Saratoga campaign of 1777 (described earlier) many a Civil War general on both sides spent much time and effort trying to gain and hold strategic points, usually forts or fortified cities, on rivers. It was due to this pressing need to control rivers that the public in the North and the South first began to hear in early 1862 of the exploits of a quiet, unassuming, somewhat disheveled Union brigadier general named Ulysses S. Grant. Riverine warfare is but one example of the greater unity of command that was exercised by the Union as opposed to the Confederacy during the Civil War. Grant's February 1862 victories at Fort Donelson and Fort Henry in northern Tennessee would have been impossible without strong support from Union river gunboats. Grant could not compel cooperation from the navy, but army-navy relations in the Union camp were good anyways, at least when Grant was commanding. The early victories at Forts Henry and Donelson made it possible for Grant, promoted Major General after the capture of Fort Donelson in February 1862, to operate deep in Confederate territory very early in the war. The Battle of Shiloh, fought on April 6–7, 1862, took place in southern Tennessee, just a few miles from the northern border of Mississippi—a Gulf Coast state.

Grant's capture of Fort Henry on the Tennessee River on February 6, 1862 was only Grant's second battle of the Civil War. Nevertheless, he and Commander Andrew Foote, USN, carried out a skillfully coordinated attack in which Grant put pressure on the Fort from the landward side while Foote's flotilla of gunboats slugged it out with Confederate artillery batteries in the Fort. The follow-up attack on nearby Fort Donelson on the Cumberland River in mid-February 1862 was far from being a perfect example of a combined operation, but this was not due to any army-navy ill will, rather to the hazards of war. Commander Foote was eager to help Grant and certainly tried his best, but all six of Foote's gunboats were disabled by Confederate artillery fire during a fierce duel between the Fort and gunboats on February 14. Foote was a brave and eager fighter who got on quite well with Grant, but after this action Foote sadly informed General Grant that he would need more than a week to effect repairs to his little fleet.[33] Testifying to the ferocity of this duel between the Union gunboats and the Donelson batteries, Navy Captain Henry Walke (a Virginian who had remained loyal to the Union), commanding the Union gunboat *Carondelet,* recorded that amongst the sailors killed in his ship were five men who had been decapitated by Confederate round shot.[34]

Then Grant got lucky in two ways. First, his opponents did not know that the Union gunboats would be out of action for such a long time and thus that the Confederates could conceivably have reinforced Fort Donelson from the river side. Second, it is no secret that during the war as a whole, Confederate troops generally enjoyed superb leadership. At Donelson, however, Grant was definitely facing the Confederate second team in regard to commanders. The deputy commander at Fort Donelson, Brigadier General Gideon J. Pillow, was a sort of southern version of Dan Sickles—i.e., a mentally unstable officer who owed his high rank solely to his political connections. The overall commander at Donelson was Confederate Brigadier General John B. Floyd, another political general. Because Floyd had served as Secretary of War under President James Buchanan before the war, he feared that he would be hanged as a traitor should he be captured by Union forces.[35] For that

---

[33] William M. Fowler, Jr. *Under Two Flags: The American Navy in the Civil War.* (New York: Norton, 1990): 146–147.

[34] Henry Walke. "The Western Flotilla at Fort Donelson, Island Number Ten, Fort Pillow and Memphis," reprinted in Stephen W. Sears, ed., *The Civil War: The Second Year Told by Those Who Lived It.* (New York: The Library of America, 2012): 57, 59.

[35] Brands, *The Man Who Saved the Union,* 161. See also Civil War Trust. "Gideon J. Pillow." http://www.civilwar.org/education/history/biographies/gideon-pillow. html. Accessed March 18, 2014.

reason, all Floyd could think of when he saw the blue uniforms of Grant's troops appear near Fort Donelson was escape. The Confederate garrison should have stayed put, but Pillow and the panicked Floyd decided they needed to break out. In the pitched battle that ensued, Grant's troops beat back the Confederate assault. With Floyd terrified that he would be hanged and Pillow not wanting to be associated with defeat, the two men bolted and it was left to Confederate Brigadier General Simon Bolivar Buckner to receive Grant's famous demand for "unconditional surrender," which Buckner heeded on February 16, 1862.[36]

The loss of Forts Henry and Donelson caused the senior Confederate general in the west, Albert Sydney Johnston, to abandon Nashville and fall back on Corinth, Mississippi, which action set the stage for the Battle of Shiloh, the bloody battle that taught officers on both sides what a brutal, bloody conflict this war was going to be.[37] With Confederate forces in the west forced down into northern Mississippi, General Grant thought that now was certainly the time for a supreme commander to be appointed to oversee the actions of all Union land forces in the western theater, much like Major General George B. McClellan was then exercising (albeit quite incompetently) overall command of the Union forces in the east. There was a de facto Union Army commander in the west in that Major General Henry W. Halleck commanded Union troops in the Department of Missouri until he was summoned to Washington to become General-in-Chief on July 11, 1862. However, Halleck's exact jurisdiction and responsibilities in the west were somewhat ambiguous. He supervised Grant's operations in Tennessee from a headquarters in St. Louis. Halleck was an overly cautious micromanager who never seemed able to see the big picture. Halleck could also be petty and he quickly became jealous of Grant as the latter's star began to rise in the spring of 1862.

After Grant's victory at Shiloh, Halleck decided to take the field personally by coming to southern Tennessee and placing himself at the head of Grant's army—a strange maneuver for a man who was supposed to

[36] Fowler, *Under Two Flags*, 146–147.

[37] Brands, *The Man Who Saved the Union*, 172.

be commanding in Missouri. Union forces under Halleck did occupy Corinth, Mississippi in late May 1862, but Grant thought that Halleck's advance had been much too slow. Grant became convinced that it was due entirely to this lack of a truly unified Union command in the west that the capture of Vicksburg was delayed for a year—that is, until Grant himself did the job in July 1863.[38]

Early in the war, the Navy Department in Washington did not realize the full value of these squadrons of river gunboats that were playing such a critical role in the reduction of Confederate strong points on western rivers. In fact, the Union riverine squadrons, while always manned by naval crews and commanded by naval officers, were technically administered by the War Department, i.e., the army, until October 1862. Prior to that date, the officers of the Union blue-water navy seemed to want to keep the small, ugly, smoke belching gunboats of the river squadrons at arm's length. The order of October 1, 1862 transferring the river gunboat squadrons to the complete control of the Navy Department was a sign that Union Secretary of the Navy Gideon Welles had finally realized that in this war, naval vessels would not always be large, graceful, ocean-going ships. Welles realized that in the industrial age warships would come in all shapes and sizes. Some would be large steam-powered ocean-going frigates; others would be small ironclads such as the legendary USS *Monitor* designed for work in coastal waters; while still others would be the river gunboats which would never see salt water at all. The acknowledgment by Welles that the river gunboats did indeed belong in the US Navy represented a beneficial streamlining of the Union war machine.[39]

Still, the fact that there was no legally defined unity of command between the US Navy and the Union Army during the Civil War meant that there were inevitably breakdowns in the Union army-navy relationship, but these usually occurred when and where Grant was not commanding. Other Union generals were not always as careful as Grant was when it came to maintaining good relations with the navy. Halleck was one of these. General Halleck compounded the muddled

---

[38] Brands, *The Man Who Saved the Union*, 157, 166–169, 188–190. Sears, ed., *The Civil War: The Second Year Told by Those Who Lived It*, 10.

[39] Symonds, *The Civil War at Sea*, 115–116.

and non-unified Federal army command situation in the west by abdicating Grant's policy of close cooperation with Union naval forces. In particular, Halleck's excessive caution caused him to refuse to cooperate with Admiral Farragut during the latter's early attempt to capture Vicksburg in the summer of 1862. According to James McPherson, in late June 1862,

> Farragut wrote to General Halleck, whose 110,000 men had recently occupied Corinth, [Mississippi] and asked for enough troops to capture Vicksburg in a combined operation. Not for the first or last time would Halleck prove himself to be General 'Can't-Be-Done' in response to such requests. 'The scattered and weakened condition of my forces,' he replied to Farragut on July 3, 'renders it impossible for me to detach any troops to cooperate with you at Vicksburg.'[40]

Halleck defining his army at that time as "weak" is certainly ironic in that he had more men then than General Meade would use to defeat Robert E. Lee at Gettysburg a year later.

During the same week that the Battle of Gettysburg was fought, army-navy cooperation would be critical to Grant's successful capture of Vicksburg on July 4, 1863.[41] The correspondence between Grant and Acting Rear Admiral David Dixon Porter during the Vicksburg campaign shows how closely the two men worked together. Grant could not issue orders to Porter, but he made many requests of Porter and the latter did everything he could to assist Grant. Relations between Grant and Porter were so good that Grant came to consider Admiral Porter a friend and confidante. During the Vicksburg campaign, Grant often combined his specific requests to Admiral Porter with somewhat "chatty" reports on the latest information regarding the land campaign. For instance, on May 1, 1863 Grant wrote:

> Admiral,
> I have to request that you will take charge of the prisoners captured to day [sic], (from 300 to 500) and issue rations to them till

---

[40] Halleck, as quoted in McPherson, *War on the Waters*, 91.

[41] McPherson, *War on the Waters*, 157–158.

they can be sent north. I am compelled to request this owing to the lack of provisions with my command in the field. . . .

Our day's work has been very creditable; we have *six* guns, 3 to 500 prisoners, killed [Confederate] Genl. Tracy and utterly routed the enemy. Our forces are on the move, and will lie very close to Port Gibson tonight—.ready for early action tomorrow.

Grierson of the cavalry, has taken the heart out of Mississippi—[42]

Porter reciprocated the good feelings and "can do" attitude fully. In April 1863, when Grant was at Millikins Bend, Louisiana and Porter was onboard a gunboat at New Carthage, Mississippi, about eight miles downstream from Vicksburg, Porter expressed his concerns to, and faith in, Grant because he (Porter) could see that Confederate troops were digging entrenchments and building fortifications in and around Vicksburg. He felt the time was ripe for taking the city right then. Porter lamented the fact that the nearest Federal troops were still too far away to assault the city directly at that time.[43] While Porter did not blame Grant for this situation, he did confide in the general that "I wish twenty times a day that Sherman was here or yourself, but I suppose we cannot have all we wish."[44]

Alfred Thayer Mahan wrote of the Vicksburg campaign that "the great service of the navy during the siege was keeping open the communications, which were entirely by the river from" late May 1863.[45] Porter's gunboats constantly patrolling the river also formed the vital left flank of Grant's siege, preventing Confederate supplies or reinforcements

---

[42] Grant to Porter, May 1, 1863, reprinted in John Y. Simon, ed.; John M. Hoffmann and David L. Wilson, Assist. Eds. *The Papers of Ulysses S. Grant.* Vol. 8. *April 1–July 6, 1863.* (Carbondale and Edwardsville, IL: Southern Illinois University Press, 1979—in conjunction with the Ulysses S. Grant Association): 139.

[43] Porter to Grant, April 20, 1863, *The Papers of Ulysses S. Grant,* Vol. 8, 103–104, *n.*

[44] Porter to Grant, April 20, 1863, *The Papers of Ulysses S. Grant,* Vol. 8, 104 *n.*

[45] Alfred Thayer Mahan. *The Gulf and Inland Waters: Campaigns of the Civil War.* (New York: Charles Scribner's Sons, 1883. Reissued 1989 by Broadfoot Publishing Company, Wilmington, NC): 173.

from getting through to Vicksburg from the river side while providing much needed offensive firepower. Porter's gunboats were in fact floating artillery batteries whose firepower Grant simply had to have in order to subdue the city.[46]

While Grant's siege of Vicksburg was underway, another similar operation was taking place downstream at Port Hudson, Louisiana. There, the Army of Union Major General Nathaniel Banks was receiving superb assistance from Union warships under the command of Rear Admiral David G. Farragut. Once again Union army-navy cooperation would achieve great things in that the Confederate garrison at Port Hudson surrendered on July 9, 1863.[47]

The most successful army-navy joint operation of the Civil War was the January 1865 Union assault on Fort Fisher, which guarded the port of Wilmington, North Carolina. By the fall of 1864, overwhelming Union naval strength had enabled Union forces to either capture or make unusable due to close blockade every southern port except Wilmington, North Carolina and Galveston, Texas. Admiral Farragut's spectacular seizure of Mobile Bay in August 1864 was a particularly harsh blow for the Confederacy. The blockade-running ships on which the South relied for imports of rifles, ammunition, and other military supplies were now almost totally dependent upon Wilmington. Galveston was too remote to ever be of much use to blockade runners, especially since Grant's capture of Vicksburg in July 1863 had given Union forces control of the entire Mississippi river; effectively isolating Texas, Arkansas, and almost all of Louisiana from the rest of the Confederacy.

The first Union attempt to seize Fort Fisher in December 1864 had been an abysmal failure, due largely to a failure to exercise unity of command. Admiral Porter and his Army counterpart for this operation, Major General Benjamin Butler, hated each other vigorously and allowed their personal animosity to prevent anything like an adequate level of army-navy cooperation. After this debacle, which was characterized by completely disjointed attacks by the army and navy respectively, Admiral Porter wrote laconically that "'if this temporary failure succeeds

---

[46] Symonds, *The Civil War at Sea*, 116.

[47] McPherson, *War on the Waters*, 167.

in sending General Butler into private life, it is not to be regretted.'"[48] This fiasco did indeed put an end to Butler's military career.

For the second attempt, General Grant supplied Porter with an infantry division from the Army of the Potomac under the command of Major General Alfred Terry. Grant made it clear to Terry that this time he expected results and that that would mean getting along with the navy. Terry took the hint and he went out of his way to establish and maintain a close and cordial working relationship with Admiral Porter. The second Union assault on Fort Fisher took place on January 15, 1865 and the Fort was taken, although Union losses were heavy, particularly amongst a force of sailors and marines that Porter had put ashore. It was General Terry's infantry which actually captured the Fort. In doing so, however, Terry's troops received excellent support from a superbly executed naval bombardment delivered by Porter's squadron of warships, the best of which was an ironclad steam-powered frigate the USS *New Ironsides*.[49] James M. McPherson writes: "In a striking example of coordination in that pre-radio age, the warships (especially the *New Ironsides*) brought down fire on each of thirteen traverses just ahead of the Union troops as they cleared one after another. . . . It was the crowning achievement of combined operations in the war."[50]

Grant had a dress rehearsal for the exercise of supreme and unified command in his most brilliant victory—the Battle of Chattanooga in October and November 1863. Indeed, it was his victory at Chattanooga that removed any lingering doubts in the mind of President Lincoln, at the War Department, and in Congress that Grant was the right man for the job of coordinating the activities of all Union land forces as supreme commander. In what was really a series of battles to secure the eastern half of Tennessee, Grant had been called in to restore order after the Union setback at Chickamauga Creek in northern Georgia in September 1863. Holding Chattanooga, to where the demoralized Union forces had fallen back after Chickamauga, Grant needed to defeat the Confederate

---

[48] Admiral Porter, as quoted in Symonds, *The Civil War at Sea*, 162.

[49] McPherson, *War on the Waters*, 217–219.

[50] McPherson, *War on the Waters*, 218–219.

Army of Tennessee, which was under the command of General Braxton Bragg. This Grant proceeded to do, and with great skill. Grant has been characterized as the cruel butcher who simply threw his men into bloody frontal assaults and simply wore down his enemies by attrition. The reality was quite different. At Chattanooga, as at Vicksburg, Grant proved that when he did not enjoy an overwhelming superiority of troops and supplies, he could be every bit as brilliant a tactician as Robert E. Lee, a man usually classified as Grant's intellectual superior.[51]

In the late-1863 Tennessee campaign, Grant coordinated the activities of troops from four different Union armies, solved a seemingly hopeless supply problem, and managed to coax a brilliant performance in the Lookout Mountain phase of the Battle of Chattanooga from the most unlikely of sources—the very mediocre Major General Joseph Hooker. Grant's presence at Chattanooga was even enough to put some backbone into the hapless Major General Ambrose Burnside, whose army was under pressure from a separate Confederate force at Knoxville in eastern Tennessee.[52]

Historian H.W. Brands provides an interesting view on Grant's rising stock post-Chattanooga and the way in which the war seemed to rejuvenate him. In contrast to the way in which many historians talk of General Grant as a late bloomer, Brands writes that

> Grant's emergence as his country's warrior hero amazed many who had scarcely heard of him before Vicksburg and even now couldn't credit that a man so young could have accomplished so much. Forty-one years old, Grant looked, if anything, younger than he had when the war began. . . . At the time of secession he appeared older than his chronological age; a decade of frustration and failure had worn him down. Now he was refreshed by his string of victories.[53]

Brands makes a good point about Grant's appearance, which is borne out in the photographic record. It is often noted that General Grant

---

[51] Brands, *The Man Who Saved the Union*, 265–280.

[52] Brands, *The Man Who Saved the Union*, 265–280.

[53] Brands, *The Man Who Saved the Union*, 281–282.

never looked like a dashing military hero. His uniforms were wrinkled and often dusty or even spattered with the mud that had been kicked up by his horse. Nevertheless, he undoubtedly looked younger in 1864, even during the terrible stress of the murderous battle at Cold Harbor, than he had in 1861. He had lost weight; not enough to look gaunt, but instead fit. Grant also looked more alert late in the war, at a time when the strains of war were making President Lincoln appear older by the day.[54] Contrary, however, to the views of some historians, Grant was not callous or oblivious to the horrors of war. He took no pleasure from the terrible battles that were fought on his orders in the spring of 1864. He wrote his wife Julia that May regarding the fighting at Spotsylvania Court House, Virginia and presumably also in regard to the immediately preceding Battle of the Wilderness that "the world has never seen so bloody or so protracted a battle as the one being fought and I hope never will again."[55] Grant was realistic about the necessity for total war, but he took no pleasure in it.

Perhaps General Grant's greatest talent was that he was a strategist, not just a commander. He knew how to think big. As stated in Chapter One in regard to Gettysburg, the critics of Major General George Gordon Meade were and are too harsh in castigating Meade for not following up the Gettysburg victory with more vigor. Meade performed superbly at Gettysburg, particularly in view of the fact that he had almost no time to prepare in advance for the battle. However, every rumor has a grain of truth in it, and it probably is true that after Gettysburg General Meade was a bit unsure of exactly how he should proceed. Grant, while getting on well with Meade, did not suffer any such hesitancy. Grant thought in terms of campaigns, not just about individual battles. According to Brands, by the time he assumed the supreme command in March 1864,

> Grant conceived of the entire South as a single battlefield. . . . Grant's strategy was simple. Union forces would pursue and capture or destroy [Joseph] Johnston's and Lee's armies and by that means

---

[54] Brands, *The Man Who Saved the Union*, 281–282.

[55] Grant to Julia, May 13, 1864, reprinted in Simon, ed., *The Papers of Ulysses S. Grant*, Vol. 10, 444.

Courtesy: U.S. National Archives photo no. 111-B-4246 (Brady Collection).

Lieutenant General Ulysses S. Grant, Commanding General of all Union Armies, at Cold Harbor, Virginia in June 1864. Note the three stars on Grant's shoulder straps.

eliminate the enemy's ability to continue fighting. As before, he considered the capture of Confederate cities secondary, although he didn't dismiss the symbolic and logistical value of Richmond, Atlanta and Mobile.[56]

Grant's strategic thinking had thus evolved in logical fashion from his earlier desire in the spring of 1862 to see one supreme Union commander named for the entire western theater of the war. Now he was that supreme commander—of the entire Union war effort on land; east, west, north, and south.

The order from President Lincoln installing General Grant as supreme commander of all Union armies is dated March 10, 1864, and reads as follows: "Under the authority of an act of Congress to revive the grade

---

[56] Brands, *The Man Who Saved the Union*, 292.

of Lieutenant General in the United States Army, approved February 29, 1864, Lieutenant General Ulysses S. Grant, U.S. Army, is assigned to the command of the armies of the United States."[57] These were Grant's marching orders. He had actually received his commission as Lieutenant General personally from the president at the White House on the previous day, March 9, 1864.[58]

In July 1864, General Grant was at his headquarters at City Point (present-day Hopewell), Virginia as the Army of the Potomac began its long siege of Lee's Army at Petersburg, some twenty miles south of Richmond. Grant had his hands full at that time directing operations against Lee, but as General-in-Chief of all Union Armies he could not allow the impudence of Confederate Lieutenant General Jubal Early to go unpunished. On July 11, 1864, a Confederate force that Early had led north through Virginia's Shenandoah Valley reached the outskirts of Washington, DC, and fought a pitched battle with the Union Army Sixth Corps, which Grant had hurriedly detached for the defense of the capital.[59] An enraged Grant decided that the time had come to close down the Shenandoah Valley once and for all as far as the Valley serving as a base of supply, and convenient north-south highway, for Confederate forces. Grant himself had to remain at Cedar Point and General Sherman was then marching towards Atlanta, but the General-in-Chief had the perfect man in mind for the job of denying the Confederacy the use of the Shenandoah Valley. Grant had become highly impressed with the

---

[57] Roy P. Basler, ed. Marion Delores Pratt and Lloyd A. Dunlap, Assist. Ed., *The Collected Works of Abraham Lincoln*. Vol. 7. (New Brunswick, NJ: Rutgers University Press, 1953—published by arrangement with the Abraham Lincoln Association; Springfield, IL): 236.

[58] Basler, ed., Pratt and Dunlap, Assist. Eds, *The Collected Works of Abraham Lincoln*, Vol. 7, 234.

[59] Grant to Meade, July 9, 1864, reprinted in John Y. Simon, ed.; David L. Wilson, Assoc. Ed.; Sue E. Dotson, Editorial Assistant. *The Papers of Ulysses S. Grant*. Vol. 11. *June 1–August 15, 1864*. (Carbondale and Edwardsville, IL: Southern Illinois University Press, 1984—in conjunction with the Ulysses S. Grant Association): 202. See also, Bruce Catton, *Grant Takes Command*. (Boston: Little, Brown and Company, 1968): 310–316.

multi-talented and aggressive young Major General Philip Sheridan, a man who was equally at home commanding cavalry or infantry. At Grant's urging, the War Department made Sheridan, aged thirty-three, the youngest army commander of the war. When he dispatched General Sheridan to the Shenandoah Valley in August 1864, Grant left Sheridan in no doubt as to the thoroughness with which Grant wanted the area to be ravaged so that it could never again be of use to the Confederacy. Grant ordered Sheridan to

> 'Carry off the crops, animals, negroes, and all men under fifty years of age capable of bearing arms.' . . . . Grant particularly wanted to neutralize the partisan forces mobilized by John Mosby. . . . 'When any of them are caught with nothing to designate what they are, hang them without trial.'[60]

While Grant expected Sheridan to be ruthless with the nation's enemies, Grant never lost sight of the fact that President Lincoln's, and his own, overriding war aim was to reunite the nation, not to settle scores. Thus, in September 1864, Grant saw fit to remind Sheridan that not every Virginian supported the rebellion and that it would not do to antagonize pro-Union sentiment where it existed. He felt that Louden (now known as Loudoun) County, Virginia, might be such a place. In regard to the people of Louden County, Grant advised Sheridan that if the latter were certain that the residents there were not providing aid and comfort to the enemy, that the men there of military age need not be placed under arrest and that loyal farmers in the county could be paid for the supplies Sheridan needed for his troops, rather than having their goods confiscated.[61]

In two pitched battles, Winchester and Cedar Creek in September and October 1864, respectively, Sheridan's army decisively defeated

---

[60] Grant to Sheridan, as quoted in Brands, *The Man Who Saved the Union*, 326.

[61] Grant to Sheridan, September 4, 1864, reprinted in John Y. Simon, ed.; David L. Wilson, Assoc. Ed.; Sue E. Dotson, Editorial Assistant. *The Papers of Ulysses S. Grant*. Vol. 12. *August 16–November 15, 1864.* (Carbondale and Edwardsville, IL: Southern Illinois University Press, 1984—in conjunction with the Ulysses S. Grant Association): 127.

the Confederate forces in the Valley. Like Winfield Scott Hancock at Gettysburg, Sheridan had all of the personal charisma of Robert E. Lee when it was time to rally demoralized troops. At Cedar Creek on October 19, 1864, Sheridan's Federals had begun to panic and retreat while under Confederate attack. Sheridan's personal presence turned a seeming defeat into a brilliant Union victory. According to H.W. Brands: "Sheridan's appearance at the front transformed the battle. His troops repulsed the Confederate attack and launched a counterattack. The dazed rebels surrendered by the hundreds; those who avoided surrender fled the field as quickly as they could."[62]

Grant was rapturous at the news in early September 1864 that General Sherman had captured Atlanta and with impish delight even decided to include, after a fashion, Lee's Confederate troops in the lines at Petersburg who were facing Grant's own Army of the Potomac in his celebration of the event. From Virginia, Grant wrote his good friend Sherman on September 4 to say that "I have just received your dispatch announcing the capture of Atlanta. In honor of your great victory I have ordered a salute to be fired with shotted guns from every battery bearing upon the enemy. The salute will be fired within an hour amidst great rejoicing."[63] The exact reaction amongst Lee's veterans in the Army of Northern Virginia at having been included in the festivities in this manner has not been recorded.

As the war drew to a close, General Grant, like Allied supreme commanders in World War II, found himself being drawn into matters that were not entirely military. In late January 1865, Grant took steps to have the army begin governing all of North Carolina as if it were now Union territory once again. At the same time, he was occupied for several days in the intricacies of what seemed to be the first credible overtures from the Confederate government toward seeking peace.

On January 31, 1865, Grant requested Secretary of War Edwin Stanton to officially designate North Carolina as a Union Army military department. Grant intended for Major General John M. Schofield

---

[62] Brands, *The Man Who Saved the Union*, 329.

[63] Grant to Sherman, September 4, 1864, reprinted in Simon, ed., *The Papers of Ulysses S. Grant*, Vol. 12, 127.

to command in North Carolina. While it was part of the Confederacy, enthusiasm for secession had never been anywhere near as strong in North Carolina as it had been in South Carolina. Grant judged that the time was ripe to attempt to detach North Carolina from the Confederacy. He also had practical logistical concerns in mind. General Sherman was marching north from Savannah and had not had a solid supply line behind him since he departed Atlanta on his march to the sea in early November 1864. Grant wanted Schofield to make Wilmington, North Carolina the port of which had recently been captured in the brilliant Union army-navy combined operation described earlier, into a fully functioning Union supply depot so that Sherman's troops would have supplies waiting for them when they got that far north.[64]

While he was drawing up a blueprint for martial law in North Carolina, Grant received at his City Point, Virginia headquarters, a letter from three high-ranking Confederate emissaries, including Alexander H. Stephens, the Vice President of the Confederacy, who were then at Petersburg. The three men wished to travel to Washington to discuss peace terms with President Lincoln. Upon being informed by Grant on January 31 of this development, a startled President Lincoln instructed Grant to "detain the gentlemen in comfortable quarters"[65] at City Point until such time as Lincoln could figure out what to do. Apparently, the president was initially disinclined to meet the Confederate delegates and it appears that Grant played a role in prodding the president to at least hear what they had to say. Grant wrote Secretary of War Edwin M. Stanton on February 1, 1865, to say that "I fear now their going back without any expression from any one in authority will have a bad

---

[64] Grant to Stanton, January 31, 1865, reprinted in John Y. Simon, ed.; David L. Wilson, Assoc. Ed.; Sue E. Dotson, Editorial Assistant. *The Papers of Ulysses S. Grant.* Vol. 13. *November 16, 1864–February 20, 1865.* (Carbondale and Edwardsville, IL: Southern Illinois University Press, 1985—in conjunction with the Ulysses S. Grant Association): 336. Grant to Schofield, January 31, 1865 (two messages), reprinted in Simon, ed.; Wilson, Assoc. Ed., *The Papers of Ulysses S. Grant,* Vol. 13, 338–341.

[65] Lincoln to Grant, January 31, 1865, reprinted in Simon, ed.; Wilson, Assoc. Ed., *The Papers of Ulysses S. Grant,* Vol. 13, 334 *n.*

influence [*sic*]."[66] Lincoln did meet with the Confederate delegates on February 2, 1865—but at Fort Monroe near Hampton, Virginia, not in Washington. Lincoln quickly became convinced that the three men were waffling on the key and closely intertwined Union demands of a united nation with no slaves. The Confederate delegates returned to Richmond empty-handed.[67]

During all this time when Grant was directing armies in several different theaters, setting up a military government for North Carolina, and handling Confederate hints towards ending the war, Robert E. Lee was still just the commander of one Confederate army, engaged in purely military matters.

In the Gulf War fought in January and February 1991 to liberate Kuwait from the Iraqi forces that had invaded in August 1990, American President George H.W. Bush saw Iraqi dictator Saddam Hussein as another Hitler and Hussein's August 2, 1990 invasion of Kuwait as another "Munich" moment. The choice was clear to Bush. The United States and its allies could not back down in the face of Iraqi aggression in the manner that Britain and France had backed down to Hitler over Czechoslovakia in 1938. George H.W. Bush was a World War II navy veteran who had flown combat missions as the pilot of a TBM Avenger torpedo plane from the deck of the aircraft carrier USS *San Jacinto*. He had even been shot down in the western Pacific in September 1944. His two crewmen were killed, but Bush was plucked from the water in a daring rescue by the crew of the submarine USS *Finback*, which was on "lifeguard" duty in the area.[68] His World War II experience was a critical factor in the way in which President Bush reacted to the invasion of

---

[66] Grant to Stanton, February 1, 1865, reprinted in Simon, ed.; Wilson, Assoc. Ed., *The Papers of Ulysses S. Grant*, Vol. 13, 345.

[67] For the details of Lincoln's meeting with the Confederate delegates, see the series of extracts of messages between Grant, Secretary of State William H. Seward, President Lincoln, and the president's personal emissary and telegrapher Thomas T. Eckert, Feb. 1–Feb. 8, 1865, as reprinted in Simon, ed.; Wilson, Assoc. Ed., *The Papers of Ulysses S. Grant*, Vol. 13, 346–347 *n*. See also Brands, *The Man Who Saved the Union*, 347–349.

[68] Tom Wicker. *George Herbert Walker Bush*. (New York: Viking/Penguin, 2004): 6.

Kuwait. His two most important priorities were that aggression cannot go unpunished, and that aggression can only be successfully combated by using the British-American World War II model—i.e., a multinational alliance in which the partners worked together closely to win a coalition war.

As such, President Bush reacted immediately to Saddam Hussein's invasion of Kuwait by initiating a massive American military buildup in Saudi Arabia both to protect Saudi Arabia from any Iraqi invasion and to use bases in Saudi Arabia as a launching point from which to expel the Iraqi Army from Kuwait. During the military buildup, Operation Desert Shield, in the fall of 1990, Bush quickly and successfully stitched together an international coalition that included European allies like Great Britain and Italy and even Arab nations such as Syria and Egypt.

President Bush did not follow the World War II blueprint completely in 1991, however, in that he did not make regime change in Iraq an American war aim. According to David R. Gergen: "It can be argued that [George H.W.] Bush set himself up with the frequent Hitler analogy: If Saddam Hussein [was] Adolf Hitler, why did Bush leave him in power?"[69] Gergen was writing in 1992. Of course, in 2014, the question of whether the cost of finally ridding the world of Saddam Hussein was actually worth it is still being actively debated.

No coalition is perfect. The commander of the 1991 Gulf War Coalition, American General H. Norman Schwarzkopf, experienced plenty of problems in the field—not all of which came from the enemy. Former US Marine Lieutenant General Bernard E. Trainor writes in regard to the issue of unity of command amongst the international coalition facing Saddam Hussein in the 1991 Gulf War that "General Schwarzkopf never quite managed to truly integrate the coalition forces, but he did the next best thing; he got all his disparate warriors to cooperate."[70] Schwarzkopf was greatly aided by the fact that the largest

---

[69] David R. Gergen. "The Unfettered Presidency," in Joseph S. Nye, Jr. and Roger K. Smith, eds. *After the Storm: Lessons from the Gulf War.* (Lanham, MD: Madison Books; in conjunction with the Aspen Institute, 1992): 183.

[70] Bernard E. Trainor, "War by Miscalculation" in Nye and Smith, eds., *After the Storm*, 203.

and most powerful piece of the coalition, the American land, sea, and air forces in-theater, were under his direct command.[71]

In addition to coordinating the activities of a multinational alliance, General Schwarzkopf had to overcome barriers to unity of command even within the American military during the 1991 Gulf War. Interestingly, in those pre-Internet days, the computers used by different branches of the American military in 1991 were surprisingly incompatible. According to Trainor, these computer problems became apparent as soon as the American-led coalition began its devastating air attacks against Iraqi installations on January 16, 1991:

> Interoperability problems . . . arose, primarily due to the incompatibility of similar equipment. Thus the thirty page daily air tasking order specifying missions for the upcoming twenty four hours had to be flown by helicopter to the navy carriers in the Gulf because air force and navy computers could not talk to one another."[72]

Even without the Internet, it is surprising that the American military did not have a better real-time interservice communications capability in 1991, especially since the American Armed Forces had been unified since September 1947. If Iraq had been a more powerful adversary and the war had lasted longer, such a deficiency could have been very damaging to American forces.

Another difference from the World War II model was that much of the target selection for the air campaign in 1991 was done at the Pentagon. That worried Schwarzkopf's air commander, US Air Force Lieutenant General Charles Horner, who reminded Schwarzkopf about the disaster that had ensued when Vietnam targets were chosen in Washington rather than in-theater. Schwarzkopf overruled Horner because Schwarzkopf was convinced that Horner simply had too much to do already and that he needed assistance. General Horner was particularly overworked early on because he had been left in Riyadh when a delegation including then Defense Secretary Dick Cheney and General Schwarzkopf had made a quick visit in to Saudi Arabia in early August 1990 to ask permission of

---

[71] Trainor, "War by Miscalculation" in Nye and Smith, eds., *After the Storm*, 203.

[72] Trainor, "War by Miscalculation," in Nye and Smith, eds., *After the Storm*, 208.

Saudi King Fahd for American forces to be sent to defend Saudi Arabia. Thus, for the first few weeks of Desert Shield, General Horner was the senior American officer in-theater.

Another alteration from the World War II model is that it appears that the major outlines for the offensive phase were outlined by General Schwarzkopf and his staff in mid-August 1990 at their stateside post at the headquarters of the US Central Command in Tampa, Florida after Schwarzkopf had returned from his flying visit to Saudi Arabia, but before he moved his headquarters to Saudi Arabia in late August 1990. At a meeting in Tampa on August 16, 1990 General Schwarzkopf decided that when the coalition took the offensive, the code name would be changed from Desert Shield to Desert Storm and he decided that half the Iraqi ground forces in Kuwait had to be destroyed by the coalition air campaign before the ground invasion could begin.[73] The latter is the type of decision that would have been made in Washington by the Combined Chiefs of Staff in World War II, rather than by a theater commander.

In addition to a unified command structure, the 1991 coalition forces brought overwhelming strength to bear against Iraq. The coalition naval forces deployed between them well over 150 warships in the Persian Gulf and the Red Sea, respectively. Six American aircraft carriers were present to supplement the already overwhelming land-based air power that General Schwarzkopf had at his disposal. There were even two World War II vintage American *Iowa* class battleships on hand to provide shore bombardment with their 16-inch guns and to serve as launching platforms for cruise missiles.[74] Schwarzkopf had more than 500,000 troops at his disposal and the hundreds of aircraft in his land-based air armada were able to use bases in Saudi Arabia and Turkey, placing them within easy reach of any target within Iraq or Kuwait.[75]

---

[73] H. Norman Schwarzkopf, with Peter Petre. *It Doesn't Take a Hero.* (New York: Bantam, 1992): 302–308, 318–321.

[74] Lawrence Freedman and Efraim Karsh. *The Gulf Conflict 1990–1991: Diplomacy and War in the New World Order.* (Princeton, NJ: Princeton University Press, 1993): 392–393.

[75] Trainor, "War by Miscalculation," in Nye and Smith, eds., *After the Storm,* 201–203.

This overwhelming power was concentrated against a relatively weak opponent. Although the Iraqi army had almost a million men under arms in 1990, making it even larger than the US active duty Army (not including reserves) at that time, the numbers were deceiving. Only a small fraction of Saddam Hussein's army consisted of the vaunted Republican Guard units. The vast bulk of the Iraqi Army was made up of unhappy conscripts whose devotion to the regime was sketchy at best. The Iraqis did have tanks, artillery, and a large air force.[76] The most important advantages enjoyed by Saddam Hussein's opponents in 1991 were that the most powerful member of the coalition, the United States, had an all volunteer military in which overall morale was quite high. Not the least of the factors responsible for high morale in the American forces was that the Americans who fought in Desert Storm knew that they were the best-armed, best-trained, and best-equipped fighting force in the World.

The overwhelming power, high morale, and excellent training of the coalition forces in 1991 meant that the difficulties of interservice and international cooperation, while present, were greatly mitigated. For example, the five week long air campaign, beginning on January 16, 1991 and which preceded the coalition ground offensive had its share of controversy, but was overwhelmingly successful nevertheless. The air commander, General Horner, was criticized for not paying enough attention to tactical, battlefield targets, but instead being preoccupied with strategic targets such as Iraqi military command and control buildings in Baghdad.[77] In his memoirs, General Schwarzkopf claims that part of the problem was that intelligence analysts were never satisfied that enough damage had been done to the Iraqi infrastructure via strategic bombing attacks, but that as a ground forces officer himself, he was acutely aware of the need to shift the emphasis of the bombing campaign away from urban targets and to the battlefield itself.[78] There was certainly some

---

[76] Schwarzkopf with Petre, *It Doesn't Take a Hero*, 300–301.

[77] Michael R. Gordon and General Bernard E. Trainor. *The Generals' War: The Inside Story of the Conflict in the Gulf.* (Boston: Little, Brown and Company, 1995): 317–323.

[78] Schwartzkopf with Petre, *It Doesn't Take a Hero*, 430–432.

interservice rivalry present in the American camp owing to the fact that the US Air Force had so much influence during five of the six weeks of the actual fighting. Officers from the other American services, army, marines, and navy, feared that Iraqi ground troops and their heavy weapons might not suffer anything close to the fifty percent reduction that was supposed to occur before the US and its Allies launched their ground offensive. However, the sheer volume of coalition air strikes and the isolation of the battlefield for the Iraqis that occurred via the destruction of those command and control buildings in Baghdad meant that the coalition was winning the air war in a big way even if not all of the right targets were being struck. To his credit, as the date (February 24, 1991) for the beginning of the ground offensive approached, General Horner did direct more and more air attacks against tactical targets so that by the time the ground offensive began, American pilots had become adept at destroying individual Iraqi tanks in the desert at night.[79]

There were certainly many differences between the Gulf War Coalition of 1991; General Grant's appointment as supreme Union land commander in 1864; and the activities of World War II Allied theater commanders such as Admiral Nimitz and General Eisenhower. However, a unified command structure is a common thread connecting each of these examples. Of course, unified command systems are never perfect. Nevertheless, unified command structures have provided great dividends for American forces in several different wars. The difficulties in establishing a unified command structure can be immense. In the British-American World War II alliance, differences between British and American war aims had to be overcome as did differences due to interservice rivalry within the branches of the British and American armed forces, respectively.[80] President George H.W. Bush and General Schwarzkopf had to grapple with similar difficulties during the 1991 Gulf War. International coalitions were not a factor in the American Civil War. Nevertheless, President Lincoln and his best general, Ulysses S. Grant, were amongst the first Americans to realize the great benefits that a unified command

---

[79] Gordon and Trainor, *The Generals' War*, 317–323.

[80] Rigby, *Allied Master Strategists*, 5–6.

structure can yield. In many ways, the moves towards a unified command structure that were initiated during the Civil War first by Grant in the field cooperating closely with the navy and then by President Lincoln in Washington bestowing the supreme command of all Union armies upon Grant in March 1864 paved the way for the official unification of the American armed forces which occurred in September 1947 with the enactment of the National Security Act. Unity of command is difficult to obtain, but it is very much worth the effort because a unified military command structure truly is a whole that is greater than the sum of its parts.

CONCLUSION

"It has been said that democracy is the worst form of Government except for all those other forms that have been tried from time to time."[1]

Winston Churchill spoke these words in the House of Commons on November 11, 1947, a time of relative quiet in his life of which he took advantage to begin working on his memoirs. Perhaps Churchill's very half-hearted praise of democracy was a reference to the deliberate inefficiency of democratic governments. Churchill was acutely aware of the extent of that deliberate inefficiency, having by 1947 been a member of Parliament for over forty years. While Churchill had exercised extraordinary powers during his five years as prime minister of Great Britain during World War II, he had also been compelled to make certain that he always retained the confidence of his colleagues in the House of Commons during that time.[2] Like his friend American President Franklin D. Roosevelt, Winston Churchill as prime minister was answerable to the public he served, even in time of war. Neither Churchill nor Roosevelt was ever a law unto himself. Their opponents in World War II—Hitler, Mussolini, and Prime Minister Tōjō Hideki were far less answerable to public opinion. In Japan, Tōjō was forced to resign after the American seizure of the Mariana Islands in the summer of 1944. Tōjō's ouster, however, was more

---

[1] Winston Churchill, Address to the House of Commons, November 11, 1947, as reprinted in Richard M. Langworth, ed., *Churchill by Himself: The Definitive Collection of Quotations.* (New York: PublicAffairs/Perseus, 2008): 573.

[2] David Rigby. *Allied Master Strategists: The Combined Chiefs of Staff in World War II.* (Annapolis, MD: Naval Institute Press, 2012): 149.

of a palace coup amongst a ruling clique than any kind of a reference to public opinion in Japan.

Well versed in American history, Winston Churchill was well aware by the time he spoke the lines quoted above that the US Constitution makes the president the Commander-in-Chief of the armed forces of the United States, but that only the Congress can declare war. Churchill also would have known that while every American commissioned military officer from a young second lieutenant up through a middle aged four-star general is a presidential appointment, each and every one of those officers must be confirmed by the US Senate. Churchill was also well aware that while the president is the Commander-in-Chief of the American armed forces, the money required to put those armed forces in the field cannot be withdrawn from the US Treasury without the approval of the Congress. In short, Churchill's statement that all types of government are far from perfect but that democracy is the least imperfect form was an expression of his knowledge that the framers of the world's great democracies tried hard to create governments that would be antithetical to dictatorship.

Checks and balances, the separation of powers; these are deliberate inefficiencies built in to democratic governments to prevent one person or one group from becoming too powerful. Far from being weaknesses, these deliberate inefficiencies in democratic governments are instead the source of their greatest strength. John Lewis Gaddis highlights a key characteristic that dictatorships have in common when he mentions George Kennan's view that one of the most important features of life in the Soviet Union under the Stalin regime was "the Russians' chronic inability to tolerate diversity."[3] Democracies, on the other hand, are quite diverse. Democracies are governments in which leaders are not afraid of their own people. When a so-called "election" is held by a dictatorial regime, such as that of Ngo Dinh Diem, the American puppet who ruled South Vietnam as an autocrat from 1955–1963, the leader usually "wins" ninety-eight percent of the popular vote. Lacking legitimacy, dictators

---

[3] John Lewis Gaddis. *Strategies of Containment: A Critical Appraisal of American National Security Policy During the Cold War.* (New York: Oxford University Press, 1982, 2005): 41.

are desperate for the appearance of popularity and rig their "elections" accordingly.

By contrast, a vote in a real democracy reflects ambiguity and diversity to the highest degree. When Churchill made his famous quote about the very real imperfections of democracy, he was aware that FDR's victory over Republican Alf Landon in the 1936 presidential election was the biggest landslide in American history since 1820—when James Monroe had run for president essentially without opposition. The 1936 presidential election was a genuine contest between two viable candidates (with two minor candidates mixed in as well) in which FDR won sixty percent of the popular vote and almost all of the electoral votes. Lyndon Johnson did achieve a slightly higher margin of victory in 1964, winning sixty-one percent of the popular vote. Nevertheless, no American president is ever likely to get much over sixty percent of the popular vote. Some presidents have received considerably less, particularly when a third party candidate draws off a significant number of votes. Despite FDR's near sweep of the Electoral College in 1936, the fact remains that almost forty percent of the people who voted in the 1936 presidential election— millions of Americans—woke up disappointed on the day after that election because their candidate lost. In fact, 16,679,683 Americans voted for Alf Landon in 1936 and *not* for the winner—FDR. These results were immediately broadcast to the world. No attempt was made to conceal the vote count. By way of contrast, no dictator would ever dare to allow it to become known that so many people did not like him. That is what Kennan meant when he said that dictators have to stamp out all vestiges and even appearances of diversity. The checks and balances of American democracy enable the millions of Americans who cast their votes for a presidential candidate who then goes down in defeat to rest assured that fundamental liberties in the United States, such as the constitutionally guaranteed right to free speech, will remain safe no matter who ends up in the White House.

Historians have often mentioned that American democracy has a deep impact on the way the United States fights its wars.[4] War is an

---

[4] Andrew Roberts. *Masters and Commanders: How Four Titans Won the War in the West, 1941–1945*. (New York: HarperCollins, 2009): 575–576.

aberration for the American people; a people who would much rather live in peace. As stated in Chapter One, Richard Overy credits Allied victory in World War II to the fact that the people of the Allied nations had "the will to win."[5] The Gulf War to liberate Kuwait from Iraqi occupation was another conflict in which the American people had the will to win and in which, like in World War II, the United States benefited greatly from the existence of a unified command structure. Unity of command in wartime requires cooperation; individual commanders have to keep their sometimes clashing egos in check and allied nations have to find a way to work together. The cooperation necessary for a unified command structure only ever exists amongst combatant nations whose people are determined to win. Likewise, total mobilization can only occur when the determination to win is present amongst the public and their leaders.[6] An interesting parallel between the combatants on both sides during World War II and the Gulf War of 1991 is that nations whose people and leaders *hate* war have the best chance of winning once they are in one. This is one of the latent strengths of a democracy in time of war. If the people of a democracy understand and support their nation's war aims, such a democracy can become an almost invincible combatant.[7] Dictators like Adolf Hitler and Saddam Hussein saw war as a sort of way of life, bearing out George Orwell's mantra in *Nineteen Eighty-Four* that "War is Peace."[8] No amount of conquest would ever have been enough to satisfy either man. After assuming undisputed control of Iraq in 1979, Saddam Hussein spent much of his twenty-four year reign engaged in armed conflict with Iran, Kuwait, the American-led coalition of 1991, Kurdish rebels at home, and then with the Americans again. Even if Hitler had been successful in Operation Barbarossa, the 1941 invasion of the Soviet Union, he had his eye on a scheme that was in some ways

---

[5] Richard Overy. *Why the Allies Won.* (New York: Norton, 1995): 325.

[6] Rigby, *Allied Master Strategists*, 105.

[7] Rigby, *Allied Master Strategists*, 105, 98.

[8] George Orwell. *Nineteen Eighty-Four.* (New York: Everyman's Library/Alfred A. Knopf, 1992): 6.

even more grandiose, namely his "Z" Plan to defeat the American and British navies in the North Atlantic and thus secure at least maritime hegemony in the western hemisphere to accompany German mastery of the European continent.

Since dictators often enjoy being at war, they tend to be in no hurry and to have war aims that are vague, at best. For them, war is the aim. The irrationality of the dictators who enjoy war is actually a serious handicap to such dictators in time of war. The victorious coalitions in World War II and the Gulf War of 1991, respectively, were comprised of nations that saw war as a necessary evil; something to be got over with as quickly as possible. The way to get a war over with quickly is to mobilize every resource to win, to have clear war aims, to work closely with allies, and to try hard to develop effective fighting strategies. Stated bluntly, Americans and other peoples who despise war will often fight harder than will a militarized dictatorship because any rational person wants to get war over with as quickly as possible. Of course, the fact that Stalin had not wanted war in 1941 when the Soviet Union was attacked by Germany proves that not every dictator enjoys war.

When the American people are united behind a war effort, such as was the case in World War II, there is nothing that cannot be accomplished because the war effort represents an act of national will. Getting the American people behind a war effort requires the political leadership, particularly the president, to articulate clear and logical war aims. When the American people are united in support of a war and the aims of that war are clear, American military forces are able to fight all out in order to get a terrible job over with as quickly as possible. At Midway in June 1942, Admiral Nimitz could stake everything on challenging the Japanese fleet with all of the resources that he, Nimitz, had at his disposal then because he knew that the American people would accept that risk.

When popular support for a war is less unanimous, such as in the American Civil War, a president needs to tread more cautiously. It took until March 1864, almost three years in to the Civil War, for President Lincoln to find the right general to command and coordinate the entire Union war effort. But Lincoln had other problems besides locating military talent. By late 1862, Lincoln realized that he needed to convince the people of the North that the nation could not be reunited until slavery was destroyed.[9]

Richard Overy's point about the importance of the American "will to win"[10] in World War II cannot be overstated, and applies to other wars in which the United States has fought. The will to win has to be fed—with victories, particularly when popular support for a war is not quite unanimous. Despite impressive victories in the Union column such as Gettysburg, Vicksburg, and Chattanooga, President Lincoln became convinced in the summer of 1864 that he was going to lose the upcoming presidential election.[11] The capture of Atlanta by General Sherman's army in September 1864 kept the Union will to win fed late in a long and bloody war and was an event that proved to be pivotal to Lincoln's re-election.

The successful American military strategies described in this volume have in common that they required American presidents and the military commanders who served them to carefully gauge the public's level of support for a war and to respond to that level of support with what Henry R. Nau has identified in the case of President Polk as "an exquisite sense of timing."[12] President Lincoln had to have Sherman's capture of Atlanta, not to satisfy the President's personal political ambition to be re-elected, but so that Lincoln could ensure (by being re-elected) that the war would continue to be prosecuted in the manner in which Lincoln knew in his gut to be the right way—i.e., until the Confederacy had been completely vanquished. Earlier, Lincoln had waited until the Army of the Potomac had finally won a partial victory over Robert E. Lee at Antietam in September 1862 before issuing the Emancipation Proclamation. In the

---

[9] Eric Foner. *The Fiery Trial: Abraham Lincoln and American Slavery.* (New York: Norton, 2010): 229.

[10] Overy, *Why the Allies Won,* 325.

[11] H.W. Brands, *The Man Who Saved the Union: Ulysses Grant in War and Peace.* (New York: Doubleday, 2012): 319.

[12] Henry R. Nau, *Conservative Internationalism: Armed Diplomacy Under Jefferson, Polk, Truman, and Reagan.* (Princeton, NJ: Princeton University Press, 2013): 134.

Mexican War, President Polk had to accept a peace treaty that was not entirely to his liking because he knew that public opinion was quite divided about the war with Mexico and that he therefore needed to end that war.[13]

American military commanders in the field are themselves far from immune from the currents of public opinion. General Meade can be excused for failing to completely destroy the Confederate Army of Northern Virginia in the immediate aftermath of the Union victory at Gettysburg. In July 1863, support for the war effort amongst the people of the North was somewhat tenuous. Had Meade's Army of the Potomac been destroyed by following up the repulse of Pickett's charge with an all-out attack (which would have meant leaving the defensive position on Cemetery Ridge which had made Union victory possible), the effect on northern public opinion could have been disastrous. By late summer 1864, General Grant realized that he may have gone a bit too far when he instructed General Sheridan to ravage the entire Shenandoah Valley in Virginia. Thus, after learning that at least one county in the Valley was heavily pro-Union, Grant amended his orders to Sheridan in September 1864 by instructing the latter to find out which farmers in the Shenandoah Valley were loyal to the Union and which ones were not and then to pay loyal farmers for supplies while confiscating supplies from farmers who supported the Confederacy.[14] Similarly, it was unthinkable that the United States would engage in armed conflict with the Soviet Union when the Russians instituted the blockade of Berlin in June 1948. What was needed then was creativity. President Truman and his advisors supplied that creativity by inaugurating the Berlin Airlift. During that Airlift Gail Halvorsen, by dropping all that candy to the children of Berlin, won a victory for the United States that was more complete than any amount of weaponry ever could have achieved.

---

[13] Nau, *Conservative Internationalism*, 134.

[14] Grant to Sheridan, September 4, 1864, reprinted in John Y. Simon, ed.; David L. Wilson, Assoc. Ed.; Sue E. Dotson, Editorial Assistant. *The Papers of Ulysses S. Grant*. Vol. 12. *August 16–November 15, 1864*. (Carbondale and Edwardsville, IL: Southern Illinois University Press, 1984—in conjunction with the Ulysses S. Grant Association): 127.

BIBLIOGRAPHY

Published Primary Sources

Basler, Roy P., ed. Pratt, Marion Delores, and Dunlap, Lloyd A., Assistant Editors. *The Collected Works of Abraham Lincoln*. Vol. 7. New Brunswick, New Jersey: Rutgers University Press, 1953—published by arrangement with the Abraham Lincoln Association; Springfield, Illinois.

Bland, Larry I., and Stoler, Mark A., eds. Ritenour Stevens, Sharon, Associate Editor. *The Papers of George Catlett Marshall*. Vol. 6. *The Whole World Hangs in the Balance: January 8, 1947–September 30, 1949*. Baltimore: The Johns Hopkins University Press, 2013.

Cutler, Wayne, ed. Rogers, James L. II, and Severance, Benjamin H., Associate Editors Rogers, Cynthia J.; Smith, Trevor A.; and William K. Bolt, Assistant Editors. *Correspondence of James K. Polk*. Volume XI: 1846. Knoxville: The University of Tennessee Press, 2009.

Grizzard, Frank E., Jr., ed. Hoth, David R., Assistant Editor. *The Papers of George Washington: Revolutionary War Series*. Vol. 12. *October–December 1777*. Charlottesville: University Press of Virginia, 2002.

Langworth, Richard M., ed. *Churchill by Himself: The Definitive Collection of Quotations*. New York: PublicAffairs/Perseus, 2008.

Lincoln, Abraham. *The Gettysburg Address and Other Writings*. New York: The Fall River Press, 2013.

Meade, George Gordon, ed. *The Life and Letters of George Gordon Meade: Major-General, United States Army*. Vol. 2. New York: Charles Scribner's Sons, 1913.

Polk, James K. *The Diary of James K. Polk During His Presidency, 1845 to 1849 (Polk Diary)*. Edited and Annototated by Milo Milton Quaife. Vols. 1 and 3. Chicago: A.C. Mclurg & Co. on behalf of the Chicago Historical Society, 1910.

Rhodehamel, John, ed. *The American Revolution: Writings from the War of Independence*. New York: The Library of America, 2001.

Sears, Stephen W., ed. *The Civil War: The Second Year Told by Those Who Lived It*. New York: Library of America, 2012.

Simon, John Y., ed.; Hoffmann, John M., and Wilson, David L., Assistant Editor. *The Papers of Ulysses S. Grant*. Vol. 8. *April 1–July 6, 1863*. Carbondale and Edwardsville, Illinois: Southern Illinois University Press, 1979—in conjunction with the Ulysses S. Grant Association.

Simon, John Y., ed. Wilson, David L., Assistant Editor. *The Papers of Ulysses S. Grant*. Vol. 10. *January 1–May 31, 1864*. Carbondale and Edwardsville, Illinois: Southern Illinois University Press, 1982—in conjunction with the Ulysses S. Grant Association.

Simon, John Y., ed. Wilson, David L., Associate Editor. Dotson, Sue E., Editorial Assistant. *The Papers of Ulysses S. Grant*. Vol. 11. *June 1–August 15, 1864*. Carbondale and Edwardsville, Illinois: Southern Illinois University Press, 1984—in conjunction with the Ulysses S. Grant Association.

——. *The Papers of Ulysses S. Grant*. Vol. 12. *August 16–November 15, 1864*. Carbondale and Edwardsville, Illinois: Southern Illinois University Press, 1984—in conjunction with the Ulysses S. Grant Association.

——. *The Papers of Ulysses S. Grant*. Vol. 13. *November 16, 1864–February 20, 1865*. Carbondale and Edwardsville, Illinois: Southern Illinois University Press, 1985—in conjunction with the Ulysses S. Grant Association.

Simpson, Brooks D., ed. *The Civil War: The Third Year Told by Those Who Lived It*. New York: Library of America, 2013.

Simpson, Brooks D.; Sears, Stephen W.; and Aaron Sheehan-Dean, eds. *The Civil War: The First Year Told by Those Who Lived It*. New York: Library of America, 2011.

War Department. *The War of the Rebellion: A Compilation of the Official Records of the Union and Confederate Armies*. Series 1, Vol. 27, Part 1—Reports. Volume Editor— Lieutenant Colonel Robert N. Scott, Third U.S. Artillery. Washington, D.C.: Government Printing Office, 1889.

Secondary Sources

Anderson, Troyer Steele. *The Command of the Howe Brothers During the American Revolution*. New York: Oxford University Press, 1936.

Bartov, Omer. *Hitler's Army: Soldiers, Nazis, and War in the Third Reich*. New York: Oxford University Press, 1992.

Beevor, Antony. *The Fall of Berlin 1945*. New York: Penguin, 2002.

Behrman, Greg. *The Most Noble Adventure: The Marshall Plan and the Time When America Helped Save Europe*. New York: Free Press, 2007.

Belote, James H., and Belote, William M. *Typhoon of Steel: The Battle for Okinawa*. New York: Harper & Row, 1970.

Berkin, Carol; Miller, Christopher L.; Cherny, Robert W.; and Gormly, James L. *Making America: A History of the United States*. Vol. 1. *To 1877*. Sixth Edition. Boston: Cengage, 2013.

Boatner, Mark Mayo III. *Encyclopedia of the American Revolution*. New York: David McKay Company, 1966.

Borneman, Walter R. *Polk: The Man Who Transformed the Presidency and America*. New York: Random House, 2008.

Brands, H.W. *The Man Who Saved the Union: Ulysses Grant in War and Peace*. New York: Doubleday, 2012.

--------------. *TR: The Last Romantic*. New York: BasicBooks, 1997.

Brighton, Terry. *Patton, Montgomery, Rommel: Masters of War*. New York: Crown Publishers, 2008.

Buell, Thomas B. *Master of Sea Power: A Biography of Admiral Ernest J. King*. Boston: Little, Brown and Company, 1980.

Buell, Thomas B. *The Quiet Warrior: A Biography of Admiral Raymond A. Spruance*. Annapolis, Maryland: Naval Institute Press, 1974, 1987.

Catton, Bruce. *The Army of the Potomac: Glory Road*. Garden City, New York: Doubleday, 1952.

--------------. *The Centennial History of the Civil War*. Vol. 3. *Never Call Retreat*. Garden City, New York: Doubleday, 1965.

--------------. *Glory Road: The Bloody Route from Fredericksburg to Gettysburg*. Garden City, New York: Doubleday, 1956.

--------------. *Grant Takes Command*. Boston: Little, Brown and Company, 1968.

--------------. *This Hallowed Ground: The Story of the Union Side of the Civil War*. Garden City, New York: Doubleday, 1956.

Chernow, Ron. *Washington: A Life*. New York: Peguin, 2010.

Cherny, Andrei. *The Candy Bombers: The Untold Story of the Berlin Airlift and America's Finest Hour*. New York: G.P. Putnam's Sons, 2008.

Churchill, Winston S. *The Second World War*. Vol. 2. *Their Finest Hour*. Boston: Houghton Mifflin Company, 1949.

----------------------. *The Second World War*. Vol. 6. *Triumph and Tragedy*. Boston: Houghton Mifflin Company, 1953.

Clark, Jane. "Responsibility for the Failure of the Burgoyne Campaign," in *American Historical Review*. Vol. 35, No. 3, April 1930, pgs. 542–559.

Clausewitz, Carl von. *On War*. Michael Howard and Peter Paret, eds. and trans. Princeton, New Jersey: Princeton University Press, 1976.

Collier, Richard. *Bridge Across the Sky: The Berlin Blockade and Airlift, 1948–1949*. New York: McGraw-Hill, 1978.

Cook, Don. *The Long Fuse: How England Lost the American Colonies, 1760–1785*. New York: The Atlantic Monthly Press, 1995.

Dalton, Kathleen. *Theodore Roosevelt: A Strenuous Life*. New York: Alfred A. Knopf, 2002.

Elson, Henry W. (text); Barnes, James (captions). *The Photographic History of the Civil War in Ten Volumes*. Vol. 2. *Two Years of Grim War*. New York: The Review of Reviews Co., 1911.

Ferling, John. *A Leap in the Dark: The Struggle to Create the American Republic*. New York: Oxford University Press, 2003.

Ferrell, Robert H. "Woodrow Wilson: A Misfit in Office?" in Dawson, Joseph G. III, ed. *Commanders in Chief: Presidential Leadership in Modern Wars*. Lawrence, Kansas: University Press of Kansas, 1993.

Flexner, James Thomas. *George Washington in the American Revolution (1775–1783)*. Boston: Little, Brown and Company, 1967, 1968.

Foner, Eric. *The Fiery Trial: Abraham Lincoln and American Slavery*. New York: Norton, 2010.

Fortescue, Sir John. *The War of Independence: The British Army in North America, 1775–1783*. London: Greenhill Books, 1911. Mechanicsburg, Pennsylania: Stackpole Books, 2001.

Fowler, William M., Jr. *Under Two Flags: The American Navy in the Civil War*. New York: Norton, 1990.

Freeman, Douglas Southall. *R.E. Lee: A Biography*. Vol. 3. New York: Charles Scribner's Sons, 1935.

Freedman, Lawrence, and Karsh, Efraim. *The Gulf Conflict 1990–1991: Diplomacy and War in the New World Order*. Princeton, New Jersey: Princeton University Press, 1993.

Furneaux, Rupert. *The Battle of Saratoga*. New York: Stein and Day, 1971.

Gaddis, John Lewis. *The Cold War: A New History*. New York: Penguin, 2005.

----------------------. *George F. Kennan: An American Life*. New York: Penguin, 2011.

----------------------. *Strategies of Containment: A Critical Appraisal of American National Security Policy During the Cold War*. New York: Oxford University Press, 1982, 2005.

Gallagher, Gary W. *The Union War*. Cambridge, Massachusetts: Harvard University Press, 2011.

Goolrick, William T.; Tanner, Ogden; and the Editors of Time-Life Books. *The Battle of the Bulge*. Alexandria, Virginia: Time-Life Books, 1979.

Gordon, Michael R., and Trainor, General Bernard E. *The Generals' War: The Inside Story of the Conflict in the Gulf*. Boston: Little, Brown and Company, 1995.

Guelzo, Allen C. *Fateful Lightning: A New History of the Civil War & Reconstruction*. New York: Oxford University Press, 2012.

Headrick, Daniel R. *The Invisible Weapon: Telecommunications and International Politics 1851–1945*. New York: Oxford University Press, 1991.

Herman, Arthur. *Freedom's Forge: How American Business Produced Victory in World War II*. New York: Random House, 2012.

Howe, Daniel Walker. *What Hath God Wrought: The Transformation of America, 1815–1848*. New York: Oxford University Press, 2007.

Iriye, Akira. *The Origins of the Second World War in Asia and the Pacific*. New York: Longman, 1987.

-------------. *Power and Culture: The Japanese-American War 1941–1945*. Cambridge, Massachusetts: Harvard University Press, 1981.

Kennan, George F. *Memoirs: 1925–1950*. Boston: Little, Brown and Company, 1967.

--------------------. "The Sources of Soviet Conduct", *in Foreign Affairs*, Vol. 25, No. 4, July 1947, pgs. 566–582.

Kernan, Alvin. *The Unknown Battle of Midway: The Destruction of the American Torpedo Squadrons*. New Haven: Yale University Press, 2005.

Ketchum, Richard M. *Saratoga: Turning Point of America's Revolutionary War*. New York: Henry Holt, 1997.

Korda, Michael. *Ike: An American Hero*. New York: HarperCollins, 2007.

Kuehn, John T. *Agents of Innovation: The General Board and the Design of the Fleet that Defeated the Japanese Navy*. Annapolis, Maryland: Naval Institute Press, 2008.

Leckie, Robert. *George Washington's War: The Saga of the American Revolution*. New York: HarperCollins, 1992.

Longford, Elizabeth. *Wellington: the Years of the Sword*. New York: Harper & Row, 1969.

Lundstrom, John B. *Black Shoe Carrier Admiral: Frank Jack Fletcher at Coral Sea, Midway, and Guadalcanal*. Annapolis, Maryland: Naval Institute Press, 2006.

Lunt, James. *John Burgoyne of Saratoga*. New York: Harcourt Brace Jovanovich, 1975.

Mahan, Alfred Thayer. *The Gulf and Inland Waters: Campaigns of the Civil War*. New York: Charles Scribner's Sons, 1883. Reissued 1989 by Broadfoot Publishing Company, Wilmington, North Carolina.

Massie, Robert K. *Castles of Steel: Britain, Germany, and the Winning of the Great War at Sea*. New York: Random House, 2003.

du Maurier, Daphne. *The Du Mauriers*. New York: The Literary Guild of America, Inc., 1937.

May, Stacy. "Measuring the Marshall Plan", *in Foreign Affairs*, Vol. 26, No. 3, April 1948, pgs. 457–466.

McMaster, H.R. *Dereliction of Duty: Lyndon Johnson, Robert McNamara, The Joint Chiefs of Staff, and the Lies that Led to Vietnam*. New York: HarperPerennial, 1997.

McNamara, Robert, and VanDeMark, Brian. *In Retrospect: The Tragedy and Lessons of Vietnam*. New York: Times Books/Random House, 1995.

McPherson, James M. *Tried by War: Abraham Lincoln as Commander-in-Chief*. New York: Penguin, 2008.

--------------------. *War on the Waters: The Union & Confederate Navies, 1861–1865*. Chapel Hill: University of North Carolina Press, 2012.

Merry, Robert W. *A Country of Vast Designs: James K. Polk, the Mexican War and the Conquest of the American Continent.* New York: Simon & Schuster, 2009.

Middlekauff, Robert. *The Glorious Cause: The American Revolution, 1763–1789.* New York: Oxford University Press, 1982, 2005.

Miller, Donald L. *D-Days in the Pacific.* New York: Simon & Schuster Paperbacks, 2001, 2005.

--------------------. *Masters of the Air: America's Bomber Boys Who Fought the Air War Against Nazi Germany.* New York: Simon & Schuster, 2006.

Morison, Samuel Eliot. *History of United States Naval Operations in World War II.* Vol. 4. *Coral Sea, Midway and Submarine Actions: May 1942–August 1942.* Edison, New Jersey: Castle Books—by arrangement with Little, Brown and Company, Inc., 1949, 2001.

-------------------------. *History of United States Naval Operations in World War II.* Vol. 7. *Aleutians, Gilberts and Marshalls.* Boston: Little, Brown and Company, 1951, 1955.

-------------------------. *History of United States Naval Operations in World War II.* Vol. 8. *New Guinea and the Marianas, March 1944–August 1944.* Boston: Little, Brown and Company, 1953.

-------------------------. *History of United States Naval Operations in World War II.* Vol 15. *Supplement and General Index.* Boston: Little, Brown and Company, 1962.

Nau, Henry R. *Conservative Internationalism: Armed Diplomacy Under Jefferson, Polk, Truman, and Reagan.* Princeton, New Jersey: Princeton University Press, 2013.

Nye, Joseph S., Jr., and Smith, Roger K., eds. *After the Storm: Lessons from the Gulf War.* Lanham, Maryland: Madison Books—in conjunction with the Aspen Institute, 1992.

Orwell, George. *Nineteen Eighty-Four.* New York: Everyman's Library/Alfred A. Knopf, 1992.

Overy, Richard. *Why the Allies Won.* New York: Norton, 1995.

Parshall, Jonathan and Tully, Anthony. *Shattered Sword: The Untold Story of the Battle of Midway.* Washington, DC: Potomac Books, 2005.

Perret, Geoffrey. *Eisenhower.* New York: Random House, 1999.

Pitt, Barrie, Consultant Editor. *The Military History of World War II.* New York: The Military Press, 1986.

Pogue, Forrest C. *George C. Marshall.* Vol. 2. *Ordeal and Hope 1939–1942.* New York: Viking, 1966.

--------------------. *George C. Marshall.* Vol. 4. *Statesman 1945–1959.* New York: Viking Penguin, 1987.

Potter, E.B. *Nimitz.* Annapolis, Maryland: Naval Institute Press, 1976, 1987.

Pratt, Julius W. "The Origin of 'Manifest Destiny'", in *The American Historical Review.* Vol. 32, No. 4, July 1927, pgs. 795–798.

Rakove, Jack. *Revolutionaries: A New History of the Invention of America.* Boston: Houghton Mifflin Harcourt, 2010.

Rigby, David. *Allied Master Strategists: The Combined Chiefs of Staff in World War II.* Annapolis, Maryland: Naval Institute Press, 2012.

Roberts, Andrew. *Masters and Commanders: How Four Titans Won the War in the West, 1941–1945.* New York: HarperCollins, 2009.

--------------------. *Waterloo, June 18, 1815: The Battle for Modern Europe.* New York: Harper Perennial, 2005.

Schwarzkopf, H. Norman, and Petre, Peter. *It Doesn't Take a Hero.* New York: Bantam, 1992.

Stafford, Edward. *The Big E: The Story of the U.S.S. Enterprise.* Annapolis, Maryland: Naval Institute Press, 1962.

Stephenson, Michael. *Patriot Battles: How the War of Independence Was Fought.* New York: HarperCollins, 2007.

Stille, Mark. *Imperial Japanese Navy Heavy Cruisers 1941–45.* Long Island City, New York: Osprey Publishing, 2011.

Stowe, Harriett Beecher. *Uncle Tom's Cabin: Or Life Among the Lowly.* Garden City, New York: International Collector's Library, 1958.

Symonds, Craig L. *The Battle of Midway.* New York: Oxford University Press, 2011.

----------------------. *The Civil War at Sea.* Denver: Praeger, 2009.

Tedder, Lord Arthur. *With Prejudice: The War Memoirs of Marshal of the Royal Air Force Lord Tedder, G.C.B.* Boston: Little, Brown and Company, 1966.

Thorne, Christopher. *Allies of a Kind: The United States, Britain and the War Against Japan, 1941–1945.* New York: Oxford University Press, 1978.

Wert, Jeffry D. *The Sword of Lincoln: The Army of the Potomac.* New York: Simon & Schuster, 2005.

Wicker, Tom. *George Herbert Walker Bush*. New York: Viking/Penguin, 2004.

Woodham-Smith, C. *The Reason Why*. New York: McGraw-Hill, 1953, 1954.

Wright, Robert K., Jr. *The Continental Army*. Washington, DC: Center of Military History, 1986.

Online Sources

Britannica Online

Civil War Trust

Harvard University web site

Hazlitt, William and Gurwood, John, eds. *The Speeches of the Duke of Wellington in Parliament: Collected and Arranged by the Late Colonel Gurwood*. (London: J. Murray, 1854): pgs. 47–49, 54, 65–67. Hathi Trust Digital Library. http://babel.hathitrust.org/cgi/pt?id=mdp.39015027329815;view=1up;seq=76.

US Navy Department. Selected Naval Documents: Spanish-American War. "Naval Battle of Manila Bay, May 1, 1898. Communications Before the Battle," from *Appendix to the Report of the Chief of the Bureau of Navigation, Annual Reports of the Navy Department for the Year 1898*. Washington: Government Printing Office, 1898. Online source: http://www.history.navy.mil/docs/spanam/manila1.htm.

Newspaper Articles and Unpublished Manuscripts

Daily Boston Globe, June 6, 1947. "2185 Harvard Graduates Join 'Fellowship of Educated Men.'" pg. 4.

Feeney, Mark. "American Sage Making History as Well as Writing It: George F. Kennan Masters a Century." *Boston Globe*, October 26, 2000, pg. D1.

MacGillis, Alec. "Uncle Wigglywings to take to skies again: Candy Dropper to help mark Berlin airlift." *Boston Globe*, May 3, 1998, pg. A2.

Rigby, David. *The C.S.S.* Alabama *and British Neutrality During the American Civil War*. Unpublished paper, 1991.

INDEX